John Roy Musick

Brother Against Brother

Or, the Tompkins mystery. A story of the great American rebellion

John Roy Musick

Brother Against Brother
Or, the Tompkins mystery. A story of the great American rebellion

ISBN/EAN: 9783337212193

Printed in Europe, USA, Canada, Australia, Japan

Cover: Foto ©ninafisch / pixelio.de

More available books at **www.hansebooks.com**

BROTHER AGAINST BROTHER

OR,

THE TOMPKINS MYSTERY.

A Story of the Great American Rebellion.

By JOHN R. MUSICK,

Author of "The Banker of Bedford," "Orland Hyde,"
"Calamity Row," Etc.

(Copyright, 1887, by J. S. Ogilvie & Co.)

FIRESIDE SERIES, No. 28. JULY, 1887.
Issued Monthly, Subscription, $3 per year.
Entered at New York Post-Office as second-class matter.

J. S. OGILVIE & COMPANY,
57 Rose Street, New York; 79 Wabash Ave., Chicago.

LIST OF POPULAR NOVELS

CONTAINED IN

THE FIRESIDE SERIES,

The Cover of which is Printed in Colors, and is very attractive. Each one contains from 200 to 480 pages.

No. 1. The Mohawks, by Miss M. E. Braddon.
" 2. Lady Valworth's Diamonds, by the Duchess.
" 3. A House Party, by Ouida.
" 4. At Bay, by Mrs. Alexander.
" 5. Adventures of an Old Maid, by Belle C. Greene.
" 6. Vice Versa, by F. Anstey.
" 7. In Prison and Out, by Hesba Stretton.
" 8. A Broken Heart, by author of Dora Thorne.
" 9. A False Vow, by author of Dora Thorne.
" 10. Nancy Hartshorn at Chautauqua, by Nancy Hartshorn.
" 11. Beaton's Bargain, by Mrs. Alexander.
" 12. Mrs. Hopkins on her Travels, by Mrs. Hopkins herself.
" 13. A Guilty River, by Wilkie Collins.
" 14. By Woman's Wit, by Mrs. Alexander.
" 15. "She," by H. Rider Haggard.
" 16. The Witch's Head, by H. Rider Haggard.
" 17. King Solomon's Mines, by H. Rider Haggard.
" 18. Jess, by H. Rider Haggard.
" 19. The Merry Men, by R. L. Stevenson.
" 20. Miss Jones' Quilting, by Josiah Allen's Wife.
" 21. Secrets of Success, by J. W. Donovan.
" 22. Drops of Blood, by Lily Curry.
" 23. Strange Case of Dr Jekyll and Mr. Hyde.
" 24. Dawn, by H. Rider Haggard.
" 25. Me. A companion to "She."
" 26. East Lynne, by Mrs. Henry Wood.
" 27. Allan Quartermain, by H. Rider Haggard.
" 28. Brother against Brother. A Story of the Rebellion, by John R. Musick.

CONTENTS.

CHAPTER.		PAGE.
I.	In the Stage-Coach and at the Inn,	5
II.	A New Arrival,	17
III.	Dinner Talk,	28
IV.	More of the Mystery,	36
V.	The Mud Man,	46
VI.	A Transition Period,	52
VII.	The Election and the Result,	62
VIII.	Mr. Diggs in a New Field,	69
IX.	The Chasm Opens,	81
X.	The Beginning of Soldier Life,	89
XI.	Mr. Tompkins' Peril,	102
XII.	Foraging,	108
XIII.	Uncle Dan Means Business,	114
XIV.	Mrs. Juniper Entertains,	120
XV.	Mr. Diggs Again in Trouble,	127
XVI.	Yellow Steve,	143
XVII.	A Soldier's Turkey Hunt,	151
XVIII.	Mr. Tompkins Receives Strange News,	158
XIX.	Irene's Dilemma—The Brothers Meet,	162
XX.	War in the Neighborhood,	174
XXI.	Crazy Joe's Mistake,	182
XXII.	Diggs Gets out of His Scrape Again,	193
XXIII.	The Abduction,	201
XXIV.	He is My Husband. Oh, Spare His Life,	209
XXV.	At Home Again,	219
XXVI.	Another Phase of Soldier Life,	223
XXVII.	A Prisoner,	227
XXVIII.	Olivia,	231
XXIX.	The Alarm—The Manuscript,	236
XXX.	Yellow Steve's Mysterious Story,	242
XXXI.	The Reconciliation,	247

BROTHER AGAINST BROTHER.

CHAPTER I.

IN THE STAGE-COACH AND AT THE INN.

Thick, misty clouds overcast the sky ; peals of thunder in the distance came rolling nearer and nearer, until they burst into one prolonged roar just above a lumbering old stage-coach slowly making its way over the muddy roads of a Virginia post route, the driver incessantly cracking his long whip over the backs of his jaded horses, and urging them, with shouts and exclamations, to accelerate their speed.

This scene occurs in what is now West Virginia. It is west of the mountain range, but where, on every hand, are frowning precipices, deep gorges and swift-flowing torrents. On the right, the jutting headlands are crowned with huge old bowlders, just peeping out from the thicket of evergreens and creeping vines which surround them. Although not called mountainous, it is a country whose picturesque heights and umbrageous valleys would excite a degree of enthusiasm in the bosom of a lover of the beautiful. Down in those lonely valleys, almost hidden in their leafy groves, was the home of many an old Virginia aristocrat. The great, gnarled oak standing upon the verge of some miniature precipice, and glooming sullenly through the misty rain, seems but part of some pictured scene. Far in the distance, faintly penciled against the misty sky, rise headlands to what seems an enormous height, about them a dark mass of clouds, like some giant's garment caught upon the peaks and blown about at the will of the wind. It envelops and conceals the highest peaks, leaving the imagination to add to the belief in their stupendous height.

It has been raining all day, and the driver of the stage-coach is anxious to reach his destination.

"Gee-up! If we don't git to Lander's Hill before dark, I be hanged if we don't stick there for the night," he exclaimed.

The stage-coach moves slowly along, and the shades of evening are closing in. Six or seven passengers are seated within, and are about as uncomfortable as stage-coach travelers could well be. There is but a single lady among them, and the chivalric spirit of the Southron has assigned to her the most comfortable place in the coach. We are interested in but one of these travelers, a man about forty-five or fifty years of age, something over medium size, whose appearance stamped him as a well-to-do Virginia planter. His face was smooth-shaven, and his hair, once dark, was silvered with the flight of years. His was a handsome face, and a pleasant one to look upon; there was something pleasing and attractive about its expression, and the mild gray eyes burned with no ambitious designs or fiery passions; his dress was plain gray homespun, commonly worn as the traveling dress of a Southerner at the time of which we write. His hat was of the finest silk, broad-brimmed and low-crowned, such as Southern planters invariably wore. Though unostentatious in manner, he was evidently a man accustomed to the manifold comforts of Southern life. He was, moreover, a man accustomed to looking at both sides of a question, and arriving at conclusions without bias or prejudice. His frame was a fine type of manhood, and his muscular arms showed him possessed of more than an ordinary degree of strength.

This man alone of all the passengers maintained a silent and thoughtful mood as the coach passed on its way. A constant conversation was kept up by the other passengers on the weather, the roads, the journey, its termination, and last, but not least, the politics of the day. However, while the gentleman whom we have more particularly described, and now introduce to our readers as George W. Tompkins, of Virginia, sat moody and silent, and seemingly utterly oblivious of the discomforts within or the gloomy prospect without, his fellow passengers were continually talking, and continually jostling against him, without rousing Mr. Tompkins from his reverie.

His mind was clouded by a horror that made him careless of present surroundings. He looked worn and weary, more so than any of the other passengers, and occasionally, when the coach rolled over smooth ground, he would lean back in his seat and close his eyes. No sooner done, however, than a thousand fantastic shapes would glide before his mental vision, that seemed to take delight in annoying him. Whenever he became unconscious to his real surroundings, shrieks seemed to sound in his ear, and he seemed to hear the cry:

"Search, search, search! Your task's not over, your task's not over!"

"And where shall I search?" he mentally asked.

"Ah, where?" the voice wailed.

Then the planter would rouse himself, and glance at the passengers and out of the window in the endeavor to keep his mind free from the annoyances. For a few moments he would succeed, but days and nights of exertion, horror and excitement were telling upon him; once more he would succumb and once more the fantastic shadows thronged about him, and the voice, mingling strangely with the grating roar of the coach's wheels, smote on his ear:

"Search, search, search! Your task's not over! Your task's not over!"

"Where shall I search?"

"Ah, where?"

"You don't seem to be well, friend," remarked a fellow-traveler, observing the startled and restless manner of Mr. Tompkins.

"Yes, I am well; that is—no, I am not; I am somewhat wearied," Mr. Tompkins answered.

"So are we all," rejoined the passenger. "This journey has been enough to wear out men of iron, and the prospects for the night are far from cheering."

"I had expected to reach home to-night," said the planter. "but I shall fail by a good dozen miles."

"You live in this State?"

"Yes, sir," answered Mr. Tompkins, settling himself in his corner.

The gentleman, evidently a Southern man, seeing that Mr. Tompkins was indisposed to carry on any further conversation, relapsed into silence. With another effort Mr. Tompkins conquered the stupor which, with all its fantastic concomitants, was once more overcoming him, and sat bolt upright in his seat.

"This has been a fearful week," he soliloquized, "but I have done all I could."

The gentleman by his side, catching the last part of the remark, and supposing it had reference to the present journey, remarked:

"Yes, it is not the fault of the passengers, but of the managers of this line. They should be prepared for such emergencies, and have a supply of fresh horses."

Observing that his exclamation, though misinterpreted, had arrested attention, Mr. Tompkins, to guard against its recurrence, lest he should divulge the subject of his disturbed thoughts, aroused himself and resisted, with determination, the stupor that was overcoming him. It was while thus combating the fatigue that weighed him down that the stage-coach came to a very sudden stop.

The driver, pressing his face to the aperture at the top of the coach, cried out:

"Here we are at Lander's Hill, and I be hanged if the hosses are able to drag ye all up. They are completely fagged out, so I guess ye men folks 'll hev to hoof it to the top, an' occasionally give us a push, or we'll stick here until mornin'."

"How far is it to where we can stop over night?" asked the passenger who had endeavored to draw Mr. Tompkins into conversation.

"After we git on top of the hill it's only 'bout three miles to Jerry Lycan's inn, where we'll stop for the night, an' it's down hill 'most all the way," replied the driver.

With much grumbling and many imprecations on the heads of the managers of the stage line, the passengers clambered out of the coach. A long, muddy hill, in places quite steep, lay before them. It was nearly half a mile to the top, and portions of the road were scarcely passable even in good weather.

"These are public roads in Virginia!" exclaimed one gentleman, as he alighted in the mud.

"We can't have railroads to every place," essayed a fellow-traveler, evidently a Virginian; "but you will find our soil good."

"Yes, good for sticking purposes," said the first speaker, trying to shake some of the mud from his boots; "I never saw soil with greater adhesive qualities."

"Now look 'ee," said the driver, "we'll hev some purty smart jogs, where the hosses 'll not be able to pull up, and you'll hev to put your shoulders agin the coach an' give us a push."

"May I be blessed!" ejaculated the Southerner. "They are not even content to make us walk, but want us to draw the coach."

"Better to do that an' hev a coach at the top to ride in than to walk three miles," said the driver.

After allowing his horses a brief rest, the driver cracked his whip and the lumbering coach moved on, the passengers slowly plodding along behind. None seemed pleased with the prospect of a walk up the long, muddy hill, but the grumbling Southerner manifested a more decided repugnance than either of the others.

"This is worse than wading through Carolina swamps waist deep," he exclaimed, as he trudged along, dragging his weary feet and mud-freighted boots after him.

The coach had not proceeded more than a dozen rods when it came to one of the "jogs" in the hill alluded to by the driver. "Now help here, or we'll stick sure. Git up!" cried the driver, and the poor, tired horses nerved themselves for the extra effort required of them. The ascent here was both steep and slippery, and it required the united strength of horses and passengers to pass the coach over the place.

Here the passengers discovered the prodigious strength which lay in the broad shoulders of Mr. Tompkins. Not a murmur had escaped his lips when required to walk up the hill, and he was the first to place his shoulder to the wheel to push the coach over the difficult passage. To still further increase the discomforts of their position they were thoroughly drenched by a passing shower which overtook them before they reach the summit of the hill. Here they again climbed into the coach, and resuming their seats, were whirled along through the gathering darkness toward the inn.

Old Jerry Lycan stood on the long porch of his old-fashioned Virginia tavern, and peered down the road through the gloom. It had been dark but a few moments. The old man's ears caught the sound of wheels coming down the road, and he knew the stage was not far off.

"The roads are just awful," said the landlord, "and no wonder it is belated."

The night was intensely dark; not a star was to be seen in the sky; an occasional flash of lightning momentarily lit up surrounding objects, only to render the blackness more complete. Far down the road the old man's eyes caught a glimpse of the coach-lights bobbing up and down as the ponderous vehicle oscillated over the rough roads. Approaching slowly, like a wearied thing of life, the cumbrous stage at last appeared, made visible only by its own lamps, which the driver had lighted. The splashing of six horses along the miry roads and the dull rolling of the huge wheels made the vehicle heard long before it was seen.

"Rube haint no outside passengers to-night," said the landlord, seeing that the top seats of the coach were vacant. "'Spose nobody'd want to ride out in the rain."

"Here ye are at Lycan's inn," called out the driver to the inmates of the coach as he reined in his weary horses in front of the roadside tavern.

Uncle Jerry as he was called, with his old, perforated tin lantern, came to open the stage door and show his guests into the house. Rube, the driver, tossing the reins to the stable-boy, climbed down from his lofty perch, and went into the bar-room to get "something hot" to warm his benumbed body.

The landlord brought the wet and weary men into the room, where a great fire was blazing, and promised that supper should be ready by the time they were dry. The Southerner declared that he was much too dry within, though he was dripping wet without. Uncle Jerry smiling invited him into the bar-room. The Southerner needed no second invitation, and soon returned, saying that Virginia inns were not so bad after all.

The lady had been shown to a private apartment, while the gentlemen were attempting to dry their clothing by the fire in the public room. The Southerner, who had been in much better humor since his visit to the bar, seemed now to look very philosophically upon his soaking and other inconveniences of travel.

Our planter, Mr. Tompkins, sat in front of the pile of blazing logs, gazing at the bright, panoramic pictures constantly forming there. Sleeping or waking, darkness of the stage-coach and in those glowing embers, he saw but one picture, and its horrors were constantly haunting his mind.

The other guests talked and laughed while their soaked clothes were drying, but Mr. Tompkins was silent, whether sitting or standing. Almost before their clothes were dry supper was announced, and they all repaired to the long, low dining room and seated themselves at the table. The supper, plain and substantial, was just suited to the needs of the hungry guests.

The evening meal over, they returned to the sitting room. The Southerner had lit a cigar, and kept up a constant flow of conversation.

"Virginia is too near the Free-soilers," he said, evidently directing his remarks to Mr. Tompkins; "don't they come over here and steal your niggers?"

"They never have," Mr. Tompkins answered.

"I take it for granted you own slaves?"

"Yes, sir; I have a number on my plantation, and never have had one stolen yet."

"Don't the 'Barnburners,' 'Wooly Heads' and Abolitionists from Ohio and Pennsylvania come over here and steal them away?"

"They have never taken any from me."

"Well, that's a wonder. I know a number of good men on the border who find it impossible to keep niggers at all."

"Perhaps they are not good masters," said Mr. Tompkins.

"They were the best of masters, and they lost their niggers, though they guarded them with watchful overseers and bloodhounds."

"But do you think that a good master needs to guard his slaves with armed overseers and dogs?" said Mr. Tompkins.

"Of course," the Carolinian answered; "how else would you keep the black rascals in subjection? Are we not horrified almost every week by reports of some of their outrages? Swamps and canebrakes have become the haunts of runaway blacks, who, having murdered their master, seek to wreck vengeance on innocent children or women."

Mr. Tompkins started at these assertions, as though he felt a pang at his heart.

"My friend, what you say is true, too true," he said; "but is the master always blameless? The negro possesses feelings, and even a beast may be goaded to madness. Is it not an unrighteous system which is crushing and cursing our beloved country?"

"What system?"

"Slavery."

"Why, sir, you are a singular slave-holder," cried the Southerner. "Are you going to turn a Martin Van Buren and join the Free-soilers?"

"There is a great deal in that question, sir, outside of politics. I believe in slavery, else I would not own a slave; but if our slaves are to be treated as animals, it were better if the institution were abolished."

"How would you treat them?"

"Discharge the overseers, to begin with."

"I am sure, you would fail."

"The plan has succeeded well on my plantation," said Mr. Tompkins, "and I do not own a single negro who would not die for me."

Here were met two men, both believing in the institution of human slavery, but carrying out its principles, how differently! The one with cool Northern blood and kindly feelings, advocating a humane mode of ruling the helpless being in his power. The other, representing the extreme type of refined cruelty and oppression. The mind of the one grew more and more in harmony with the idea of abolition, while the other came to hate, with all the fierceness of his Southern heart, the idea of universal freedom; became willing, even, to strike at that flag which had failed to protect his interests and his opinions.

The date at which we write was directly after the election and inauguration of Taylor as President of the United States. The opposition to human slavery had steadily been gaining ground, regardless of taunts and sneers, and the ranks of the Abolitionists were hourly on the increase. Slavery was peculiarly a selfish institution. It is folly to say that only men born and reared in the South could be numbered among the upholders of this "peculiar institution," for many Northern men went South and purchased plantations and slaves, and in 1861 many of these enlisted on the Confederate side, and fought under the Confederate flag, not from principle, but from self-interest.

Mr. Tompkins, who was Northern born, believed in slavery simply because he owned slaves, and not from any well defined principle. Even now the same conflict that later convulsed the Nation was raging in his heart—the conflict between self-interest and the right. Press and pulpit, the lecturer's rostrum and the novelist's pen, had almost wrought out the doom of slavery, when the politician took up the stormy dispute.

The discussion in the Virginia inn was warm but friendly, the Carolinian declaring that God and Nature had ordained the negro for slavery; that his diet should be the ash-cake, his stimulant the whip, his reward for obedience a blanket and a hut, his punishment for rebellion chains and death. Doubtless his passion over-reached his judgment in the heat of argument, and his brain, perhaps, was not so cool since his visit to the bar-room.

"My dear sir," Mr. Tompkins finally said, hoping to end the discussion, which was drawing to them the attention of all, "the policy you suggest will, I fear, plunge our whole country into trouble. Few men are born rulers, and history has never shown one successful who ruled by harsh measures only. Admitting that a negro is not a rational being, kindness with a beast can accomplish more than harshness. It is cruel masters who make runaway slaves. The parting of parent and child, husband and wife, torn ruthlessly asunder, never to see each other again, will make even a negro furious. I fear, sir, that slavery is a bad institution, but it is firmly established among us, and I see no way at present to get rid of it."

The other guests at Jerry Lycan's inn had gathered in groups of two and three, and were listening silently to the differing views of these two upholders of slavery, for there were factions in those days among the slavery men. The landlord had entered the room, and, being a politician himself, drank in the discussion with deepest interest.

Just as the argument was at its height the outer door of the inn opened and a boy, wild-eyed, but handsome, entered. A glance at the strangely wild eyes and disheveled hair convinced all present that he was insane. He was about twelve years of age, with a slender figure and a well-shaped head, but some great shock had unseated his reason. His mania was of a mild, harmless type. Walking directly up to Mr. Tompkins, he said:

"Have you seen my father? You look very much like my father, but I know he has not yet come into Egypt."

The voice was so plaintive and sad that it touched at once the hearts of all, and happily put an end to the conversation.

"Who is your father?" asked Mr. Tompkins.

"Jacob is my father. I am his favorite son. My brothers sold me a slave into Egypt, and told my father I had been slain by wild beasts. Have you seen my father?"

"He is crazy. Humor him, say something to him," whispered the landlord.

"Your father is not yet ready to come into Egypt," said Mr. Tompkins.

"And my brother Benjamin—did you see him?" the lad asked.

"Yes."

"Is the famine sore in the land where my father dwells?"

"Yes."

"And does he suffer—is he old? Oh, yes, I remember; my father must be dead." He seated himself on a low stool by the fireside, and, bowing his head in his hands, seemed lost in thought.

"He does that twenty times a day," said the landlord.

"Who is he?" asked one of the travelers, "and where does he come from?"

"He has been here only a few days, and I know nothing about him. His first question was, 'Have you seen my father Jacob?'"

"Have you tried to find out about him?" asked Mr. Tompkins.

"Yes, but to no purpose," answered Uncle Jerry. "He came one morning and said he was fleeing from Potiphar's wrath. After inquiring for his father, he remained silent for some time. I tried to find where he came from, but no one knows and he can not tell. I should judge by the clothes he wore that he was from the South, and, from the worn condition of his shoes, that he came a great way. He is of some respectable family, for he has been well educated, and I fancy it's too much book learning that has turned the boy's head. He talks of Plato and Socrates and Aristotle, and all the ancient philosophers, and his familiarity with historical events shows him to have been a student; but he always imagines that he is Joseph."

"Where does he live?" asked Mr. Tompkins.

"Oh, he stays here at the inn, and shows no disposition to leave. He makes himself useful by helping the stable-boy and carries in fuel, imagining himself a servant of the high priest."

"Has he lucid intervals?" asked Mr. Tompkins.

"No, not what could be called lucid intervals. Once he said to a girl in the kitchen that it was books that made his head dizzy, and said something of a home a great ways off, from which he had fled to escape great violence. They hoped then to clear up the mystery, but the next moment his mind wandered again and he was Joseph sold into Egypt, bewailing his father Jacob and his brother Benjamin."

"What is his name?" asked Mr. Tompkins.

"We can't get any other name than Joseph, and the boys here call him Crazy Joe."

"His malady may be curable; have you consulted a physician about it?" inquired the Californian, who was very much interested in the strange case.

"Yes, sir; a doctor from the State Lunatic Asylum was here day before yesterday, but he pronounced him incurable."

"Could not the doctor tell how long he had been in this condition?" asked Mr. Tompkins.

"Not with certainty, but thought it only a few weeks or months. He said he had probably escaped from his guard and ran away."

At this moment the subject of conversation rose from the low stool and looked about with a vacant stare.

"Do you want to go home to your parents?" Mr. Tompkins asked.

"When the famine is sore in the land they will come for me."

"Why did you run away?"

"My brothers sold me to the merchants with their camels. They made my father believe I was killed, and brought me here and sold me; but I know it is written that my brother Benjamin will come and bring my father to me."

"Is it not written that Jacob did go down into Egypt with his whole family, and that he wept on Joseph's neck, and said he was willing to die?" said Mr. Tompkins, to lead him out of this strange hallucination.

"Yes, yes—oh, yes!" the boy cried, eagerly.

"Did not Moses deliver the children of Israel from bondage long after Jacob's death?"

"I remember now that he did," said Joe.

"Then how can you be Joseph, when he died three or four thousand years ago?"

The boy reflected a moment, and then said:

"Who can I be, if I am not Joseph?"

"Some one who imagines himself Joseph," said Mr. Tompkins. "Now, try to think who you really are and where you came from."

"I am not Socrates, for he drank the hemlock and died, nor am I Julius Cæsar, for he was killed by Brutus," the poor lunatic replied.

"Try to think what was you father's name," persisted Mr. Tompkins, hoping to discover something.

"My father's name was Jacob, and I was sold a slave into

Egypt by my brothers; but there must be something wrong; my father must be dead."

Again he seated himself on the low stool and buried his face in his hands.

"It's no use," said the landlord; "that's as near as you'll ever come to knowing who he is from him. I have advertised him in the Pittsburg daily, but no one has come yet to claim him."

"A very strange hallucination," said the Carolinian. "Is he always mild?"

"Yes; he is never cross or sullen, and seems delighted with children. He answers them in many ways."

It was growing late, and the weary travelers were ready to go to bed. The landlord assisted by Crazy Joe and another boy, took lighted candles to the various rooms for the guests.

By the combined aid of a good supper, a warm discussion on slavery, and his interest in the insane boy, Mr. Tompkins had succeeded in fighting away the legion of gloomy thoughts that harassed his mind, and a few minutes after retiring was sleeping peacefully.

CHAPTER II.

A NEW ARRIVAL.

Forty years ago a Virginia planter was a king, his broad acres his kingdom, his wife his queen, his children heirs to his throne, and his slaves his subjects. True, it was a petty kingdom and he but a petty monarch; but, as a rule, petty monarchs are tyrannical, and the Southern planter was not always an exception. In those days men were measured, not by moral worth, mental power, or physical stature, but by the number of acres and slaves they owned. The South has never possessed that sturdy class of yeomanry that has achieved wonders in the North. Before the war labor was performed by slaves, now it is done by hired help, the farmer himself there seldom cultivating his soil.

The home of Mr. George W. Tompkins, our acquaintance, was a marvel of beauty and taste. Located in the Northwestern portion of the State, before its division, it was just where the heat of the South was delightfully tempered by the cool winds of the North. No valley in all Virginia was more lovely. To the east were hills which might delight any mountain lover, all clothed and fringed with delicate evergreens, through which could be caught occasional glimpses of precipitous bald rocks. Over the heights the sun climbed every morning to illuminate the valley below with a radiance of glory. Mountain cascades came tumbling and plunging from mossy retreats to swell a clear pebble-strewn stream which afforded the finest trout to be found in the entire State.

The great mansion, built after the old Virginia plan, with a long stone piazza in front, stood on an eminence facing the post-road, which ran within a few rods of it. The house was substantial, heavy columns, painted white as marble, supporting the porch, and quaint, old-fashioned gables, about which the swallows twittered, breaking the lines of the roof. In the front yard grew the beach and elm and chestnut tree, their wide-spreading branches indicating an existence for centuries. A little below the structure, and south-west from it, was a colony of low, small buildings, where dwelt the slaves of Mr. Tompkins. One or two were nearer, and in these the domestics lived. These were a higher order of servants than the field-hands, and they never let an opportunity pass to assert their superiority over their fellow slaves.

Socially, as well as geographically, Mr. Tompkins' home combined the extremes of the North and South. He, with his calm face and mild gray eyes, was a native of the green hills of New Hampshire, while his dark-eyed wife was a daughter of sunny Georgia.

Mrs. Tompkins was the only child of a wealthy Georgia planter. Mr. Tompkins had met her first in Atlanta, where he was spending the Winter with a class-mate, both having graduated at Yale the year before. Their meeting grew into intimacy, from intimacy it ripened into love. Shortly after the marriage of his daughter, his only child, the planter exchanged his property for more extensive possessions in Virginia, but he never occupied this new home. He and his wife were in New Orleans, when the dread malady, yellow-fever, seized upon them, and they died before their daughter or her husband could go to them.

Mr. Tompkins, a man who had always been opposed to slavery, thus found himself the owner of a large plantation in Virginia, and more than a hundred slaves. There seemed to be no other alternative, and he accepted the situation, and tried, by being a humane master, to conciliate his wounded conscience for being a master at all.

He and his only brother, Henry, had inherited a large and valuable property from their father, in their native State. His brother, like himself, had gone South and married a planter's daughter, and become a large slave-holder. He was a far different man from his brother. Naturally overbearing and cruel, he seemed to possess none of the other's kindness of heart or cool, dispassionate reason. He was a hard task-master, and no "fire-eating" Southerner ever exercised his power more remorselessly than he, and no one hated the Abolition party more cordially. But it is not with Henry Tompkins we have to deal at present.

It was near noon the day after the travelers reached Jerry Lycan's inn. Mrs. Tompkins sat on the piazza, looking down the road that led to the village. She was one of those Southern beauties who attract at a first glance; her eyes large, and dark, and brilliant; her hair soft and glossy, like waves of lustrous silk. Of medium height, though not quite so slender as when younger, her form was faultless. Her cheek had the olive tint of the South, and as she reclined with indolent grace in her easy chair, one little foot restlessly tapping the carpet on which it rested, she looked a very queen.

The Tompkins mansion was the grandest for many miles around, and the whole plantation bore evidence of the taste and judgment of its owner. There seemed to be nothing, from the crystal fountain splashing in front of the white-pillared dwelling to the vast fields of corn, wheat and tobacco stretching far into the back-ground, which did not add to the beauty of the place.

On the north were barns, immense and well filled granaries and stables. Then came tobacco houses, covering acres of ground. One would hardly have suspected the plain, unpretentious Mr. Tompkins as being the possesser of all this wealth. But his house held his greatest treasures—two bright little boys, aged respectively nine and seven years.

Abner, the elder, had bright blue eyes and the clear Saxon complexion of his father. Oleah, the younger, was of the same dark Southern type as his mother. They were two such children as even a Roman mother might have been proud to call her jewels. Bright and affectionate, they yielded a quick obedience to their parents, and—a remarkable thing for boys—were always in perfect accord.

"Oh, mamma, mamma!" cried Oleah, following close after his brother, and quite as much excited.

"Well, what is the matter?" the mother asked, with a smile.

"It's coming! it's coming! it's coming!" cried Oleah.

"He's coming! he's coming!" shouted Abner.

"Who is coming?" asked the mother.

"Papa, papa, papa!" shouted both at the top of their voices. "Papa is coming down the big hill on the stage-coach."

Mrs. Tompkins was now looking for herself. Sure enough there was the great, old-fashioned stage-coach lumbering down the hill, and her husband was an outside passenger, as the sky was now clear and the sun shone warm and bright. The clumsy vehicle showed the mud-stains of its long travel, and the roads in places were yet filled with water.

The winding of the coachman's horn, which never failed to set the boys dancing with delight, sounded mellow and clear on the morning air.

"It's going to stop! it's going to stop!" cried Oleah, clapping his little hands.

"It's going to stop! it's going to stop!" shouted Abner, and both kept up a frantic shouting, "Whoa, whoa!" to the prancing horses as they drew near the house.

It paused in front of the gate, and Mrs. Tompkins and her two boys hurried down the walk.

Mr. Tompkins' baggage had just been taken from the

boot and placed inside the gate, and the stage had rolled on, as his wife and two boys came up to the traveler.

"Mamma first, and me next," said Oleah, preparing his red lips for the expected kiss.

"And I come after Oleah," said Abner.

Mr. Tompkins called to a negro boy who was near to carry the baggage to the house, and the happy group made their way to the great piazza, the two boys clinging to their father's hands and keeping up a torrent of questions. Where had he been? What had he seen? What had he brought home for them? The porch reached, Mrs. Tompkins drew up the arm-chair for her tired husband.

"Rest a few minutes," she said, "and then you can take a bath and change your clothes, and you will feel quite yourself once more."

The planter took the seat, with a bright-faced child perched on each side of him.

"You were gone so long without writing that I became uneasy," said his wife, drawing her chair close to his side.

"I had a great deal to do," he answered, shaking his head sadly, "and it was terrible work, I assure you. The memory of the past three weeks, I fear, will never leave my mind."

"Was it as terrible as the message said?" asked Mrs. Tompkins, with a shudder.

"Yes, the horrible story was all true. The whole family was murdered."

"By whom?"

"That remains a mystery, but it is supposed to have been done by one of the slaves, as two or three ran away about that time."

"How did it happen? Tell me all."

The little boys were sent away, for this story was not for children to hear, and Mr. Tompkins proceeded.

"We could hardly believe the news the dispatch brought us, my dear, but it did not tell us the worst. The roads between here and North Carolina are not the best, and I was four or five days making it, even with the aid of a few hours occasionally by rail. I found my brother's next neighbor, Mr. Clayborne, at the village waiting for me. On the way he told all that he or any one seemed to know of the affair. My brother had a slave who was half negro and part Indian, with some white blood in his veins. This slave had a quadroon wife, whom he loved with all his wild, passionate heart. She was very beautiful, and a belle among the negroes. But Henry, for some disobedience on the part of the husband, whose Indian and white blood revolted against slavery, sold the wife to a Louisiana sugar planter. The half breed swore he would be revenged, and my brother, unfortunately possessing a hasty temper, had him tied up and severely whipped—"

"Served the black rascal quite right," interrupted the wife, who, being Southern born, could not endure the least self-assertion on the part of a slave.

"I think not, my dear, though we will not argue the question. After his punishment the black hung about for a week or two, sullen and silent. Several friends cautioned my brother to beware of him, but Henry was headstrong and took no man's counsel. Suddenly the slave disappeared, and although the woods, swamps and cane-breaks were scoured by experienced hunters and dogs he could not be found. Three weeks had passed, and all thought of the runaway had passed from the minds of the people. Late one night the man who told me this was passing my brother's house, when he saw flames shooting about the roof and out of the windows. He gave the alarm, and roused the negroes. As he ran up the lawn toward the house a bloody ax met his view. On entering the front door my brother Henry was found lying in the hall, his skull cleft in twain. I cannot repeat all that met the man's horror-stricken gaze. They had only time to snatch away the bodies of my brother, his wife and two of the children when the roof fell in.

"And the other two children?" asked Mrs. Tompkins.

"Were evidently murdered also, but their bodies could not be found. It is supposed they were burned to ashes amid the ruins."

"Did you cause any extra search to be made?"

"I did, but it was useless. I have searched, searched, searched—mountain, plain and swamp. The rivers were dragged, the wells examined, the ruins raked, but in vain.

The oldest and the youngest of the children could not be found. A skull bone was discovered among the ruins, but so burned and charred that it was impossible to tell whether it belonged to a human being or an animal. I have done everything I could think of, and yet something seems to tell me my task in not over—my task is not over."

"What has been done with the plantation?" Mrs. Tompkins asked.

"The father of my brother's wife is the administrator of the estate, and he will manage it."

"And the murderer?"

"No trace of him whatever. It seems as though, after performing his horrible deed, he must have sank into the earth."

Mrs. Tompkins now, remembering that her husband needed a bath and a change of clothes, hurried him into the house. The recital of that horrible story had cast a shadow over her countenance, which she tried in vain to drive away, and had reawakened in Mr. Tompkins' soul a longing for revenge, though his better reason compelled him to admit that the half-breed was goaded to madness and desperation.

The day passed gloomily enough after the first joy of the husband and father's return. The next morning, just as the sun was peeping over the gray peaks of the eastern mountains and throwing floods of golden light into the valley below, dancing upon the stream of silver which wound beneath, or splintering its ineffectual lances among the branches and trunks of the grand old trees surrounding the plantation, Mr. Tompkins was awakened from the dreamless sleep of exhaustion.

"What was that?" he asked of his wife.

Both waited a moment, listening, when again the feeble wail of an infant reached their ears.

"It is a child's voice," said Mrs. Tompkins; "but why is it there?"

"Some of the negro children have strayed from the quarters; or, more likely, it is the child of one of the house servants," said Mr. Tompkins.

"The house servants have no children," answered Mrs. Tompkins, "and I have cautioned the field women not to allow their children to come here especially in the early morning, to annoy us."

Mr. Tompkins, whose morning nap was not yet over, closed his eyes again. The melodious horn of the overseer, calling the slaves to the labors of the day, sounded musical in the early morning air, and seemed only to soothe the wearied master to sleep again. Footsteps were heard upon the carpeted hallway, and then three or four light taps on the door of the bedroom.

"Who is there?" asked Mrs. Tompkins.

"It's me, missus, if you please." The door was pushed open and a dark head, wound in a red bandana handkerchief, appeared in the opening.

"What is the matter, Dinah?" Mrs. Tompkins asked, for she saw by the woman's manner that something unusual had occurred. Dinah was her mistress' handmaid and the children's nurse.

"If you please, missus," she said, "there is a queerest little baby on the front porch in the big clothes-basket."

"A baby!" cried the astonished Mrs. Tompkins.

"Yes'm, a white baby."

"Where is its mother?"

"I don't know, missus. It must a been there nearly all night, an' I suppose they who ever left it there wants you to keep it fur good."

"Bring the poor little thing here," said Mrs. Tompkins, rising to a sitting position in the bed.

In a few minutes Dinah returned with a baby about six months old, dressed in a faded calico gown, and hungrily sucking its tiny fist, while its dark brown eyes were filled with tears.

"It was in de big basket among some ole clothes," said Dinah.

"Poor, dear little thing! it is nearly starved and almost frozen. Prepare it some warm milk at once, Dinah," said the kind-hearted mistress.

The girl hurried away to do her bidding, leaving the baby with Mrs. Tompkins, who held the benumbed child in her arms and tried to still its cries.

Mr. Tompkins was wide awake now, and his mind busy

with conjecture how the child came to be left on their piazza.

"What is that?" called Oleah, from the next room.

"Why, it's a baby," answered Abner, and a moment later two pairs of little bare feet came pattering into their mother's room.

"Oh, the sweet little thing!" cried Oleah; "I want to kiss it."

His mother held it down for him to kiss.

"Isn't it pretty!" said Abner. "Its eyes are black, just like Oleah's. Let me kiss it, too."

The little stranger looked in wonder at the two children, who, in their joy over this treasure-trove, were dancing frantically about the room.

"Oh, mamma, where did you get it?" asked Oleah.

"Dinah found it on the porch," the mother answered.

"Who put it there?"

"I don't know, dear."

"Why, Oleah," said Abner, "it's just like old Mr. Post. Don't you know he found a baby at his door? for we read about it in our First reader."

"Oh, yes; is this the same baby old Mr. Post found?" asked Oleah.

"No," answered the mother; "this is another."

"Oh, isn't it sweet?" said Oleah, as the child cried and stretched out its tiny hands.

"It's just as pretty as it can be," said Abner.

"Mamma, oh, mamma!" said Oleah, shaking his mother's arm, as she did not pay immediate attention to his call.

"What, dear?" she asked.

"Are we goin' to keep it?"

"Yes, dear; if some one who has a better right to it does not come to claim it."

"They shan't have it," cried Oleah, stamping his little, bare foot on the carpet.

"No," added Abner; "it's ours now. They left it there to starve and freeze, and now we will keep it."

"You think, then, that the real owner has lost his title by his neglect?" said the father, with a smile.

"Yes, that's it," the boy answered.

"It's a very good common law idea, my son."

Dinah now came in with warm milk for the baby, and Mrs. Tompkins told her to take the two boys to their room and dress them; but they wanted to wait first and see the baby eat.

"Oh, don't it eat; don't it eat!" cried the boys.

"The poor little thing is almost starved," said the mother.

"Missus, how d'ye reckin it came on the porch?" Dinah asked.

"I cannot think who would have left it," answered Mrs. Tompkins.

"That is not a very young baby," said Mr. Tompkins, watching the little creature eat greedily from the spoon, for Dinah had now taken it and was feeding it.

"No, marster, not berry, 'cause it's got two or free teef," said the nurse. "Spect it's 'bout six months old."

As soon as the little stranger had been fed, Dinah wrapped it in a warm blanket and laid it on Mrs. Tompkin's bed, where it soon fell asleep, showing it was exhausted as well as hungry. Dinah then led the two boys to the room to wash and dress them.

"Strange, strange!" said Mrs. Tompkins, beginning to dress. "Who can the little thing belong to, and what are we to do with it?"

"Keep it, I suppose," said Mr. Tompkins; and, stumbling over a boot-jack, he exclaimed in the same breath, "Oh, confound it!"

"What, the baby?"

"No, the boot-jack. I've stubbed my toe on it."

"We have no right to take upon ourselves the rearing of other people's children," said Mrs. Tompkins, paying no attention to her husband's trifling injury.

"But it's our Christian duty to see that the little thing does not die of cold and hunger," said Mr. Tompkins, caressing his aching toe.

Soon the boys came in, ready for breakfast, and inquired for the baby; when told that it was sleeping, they wanted to see it asleep, and stole on tiptoe to the bed, where the wearied little thing lay, and nothing would satisfy them until they were permitted to touch the pale, pinched, tear-stained cheek with their fresh, warm lips.

The breakfast bell rang, and they went down to the dining-room, where awaiting them was a breakfast such as only Aunt Susan could prepare. They took their places at the table, while a negro girl stood behind each, to wait upon them and to drive away flies with long brushes of peacock feathers. The boys were so much excited by the advent of the strange baby that they could scarcely keep quiet long enough to eat.

"I am going to draw it on my wagon," said Oleah.

"I'm going to let it ride my pony," said Abner.

"Don't think too much of the baby yet, for some one may come and claim it," said their mother.

"They shan't have it, shall they, papa?" cried Oleah.

"No, it is our baby now."

"And we are going to keep it, ain't we, Aunt Susan!" he asked the cook, as she entered the dining-room.

"Yes, bress yo' little heart; dat baby am yours," said Aunt Susan.

"It's a Christmas gift, ain't it, Maggie?" he asked the waiter behind him. Oleah was evidently determined to array everyone's opinion against his mother's supposition.

"Yes, I reckin it am," the negro girl answered with a grin.

"Ha, ha, ha!" laughed Abner. "Why, Oleah, this ain't Christmas."

Seeing his mistake, Oleah joined in the laugh, but soon commenced again.

"We're goin' to make the baby a nice, new play-house, ain't we, Abner?"

"Yes, and a swing."

The baby slept nearly all the forenoon. When she woke (for it was a girl) she was washed, and dressed in some of Master Oleah's clothes, and Mrs. Tompkins declared the child a marvel of beauty, and when the little thing turned her dark eyes on her benefactor with a confiding smile the lady resolved that no sorrow that she could avert should cloud the sweet, innocent face.

When the boys came in they began a war dance, which

made the baby scream with delight. Impetuous Oleah snatched her from his mother's lap, and both boy and baby rolled over on the floor, fortunately not hurting either. His mother scolded, but the baby crowed and laughed, and he showered a hundred kisses on the little white face.

A boy about twelve years of age was coming down the lane. He entered the gate and was coming towards the house. Mr. Tompkins, who was in the sitting-room, in a moment recognized the boy as Crazy Joe, and told his wife about the unfortunate lad. He met the boy on the porch.

"How do you do, Joe?" he asked, extending his hand.

"I am well," Joe answered. "Have you seen my father Jacob or my brother Benjamin?"

"No, they have not yet come," answered the planter.

For several years after, Joe was a frequent visitor. There was no moment's lapse of his melancholy madness, which yet seemed to have a peculiar method in it, and the mystery that hid his past but deepened and intensified.

CHAPTER III.

DINNER TALK.

America furnishes to the world her share of politicians. The United States, with her free government, her freedom of thought, freedom of speech and freedom of press, is prolific in their production. One who had given the subject but little thought, and no investigation, would be amazed to know their number. Nearly every boy born in the United States becomes a politician, with views more or less pronounced, and the subject is by no means neglected by the feminine portion of the community. That part of Virginia, the scene of our story, abounded with "village tavern and cross-roads politicians." Snagtown, on Briar creek, was a village not more than three miles from Mr. Tompkins'. It boasted of two taverns and three saloons, where loafers congregated to talk about the weather, the doings in Congress, the terrible state of the country, and their exploits in catching "runaway niggers." A large per cent of our people pay more attention to Congressional matters than to their own affairs. We do not deny that it is every man's right to understand the grand machinery of this Government, but he should not devote to it the time which should be spent in caring for his family. Politics should not intoxicate men and lead them from the paths of honest industry, and furnish food for toughs to digest at taverns and street corners.

Anything which affords a topic of conversation is eagerly welcomed by the loafer; and it is little wonder that politics is a theme that rouses all his enthusiasm. It not only affords him food, but drink as well, during a campaign. Many are the neglected wives and starving children who, in cold and cheerless homes, await the return of the husband and father, who sits, warm and comfortable, in some tavern, laying plans for the election of a school director or a town overseer.

Snagtown could tell its story. It contained many such neglected homes, and the thriftless vagabonds who constituted the voting majority never failed to raise an excitement, to provoke bitter feelings and foment quarrels on election day.

Plump, and short, and sleek was Mr. Hezekiah Diggs, the justice of the peace of Snagtown. Like many justices of the peace, he brought to the performance of his duties little native intelligence, and less acquired erudition; but what he lacked in brains he made up in brass. He was one of the foremost of the political gossipers of Snagtown, and had filled his present position for several years.

'Squire Diggs was hardly in what might be termed even moderate circumstances, though he and his family made great pretension in society. He was one of that rare class in Virginia—a poor man who had managed by some inexplicable means, to work his way into the better class of society. His wife, unlike himself, was tall, slender and sharp visaged. Like him, she was an incessant talker, and her gossip frequently caused trouble in the neighborhood. Scandal was seized on as a sweet morsel by the hungry Mrs. Diggs, and she never let pass an opportunity to spread it, like a pestilence, over the town.

They had one son, now about twelve years of age, the joy and pride of their hearts, and as he was capable of declaiming, "The boy stood on the burning deck," his proud father discovered in him the future orator of America, and determined that Patrick Henry Diggs should study law and enter the field of politics. The boy, full of his father's conviction, and of a conceit all his own, felt within his soul a rising greatness which one day would make him the foremost man of the Nation. He did not object to his father's plan; he was willing to become either a statesman or a lawyer, but having read the life of Washington, he would have chosen to be a general, only that there were now no redcoats to fight. Poor as Diggs' family was, they boasted that they associated only with the *elite* of Southern society.

'Squire Diggs had informed Mr. Tompkins that he and his family would pay him a visit on a certain day, as he wished to consult him on some political matters, and Mr. Tompkins and his hospitable lady, setting aside social differences, prepared to make their visitors welcome. On the appointed day they were driven up in their antiquated carriage, drawn by an old gray horse, and driven by a negro coachman older than either. Mose was the only slave that the 'Squire owned, and though sixty years of age, he served the family faithfully in a multiform capacity. He pulled up at the door of the mansion, and climbing out somewhat slowly, owing to age and rheumatism, he opened the carriage door and assisted the occupants to alight.

Though Mrs. Tompkins felt an unavoidable repugnance for the gossiping Mrs. Diggs, she was too sensible a hostess to treat an uninvited guest otherwise than cordially.

"I've been just dying to come and see you," said Mrs. Diggs, as soon as she had removed her wraps and taken her seat in an easy chair, with a bottle of smelling salts in her hand and her gold-plated spectacles on her nose, "you have been having so many strange things happen here; and I told the 'Squire we must come over, for I thought the drive might do me good, and I wanted to hear all about the murder of your husband's brother's family, and see that strange baby and the crazy boy. Isn't it strange, though? Who could have committed that awful murder? Who put that baby on your piazza, and who is this crazy boy?"

Mrs. Tompkins arrested this stream of interrogatories by saying that it was all a mystery, and they had as yet been unable to find a clew. Baffled at the very onset in the chief object of her visit, Mrs. Diggs turned her thoughts at once into new channels, and, graciously overlooking Mrs. Tompkins' inability to gratify her curiosity, began to recount the news and gossip and small scandals of the neighorbood.

'Squire Diggs was in the midst of an animated conversation on his favorite theme, the politics of the day. The slavery question was just assuming prominence. Henry Clay, Martin Van Buren, and others, had at times hinted at emancipation, while John Brown and Jared Clarkson, and a host of lesser lights, were making the Nation quake with the thunders of their eloquence from rostrum and pulpit. 'Squire Diggs was bitter in his denunciations of Northerners, believing that they intended "to take our niggers from us." He invariably emphasized the pronoun, and always spoke of *niggers* in the plural, as though he owned a hundred instead of one. 'Squire Diggs was one of a class of people in the South known as the most bitter slavery men, the small slaveholders—a class that bewailed most loudly the freedom of the negro, because they had few to free. At dinner he said :

"Slavery is of divine origin, and all John Brown and Jared Clarkson can say will never convince the world otherwise."

"I sometimes think," said Mr. Thompkins, "that the country would be better off with the slaves all in Siberia."

"What? My dear sir, how could we exist?" cried 'Squire Diggs, his small eyes growing round with wonder. "If the slaves were taken from us, who would cultivate these vast fields?"

"Do it ourselves, or by hired help," answered the planter.

"My dear sir," the idea is impracticable," said the 'Squire, hotly. "We cannot give up our slaves. Slavery is of divine origin. The niggers, descending from Ham, were cursed into slavery. The Bible says so, and no nigger-loving Abolitionist need deny it."

"I believe my husband is an emancipationist," said Mrs. Tompkins, with a smile.

"I am," said Mr. Tompkins; "not so much for the slaves' good as for the masters'. Slavery is a curse to both white and black, and more to the white than to the black. The two races can never live together in harmony, and the sooner they are separated the better."

"How would you like to free them and leave them among us?" asked the 'Squire.

"That even would be better than to keep them among us in bondage."

"But Henry Clay, in his great speech on African colonization in the House of Representatives, says: 'Of all classes of our population, the most vicious is the free colored.' And, my dear sir, were this horde of blacks turned loose upon us, without masters or overseers to keep them in restraint, our lives would not be safe for a day. Domineering niggers would be our masters, would claim the right to vote and hold office. Imagine, my dear sir, an ignorant nigger holding an important office like that of justice of the peace. Consider for a moment, Mr. Tompkins, all of the horrors which would be the natural result of a lazy, indolent race, incapable of earning their own living, unless urged by the lash, being turned loose to shift for themselves. Slavery is more a blessing to the slave than to the master. What was the condition of the negro in his native wilds? He was a ruthless savage, hunting and fighting, and eating fellow-beings captured in war. He knew no God, and worshiped snakes, the sun and moon, and everything he could not understand. Our slave-traders found him in this state of barbarism and misery. They brought him here, and taught him to till the soil, and trained him in the ways of peace, and led him to worship the true and living God. *Our* niggers now have food to eat and clothes to wear, when in their native country they were hungry and naked. They now enjoy all the blessings of an advanced civilization, whereas they were once in the lowest barbarism. Set them free, and they will drift back into their former state."

"A blessing may be made out of their bondage," replied Mr. Tompkins. "As Henry Clay said in the speech from which you have quoted, 'they will carry back to their native soil the rich fruits of religion, civilization, law and liberty. And may it not be one of the great designs of the Ruler of the universe (whose ways are often inscrutable by short-sighted mortals) thus to transform original crime into a single blessing to the most unfortunate portions of the globe? But I fear we uphold slavery rather for our own mercenary advantages than as a blessing either to our country or to either race."

"Why, Mr. Tompkins, you are advocating Abolition doctrine," said Mrs. Diggs.

"I believe I am, and that abolition is right."

"Would you be willing to lose your own slaves to have the niggers freed?" asked the astonished 'Squire.

"I would willingly lose them to rid our country of a blighting curse."

"I would not," said Mrs. Tompkins, her Southern blood fired by the discussion. "My husband is a Northern man, and advocates principles that were instilled into his mind from infancy; but I oppose abolition from principle. Slaves should be treated well and made to know their place; but to set them free and ruin thousands of people in the South is the idea of fanatics."

"I'm mamma's Democrat," said Oleah, who, seated at his mother's side, concluded it best to approve her remarks by proclaiming his own political creed.

"And I am papa's Whig," announced Abner, who was at his father's side.

"That's right, my son. You don't believe that people, because they are black, should be bought and sold and beaten like cattle, do you?" asked the father, looking down, half in jest and half in earnest, at his eldest born.

"No; set the negroes free, and Oleah and I will plow and drive wagons," he replied, quickly.

"You don't believe it's right to take people's property from them for nothing and leave people poor, do you, Oleah?" asked the mother, in laughing retaliation

"No, I don't," replied the young Southern aristocrat.

"You are liable to have both political parties represented

in your own family," said 'Squire Diggs. "Here's a difference of opinion already."

"Their differences will be easy to reconcile, for never did brothers love each other as these do," returned Mr. Tompkins, little dreaming that this difference of opinion was a breach that would widen, widen and widen, separating the loving brothers, and bringing untold misery to his peaceful home.

"What are you in favor of, Patrick Henry?" Mrs. Diggs asked, in her shrill, sharp tones, of her own hopeful son.

"I'm in favor of freedom and the Stars and Stripes," answered Patrick Henry, gnawing vigorously at the chicken bone he held in his hand.

"He is a patriot," exclaimed the 'Squire. "He talks of nothing so much as Revolutionary days and Revolutionary heroes. He has such a taste for military life that I'd send him to West Point, but his mother objects."

"Yes, I do object," put in the shrill-voiced, cadaverous Mrs. Diggs, "They don't take a child of mine to their strict military schools. Why, what if he was to get sick, away off there, and me here? I wouldn't stop day or night till I got there."

Dinner over, the party repaired to the parlor, and 'Squire Diggs asked his son to speak "one of his pieces" for the entertainment of the company.

"What piece shall I say?" asked Patrick Henry, as anxious to display his oratorical talents as his father was to have him.

"The piece that begins, 'I come not here to talk,'" said Mrs. Diggs, her sallow features lit up with a smile that showed the tips of her false teeth.

Several of the negroes, learning that a show of some kind was about to begin in the parlor, crowded about the room, peeping in at the doors and windows. Patrick Henry took his position in the centre of the room, struck a pompous attitude, standing high as his short legs would permit, and, brushing the hair from his forehead, bowed to his audience and, in a high, loud monotone, began:

"I come not to talk! You know too well
The story of our thraldom. We—we—"

He paused and bowed his head.

"We are slaves," prompted the mother, who was listening with eager interest. Mrs. Diggs had heard her son "say his piece" so often that she had learned it herself, and now served as prompter. Patrick Henry continued:

         "We are slaves.
The bright moon rises——"

"No, sun," interrupted his mother.

    "The bright sun rises in the East and lights
    A race of slaves. He sets—and the—last thing"—

The young orator was again off the track.

"And his last beam falls on a slave," again the fond mother prompted.

By being frequently prompted, Patrick Henry managed to "speak his piece through."

While the mother, alert and watchful, listened and prompted, the father, short, and sleek, and fat, leaned back in his chair, one short leg just able to reach across the other, listening with satisfied pride to his son's display.

"The poor child has forgotten some of it," said the mother, at the conclusion.

"Yes," added the father; "he don't speak much now, and so has forgotten a great deal that he knew."

Mr. Tompkins and his wife, inwardly regretting that he had not forgotten all, willingly excused Patrick Henry from any further efforts. And though they had welcomed and entertained their guests with the cordial Southern hospitality, they felt somewhat relieved when the Diggs carriage, with its ancient, dark-skinned coachman, rolled away over the hills towards Snagtown.

CHAPTER IV.

MORE OF THE MYSTERY.

We have seen the perfect harmony which prevailed in the household of Mr. Tompkins, though his wife and himself were of totally different temperaments, and, on many subjects, held opposite opinions. He, with his cool Northern blood, was careful and deliberate, slow in drawing conclusions or forming a decision; but, once his stand was taken, firm as a rock. She had all the quick Southern impetuosity, that at times found rash expression, though her head was as clear and her heart as warm as her husband's. Her prejudices were stronger than his, and her reason was more frequently swayed by them.

The great Missouri Compromise was supposed to have settled the question of slavery forever, and abolition was regarded only as the dream of visionary fanatics. Though a freeholder by birth and principle, circumstances had made Mr. Tompkins a slave-holder. He seldom expressed his sentiments to his Southern neighbors, knowing how repugnant they were to their feelings; but when his opinions were asked for he always gave them freely. The movements on the political checker-board belong rather to history than to a narrative of individual lives, yet because of their effect on these lives, some of the most important must be mentioned. While the abolition party was yet in embryo, the Southern statesmen, or many of them, seeming to read the fate of slavery in the future, had declared that the Union of States was only a compact or co-partnership, which could be dissolved at the option of the contracting parties. This gave rise to the principle of States' rights and secession, and when the emancipation of the slaves was advocated, Southern politicians began to talk more and more of dissolution.

Not only in political assemblies was the subject discussed, but even in family circles, as we have seen. Mrs. Tompkins, of course, differed from her husband on the subject of "State" rights, as she did on slavery, and many were their debates on the theme. Their little sons, observing their parents' interest in these questions, became concerned themselves, and, as was very natural, took sides. Abner was the Whig and Oleah his mother's Democrat. Still, love and harmony dwelt in that happy household, though the prophetic ear might have heard in the distant future the rattle of musketry on that fair, quiet lawn, and the clash of brothers' swords in mortal combat beneath the roof which had sheltered their infancy.

Little did these fond parents dream of the deep root those seeds of political difference had taken in the breasts of their children, and the bitter fruit of misery and horror they would bear. Their lives now ran as quietly as a meadow brook. All the long Summer days they played without an angry word or thought, or if either was hurt or grieved a kiss or a tender word would heal the wound.

The tragic fate of his brother's family, and his unavailing efforts to bring the murderers to justice, directed Mr. Tompkins' thoughts into new channels. The strange baby grew in strength and beauty every day. Its mysterious appearance among them continued to puzzle the family, and all their efforts failed to bring any light on the subject. The servant to whom was assigned the washing of the clothes the baby had on when found was charged by her mistress to look closely for marks and letters upon them. When her work was done, she came to Mrs. Tompkins' room, and that lady asked:

"Have you found anything, Hannah?"

"Yes, missus; here am a word wif some letters in it," the woman answered, holding up a little undershirt and pointing to some faint lines.

Mrs. Tompkins took the garment, which, before being washed, had been so soiled that even more legible lines than these would have been undistinguishable; it was of the finest linen, and faintly, yet surely, was the word "Irene" traced with indelible ink.

"As soon as all the clothes had been washed and dried, bring them to me," said Mrs. Tompkins, hoping to find some other clew to the child's parentage.

"Yes, missus," and Hannah went back to her washing.

"Irene," repeated Mrs. Tompkins aloud, as she looked down on the baby, who was sitting on the rug, making things lively among a heap of toys Abner and Oleah had placed before her.

The baby looked up and began crowing with delight.

"Oh, bless the darling; it knows its name!" cried Mrs. Tompkins. "Poor little thing, it has seldom heard it lately. Irene! Irene! Irene!"

The baby, laughing and shouting, reached out its arms to the lady, who caught it up and pressed it to her heart.

"Oh, mamma!" cried Oleah, running into the room, with his brother at his heels, "me and Abner have just been talking about what to call the baby. He wants to call it Tommy, and that's a boy's name, ain't it, mamma?"

"Of course it is—"

"And our baby is a girl, and must have a girl's name, musn't it, mamma?"

"Yes."

"I just said Tommy was a nice name; if our baby was a boy we'd call it Tommy," explained Abner.

"But the baby has a name—a real pretty name," said the mother.

"A name! a name! What is it?" the brothers cried, capering about, and setting the baby almost wild with delight.

"Her name is Irene," said Mrs. Tompkins.

"Oh, mamma, where did you get such a pretty name?" asked Abner.

Who said it was Irene?" put in Oleah.

"I found it written on some of the clothes it wore the morning we found it," answered the mother.

"Then we will call it Irene," said Abner, decisively.

"Irene! Irene! Little Irene! ain't you awful sweet?" cried the impetuous Oleah, snatching the baby from his mother's arms and smothering its screams of delight with kisses. So enthusiastic was the little fellow that the baby was in peril, and his mother, spite of his protestations, took it from him. As soon as released, little Irene's feet and hands began to play, and she responded, with soft cooing and baby laughter, to all the boys' noisy demonstrations.

A youth, with large sad eyes and pale face, now entered the door.

"Oh, come, Joe, come and see the baby!" cried Oleah. "Isn't it sweet? Just look at its pretty bright eyes and its cunning little mouth."

Joe had visited the plantation frequently of late, and Mr. Tompkins having given orders that he should always be kindly treated, had finally established himself there, and was now considered rather a member of the household than a guest.

The poor, insane boy came close to Mrs. Tompkins' side and looked fixedly at the baby for a few moments. An expression of pain passed over his face, as though some long forgotten sorrow was recalled to his mind.

"I remember it now," he finally said. "It was at the great carnival feast, and after the gladiators fought, this babe, which was the son of the man who was slain, was given to the lions to devour, but although it was cast in the den, the lions would not harm a hair of its head."

"Oh, no, Joe; you are mistaken," said Abner; "it was Daniel who was cast into the lions' den."

"You are right," said Crazy Joe. "It was Daniel; but I remember this baby. It was one of the two taken by the cruel uncle and placed in a trough and put in the river. The river overflowed the banks and left the babes at the root of a tree, where the wolf found them, and taking compassion on the children, came every day and furnished them nourishment from his own breast."

"No, no," interrupted Abner, who, young as he was, knew something of Roman mythology. "You are talking about Romulus and Remus."

"Ah, yes," sighed the poor youth, striving in vain to gather up his wandering faculties; "but I have seen this child before. If it was not the one concealed among the bulrushes, then what can it be?"

"It's our baby," put in Oleah, "and it wasn't in no bulrushes; it was in the clothes-basket on the porch."

"It was a willow ark," said Joe; "its mother hid it there, for a decree had gone forth that all male children of the Israelites should be exterminated—"

"No; it was a willow basket," interrupted Oleah. "Its mother shan't have it again. It's our little baby. This baby ain't a liverite, and it shan't be sterminated, shall it, mamma?"

"No, dear; no one shall harm this baby," said Mrs. Tompkins.

"It's our baby, isn't it mamma?"

"Yes, my child, unless some one else comes for it who has a better right to it."

"Who could that be, mamma?"

"Perhaps its own father or mother might come—"

"They shan't have it if they do," cried Oleah, stamping his little foot resolutely on the floor."

Joe rose from the low chair on which he had been sitting, and went out, saying something about his father coming down into Egypt.

"Mamma," said Abner, when Joe had gone out, "what makes him say such strange things?" He says that he is Joseph, and that his brothers sold him into Egypt, and he calls papa the captain of the guard. He goes out into the fields and watches the negroes work, and says he is Potiphar's overseer, and must attend to his household."

"Poor boy, he is insane, my son," answered Mrs. Tompkins; "he is very unfortunate, and you must not tease him. Let him believe he is Joseph, for it will make him feel happier to have his delusion carried out by others."

"The other day, when we were playing in the barn, Joe and Oleah and me, I saw a great scar and sore place on poor Joe's head, just like some one had struck him. I asked him what did it, and he said he fell with his head on a sharp rock when his brothers threw him into the pit."

Oleah now was anxious to go back to his play, and dragged his brother out of the house to the lawn, leaving Mrs. Tompkins alone with the baby.

Several weeks after the baby and Crazy Joe became inmates of Mr. Tompkins' house, a man, dressed in trowsers of brown jeans and hunting shirt of tanned deer skin, wearing a broad-brimmed hat and heavy boots, came to the mansion. The Autumn day was delightful; it was after the Fall rains. The Indian Summer haze hung over hill, and mountain, and valley, and the sun glowed with mellowed splendor. The stranger carried a rifle, from which a wild turkey was suspended, and wore the usual bullet-pouch and powder-horn of the hunter slung across his shoulder. He was tall and wiry, about thirty-five years of age, and, to use his own expression, as "active as a cat and strong as a lion."

Daniel Martin, or "Uncle Dan," as he was more generally known, was a typical Virginia mountaineer, whose cabin was on the side of a mountain fifteen miles from Mr. Tompkins' plantation. He was noted for his bravery and his bluntness, and for the unerring aim of his rifle.

He was the friend of the rich and poor, and his little cabin frequently afforded shelter for the tourist or the sportsman. He was called "Uncle Dan" by all the younger people, simply because he would not allow himself to be called Mr. Martin.

"No, siree," he would say; "no misterin' fur me. I was never brought up to it, and I can't tote the load now." He persisted in being called "Uncle Dan," especially by the children. "It seems more home-like," he would say.

Why he had not wife and children to make his cabin "home-like" was frequently a theme for discussion among the gossips, and, as they could arrive at no other conclusion, they finally decided that he must have been crossed in love.

Mr. Tompkins, who chanced to be on the veranda, observed the hunter enter the gate, and met him with an extended hand and smile of welcome, saying:

"Good morning, Dan. It is so long since you have been here that your face is almost the face of a stranger."

"Ya-as, it's a'most a coon's age, and an old coon at that, since I been on these grounds. How's all the folks?" he answered, grasping Mr. Tompkins' out-stretched hand.

"They are all well, and will be delighted to see you Dan. Come in."

"Ye see I brought a gobbler," said Dan, removing the turkey from his shoulder. "I thought maybe ye'd be wantin' some wild meat, and I killed one down on the creek afore I came."

Mr. Tompkins took the turkey, and calling a negro boy, bade him take it to the cook to be prepared for dinner.

Then he conducted his guest to the veranda. Uncle Dan placed his long rifle and accoutrements in a far corner, and sat down by Mr. Tompkins.

"Wall, how's times about heah, any how, and how's politicks?" he asked, as soon as seated.

The mountain air in America, as in Switzerland, seems to inspire those who breathe it with love of liberty. The dwellers on the mountains of Virginia, North Carolina and Tennessee were chiefly Abolitionists, who hated the slaveholder as free men do tyrants, and when the great struggle came on they remained loyal to the Government. As a rule, they were poor, but self-respecting, possessing a degree of intelligence far superior to that of most of the lower class of the South.

The secret of the friendship between the planter and the hunter was that both were, at heart, opposed to human bondage, and though they seldom expressed their real sentiments, even when alone, each knew the other's feelings.

Before Mr. Tompkins could reply to the mountaineer's question, Abner and Oleah ran up to the veranda with shouts of joy and noisy demonstrations of welcome. Uncle Dan placed one on each knee, and for some time the boys claimed all his attention.

"Oh, Uncle Dan, you can't guess what we've got," Oleah cried.

"Why, no; I can't. What is it?" asked Uncle Dan, abandoning attempt to return to the social chat the boys had interrupted.

"A baby! a baby!" cried Oleah, clapping his hands.

"A baby?" repeated Uncle Dan, in astonishment.

"Yes, sir; a bran new baby, just as sweet as it can be, too."

The puzzled mountaineer, with a suspicious look at Mr. Tompkins, said: "Thought ye said the folks was all well?"

"They are," answered Mr. Tompkins, with an amused smile.

"Dinah found the baby in a clothes-basket," put in Abner.

"Oh, it's a nigger baby, is it?" asked Uncle Dan.

"No, no, no; its a white baby—a white baby," both boys quickly replied.

"What do the children mean?" asked Uncle Dan, bewildered, looking from the boys to their father.

"They mean just what they say," said Mr. Tompkins. "A baby was left at our door a short time ago in the clothes-basket by some unknown person."

"Don't you want to see it, Uncle Dan?" Master Oleah eagerly asked.

"To be sure I do. I always liked babies; they are the perfection o' innocence."

Before he had finished his sentence, Oleah had climbed down from his knee, and was scampering away toward the nursery. Abner was not more than two seconds in following him.

"Wall, now, see heah," said the hunter; "while them young rattletraps is gone, jest tell me what all this means. Hez someone been increasin' yer family by leavin' babies a layin' around loose, or is it a big doll some one haz give the boys?"

"It's just as the boys say," Mr. Tompkins answered. "Some one did actually leave a baby about six months old on this porch, and no one knows who he was, where he came from, or where he went."

"That's mighty strange. How long ago was it?"

"About six weeks."

"Wall, now, ain't that strange?" Have you any suspicion who done it?"

"Not the least."

"Wall, it is strange. Never saw no un sneakin' about the house, like?"

"No one at all."

"Humph! Well, it's dog gone strange."

At this moment the two boys, with Dinah in attendance, came out, bearing between them little Irene.

"Here it is; here is our baby! Ain't she sweet, though?" cried Oleah, as they bore their precious burden toward the mountaineer.

"Why it's a spankin' big un, by jingo! Ya-as, an' I be blessed ef I ain't seen that baby before," cried Uncle Dan.

"Where?" asked Mr. Tompkins, eagerly.

Uncle Dan took the little thing on his lap, and, as it turned its large dark-gray eyes up to his in wonder, he reflected a few minutes in silence and then said:

"I saw a baby what looked like this, and I'll bet a good deal it is the same one, too."

"Where did you see it?" again demanded the planter.

"That's jest what I'm tryin' to think up," said Uncle Dan. "Oh, yes; it war in the free nigger's cabin, on the side o' the east Twin Mountain. You know where the old cabin stands, where we used to camp when we war out huntin'!"

"Yes."

"Wall, I war roamin' by there one day, and found two nigger men and a woman livin' there. They had this baby with them, and I questioned them as to where they war gwine, but one nigger, who had a scar slaunch-ways across his face," here the narrator made an imaginary mark diagonally across his left cheek to indicate what he meant by "slaunch-ways," "said they war gwine to live thar. I asked 'em whar they got the baby, and they said its people war dead, and they war to take it to some of its relations. I left 'em soon, for I couldn't git much out o' them, but I detarmined to keep an eye on 'em. The next time I came by that way they were gone, bag and baggage."

"The free nigger's cabin is at least twenty miles from here," said Mr. Tompkins. "It is strange why they should bring the baby all that way here and leave it."

"It do look strange, but I guess they war runaway niggers what had stole the child out of spite, and when they got heah give out an' left it. I kinder think these niggers war from the South."

"Have you ever seen or heard of them since?" asked Mr. Tompkins.

"Neither har nor hide."

At this moment a stranger to Uncle Dan came sauntering up the lawn, and, stepping on the porch, addressed them with:

"Can you tell me where my brothers feed their flocks?"

"He's crazy," whispered Abner to the hunter. "He's crazy, and mamma says pretend as if he was talking sense."

"Oh, they are out thar somewhar on the hills, I reckin'," Uncle Dan answered.

Joe looked at the mountaineer for a moment, carefully examining the hunting jacket of tanned skins, the hair of which formed an ornamental fringe, and then said:

"I know you now. You are my Uncle Esau; but why should you be here in Egypt? It was you who grew angry with my father because he got your birthright for a mess of potage. You sought to slay him and he fled. Have you come to mock his son?"

"Oh, no, youngster; yer pap and me hev made up that little fuss long ago. I forgive him that little steal, an' now we ar' all squar' agin."

"But why are you in Egypt? You must be very old. My father, who is younger than you, is old—bowed down—"

"Poor boy," said Mr. Tompkins, with a sigh, "he has been a close student, and perhaps that was what turned his head."

"Does he ever git rantankerous?" asked Uncle Dan.

"No; he is always mild and harmless."

"Have you seen my father?" Joe now asked. He has long white hair and snowy beard."

"No, youngster; I ain't got a sight o' the old man fur some time," said Uncle Dan.

"Potiphar resembles my father, but my father must be dead," and he sank into a chair, with a sad look of despair, and, burying his face in his hands, groaned as if in pain.

"He does that way a dozen times a day," Abner whispered to Uncle Dan.

"It's maughty strange," said Uncle Dan, shaking his head in a puzzled manner.

The next day, when the mountaineer was about to return to his lonely cabin, Crazy Joe asked permission to accompany his Uncle Esau. Consent was given, and he went and stayed several weeks. For years afterward he stayed alternate on Mr. Tompkins' plantation and at the home of the mountaineer.

CHAPTER V.

THE MUD MAN.

Sixteen years, with all their joys and sorrows, all their pleasures and pains, have been numbered with the dead past. Boys have grown to be men, men in the full vigor of their prime have grown old, and creep about with bent forms and heads whitening, while men who were old before now slumber with the dead. Girls are women, and women have grown gray, yet father Time has touched gently some of his children.

Abner and Oleah Tompkins are no longer boys. Only the memory is left them of their childhood joys, when they played in the dark, cool woods, or by the brook in the wide, smooth lawn. Happy childhood days, when neither care nor anxiety weighed on their young hearts, or shadowed their bright faces.

Abner is twenty-five—a tall, powerful man, with dark-blue, fearless eyes, light-haired, broad-chested and muscular.

Oleah, two years younger, and not quite so tall, is yet in physical strength his brother's equal. He has the dark hair and large, dark, lustrous eyes of his Southern mother.

The brothers were alike and yet dissimilar. They had shared equally the same advantages; they had played together and studied together. Playmates in their childhood, friends as well as brothers in their young manhood, no one could question a doubt of their brotherly love. Where one had been, the other had always been at his side. No slightest difference had ever yet ruffled the smooth surface of their existence. Yet they were dissimilar in temperament. Abner was slow and cool, but perhaps more determined than his brother, and his reason predominated over his prejudice. Oleah was rash, impetuous and bold, and more liable to be moved by prejudice or passion than by reason. Abner was the exact counterpart of his Northern father, Oleah of his Southern mother.

Their political sympathies were different as their dispositions. Although of the same family, they had actually been taught opposite political creeds—one parent in a half-playful way, unconsciously advocating one idea; the other as firmly and unconsciously upholding another, and it was quite natural that the children should follow them. But this difference of opinion had bred no discord.

Sixteen years have wrought a wonderful change in Irene, the foundling. Her parentage is still a mystery, and she bears the name of her foster parents. She is just budding into womanhood, and a beautiful woman she promises to make—slender and graceful, her small, shapely head crowned with dark brown hair, her cheeks dimpling with smiles, mouth and chin firm and clear-cut and large, dark-gray eyes beneath arching brows and long silken lashes filled with a world of tenderness.

Irene could not have been loved more tenderly by the planter and his wife had she been their own child. They lavished care and affection upon her and filled her life with everything that could minister to her comfort and delight, and every one knew that they would make generous provision for the little waif who had gained so sure a place in their hearts.

Sixteen years had made some change in the planter. His hair had grown whiter, his brow more furrowed with care, and he went about with a heavy cane; yet he was vigorous and energetic. He had grown more corpulent, and his movements were less brisk than of yore. Father Time had dealt leniently with his wife. Her soft, dark hair was scarcely touched with silver; her cheeks were smooth and her eyes were still bright and lustrous. Her voice had lost none of its silver ring, her manner none of its queenly grace.

No ray of light had pierced the darkened mind of Crazy Joe. All these long, weary years he had been waiting, waiting, waiting, for his father Jacob to come down into Egypt, but he came not. He still talked as if it was but yesterday that he had been cast into the pit by his brethren, and then taken out and sold into Egypt. He spent his time in turns at the planter's and Uncle Dan's cabin. He was well known throughout the neighborhood, and pitied and kindly treated by all. His strange hallucination, although causing pain and perplexity to his shattered mind, worked no change in his gentle disposition ; his sad eyes never flashed with anger ; no emotion varied the melancholy monotone of his voice. When at the home of the planter, Joe divided his time between the stables, the garden and the library. He would have been a constant reader of the Bible, Josephus, Socrates, Milton's " Paradise Lost," had it not been discovered by Mrs. Tompkins that these books only tended to increase the darkness in which his mind was shrouded, and she had them kept from him. At Uncle Dan's mountain home he passed his time in hunting and trapping, becoming expert in both.

Sixteen years had wrought a great change in Uncle Dan, bowing his tall an sinewy form. His face, which he had always kept smooth shaven, had grown sharper and thinner, and his long hair hanging about his shoulders, had turned from black to gray ; yet his eyes was as true and his hand as steady as when, in his youthful days, he carried away the prize at the shooting match. His visits to the plantation became more frequent and his stays longer, for the old man grew lonesome in his hut, and he was ever a welcome guest at the Tompkins mansion.

Sixteen years had made a wonderful transformation in the politics of the country. The Whig party had been swallowed up by the Republican or Abolition organization. The seeds of freedom, sown by Clarkson, Brown and others, had taken root, and, in the Fall of 1860, bade fare to ripen into a bounteous harvest. The Southern feeling against the North had grown more and more bitter, and the low, rumbling thunders of a mighty storm might have been heard—a storm not far distant, and whose fury naught but the blood of countless thousands could assuage.

" In the beginning, God created Heaven and the earth, and all that was in them, in six days, and rested on the seventh."

The speaker was Crazy Joe, the time, midsummer of 1860, the place the banks of a creek at the foot of the mountains, not more than two or three hundred feet from Uncle Dan's cabin.

"Then the book says God made man out of clay. Josephus says he called the first man Adam, because Adam means red, and He made him out of red clay. Now, if man could once be made out of clay, why not now? Maybe God will let me make a man, too."

Filling his hands with mud, he set vigorously to work. No sculptor could have been more in earnest than was Crazy Joe. He rolled and patted the mud into shape, first the feet, then the legs, than the body. Occasionally the body would tumble down, but he patiently set to work again, persevering until he had body, arm and head all completed. His mud and man was a little over five feet in height, and greatly admired by his maker and owner.

"Now I have accomplished almost as much as God did," soliloquized Joe. "I have made a man of clay; it only remains for him to speak and move, and he will be equal to any of us."

He went to the cabin and acquainted Uncle Dan with the wonderful work he had performed, and asked him to come and see it. The next day he went to view the object of poor Joe's two days' labor, greatly to Joe's delight. Uncle Dan then returned to his cabin for his gun, and Joe went to Snagtown, which was between Mr. Tompkins' plantation and the hunter's cabin.

Joe there informed the storekeeper, the village postmaster, and a few others, of his remarkable piece of handiwork, and asked them to come and see it. They promised to go the next day, if Joe would stay all night in the village.

Joe stayed, and that night there came a heavy rain. The creek overflowed aud Joe's mud man was washed away. He conducted a party of hunters to the spot next morning, but the man of clay had vanished.

"He must have walked away," said Joe shaking his head in a puzzled manner. "He has gone off, though I cautioned him to wait until I came back."

The hunting party explained to Joe that his mud man had become tired of waiting, and left, and went off themselves, leaving the mortified Joe searching about the soft soil for tracks of the missing mud man. His search for the trail took him to Snagtown.

Patrick Henry Diggs, whom we met in his boyhood as the youthful orator at Mr. Tompkins' was, in 1860, a lawyer. His parents were dead, leaving him a limited education, a superficial knowledge of law, and a very small property. The paternal homestead was mortgaged, but Mr. Diggs still kept old Mose, for the sake of being a slaveholder and maintaining aristocratic appearance. Mr. Diggs had but little practice, and found it a difficult thing to make his own living. He was about twenty-eight years old, short and plump like his father. The most peculiar portion of his anatomy was his head. The forehead was low, and the small round head more nearly resembled a cocoanut painted white, with hair on its top, than anything else to which we can compare it. The hair was very thick and cut very short. The eyebrows were heavy and close together, the eyes dark gray and restless, the nose small and straight. The most admirable portion of his physiognomy, Mr. Diggs thought, were his side-whiskers, which were short and dark, growing half-way down his small, red cheeks and coalescing with his short mustache. Mr. Diggs was exceedingly aristocratic, and wore gold-rimmed spectacles on his short nose. These glasses, which gave him a ridiculous appearance, were removed when he wanted to read or exercise his unobstructed vision. His friends tried to persuade him to give them up, but in vain. And with his glasses on his nose, his head thrown back in order to see persons of ordinary height, and his fat little hands in his pockets, he strutted about the streets of Snagtown.

Mr. Diggs, like his father, was a politician. In the campaign of 1860 he was a candidate for the district attorneyship of his county. His dingy little office, with its scant furniture and exceedingly small library, was deserted, and he spent most of his time on the streets, discussing the political issues. On the day that Crazy Joe was in search of his mud man, Mr. Diggs, as usual was strutting about the streets, his hands in his pockets, his glasses mounted on his nose, wherefrom a very evident string extended to his neck.

"I tell you," said Mr. Diggs, closing his little fat right

hand and striking therewith the palm of his little fat left hand, "I tell you, sir, I—I do not favor outlawry, but I do believe one would be doing our country a service by hanging every man who votes or attempts to vote the Abolition ticket."

"Oh, no, Mr. Diggs," said Abner Tompkins, who chanced that day to be in Snagtown, and overheard the remark; "the ballot is a constitutional privilege, and no man should be deprived of his right."

"Yes—ahem—ahem! but you see, when there is a man on the track who, if elected, will set all *our* niggers free, we should object. You know—no, you don't know, but *we lawyers* all know—that private property can not be taken for public use without a just compensation, and still the Abolition candidate will violate this portion of our constitutional law."

"You don't know yet; Mr. Lincoln has not yet declared what he will do," replied Abner.

"Has not? Hem, hem, hem!" Mr. Diggs stumped about furiously, his head inclined backward in order to see his companion's face through his ornamental glasses, while he cleared his throat for a fresh burst of thunder. "Has not, hey? Hem, hem! He might as well. We all know what he will do if elected. And I'll tell you something more," he added, walking back and forth, his hands plunged in his pockets, while seeming to grow more and more furious, "if Lincoln is elected there will be *war!*" (Great emphasis on the last word.)

At this moment Crazy Joe, who had reached the village in search of his mud man, came up to the excited Diggs, and, laying his hand on his arm, in a very serious voice said, said:

"Say, why didn't you stay where I put you until I showed you?"

"What do you mean?" demanded Mr. Diggs, pausing in his agitated walk, and gazing furiously into the lunatic's face, for he suspected some one of attempting to play a joke on him.

"What made you go away before I showed you?" said Joe, earnestly, gazing down upon the furious little fellow.

"I—I don't understand what you mean," said the puzzled

Mr. Diggs, drawing himself up to his full height, which was hardly imposing.

"When I make a man of mud, and go off and leave him, to get people to come and look at him, I don't want him to go off, as you did, before I come back."

Abner Tompkins, and several others, who had heard the story of Joe's mud man, were now almost bursting with suppressed merriment.

"I can't tell what the deuce you mean?" said the angry Mr. Diggs.

"I made you out of mud and clay, and left you standing by the big tree at the creek while I went to get some people to show you to, that I might convince them that man was made out of clay, but before I got back you walked of. Now, why didn't you stay until I showed you?"

The men gathered about Mr. Diggs could no longer restrain themselves, and burst into peals of laughter, which made Mr. Diggs furious.

"This is some trick you are playing," he cried, and, turning upon his heel, he strutted away to his office, where he shut himself up for the next two hours.

"The joke spread rapidly, and in two hours every one in the village knew that Crazy Joe claimed Mr. Diggs as his mud man; while poor Joe, satisfied that he had found the object of his creation, consented to go home with Abner.

CHAPTER VI.

A TRANSITION PERIOD.

All Snagtown was astonished one day when a flaring handbill announcing that Abraham Lincoln and Stephen A. Douglas would speak in that unpretentious little village. Their presence there was due to the accident of missing connections in passing from one city to another.

It would have been hard to say whether the citizens of

Snagtown were more astonished or indignant. A public meeting was called the day before the Abolitionists were advertised to speak, to determine what means could be taken in this emergency. The Mayor presided, and the residents, not only of the village, but of all the surrounding country, urged to be present.

"I tell you, gentlemen—hem! hem!—it will never do," said Mr. Diggs, as he strutted about, his glasses on his nose, casting upward glances into the faces of those who were discussing the question. "Hem! hem! hem! I tell you it will not do at all," and he expectorated spitefully upon the pavement. "We must prevent Lincoln's speaking here, if we have to mob him. He comes not only to deprive us of our slaves, but to destroy the flag of Washington and Marion, the glorious Stars and Stripes! I, for one, am in favor of saying he shall not speak."

"So am I," said another.

"And so am I," said a third.

"And I, and I, and I," came responses from many voices.

"Hem, hem, hem!" began Mr. Diggs, shrugging his shoulders, and moving about furiously, indicating thereby how much in earnest he had become. "I tell you we must not permit it. Why, it's treason. Yes, sir; he teaches treason, and it's our duty, as law-abiding citizens, not to permit him to speak."

"Well, now, do you make them pints, when we have our meetin' to-morrow night," said an illiterate Virginian.

"Hem, hem, hem!" began Mr. Diggs, thrusting his hands deep into his pockets, his head on one side, kicking his feet alternately one against the other. "I will. Hem, hem! I am going to make a speech just about an hour long—ha! ha! ha!—so that no one else will get a chance to put in a word, and we shall have it all our own way." The young lawyer, highly pleased with the favor that he flattered himself he was gaining politically, finished his sentence with a gleeful chuckle, and strutted about, swelling with his own importance.

All over the village could be seen groups of men, from five to twenty in number, discussing the propriety of allowing "Abe Lincoln" to speak in the village. A majority seemed opposed to it, and a few of the more reckless spirits talked of tar and feathers and fence rails.

The evening for the public meeting, which was to decide the all-important question, arrived. The town hall was crowded to its utmost capacity. Mr. Tompkins and his two sons were present, and so was Uncle Dan, the mountaineer. The meeting was called to order and the Mayor took the chair. He was a man past the meridian of life, a slaveholder and a royal Southerner. The long, white beard falling down upon his breast gave him a patriarchal look.

The uproar and confusion of tongues were hushed, and all awaited the speaker in anxious silence.

A call was made on any one present to state the object of the meeting. A man sprang at once to his feet, and succinctly informed the chairman that the "object of th's meetin' is to determine the question whether or not it is best to 'low Abraham Lincoln, the great Abolitionist, to speak in the town. I believe them's all the pints to be discussed," and he sat down. Another and more voluble speaker arose and addressed the meeting. He was of the class called "fire-eaters," and was strongly and directly opposed to Lincoln's visit to Snagtown. His speech was replete with the vilest vituperations his brain could conceive, or his tongue utter, against the Republican party. He regarded them as robbers, as enemies who should be shot down at sight, and he was in favor of greeting Abe Lincoln with tar and feathers if he dared show himself in Snagtown.

Several others spoke in the same vein, and then Mr. Diggs rose. His speech of an hour proved not half so long. It was full of empty-sounding words and borrowed ideas, for there was little originality about Mr. Diggs.

All, so far, had been against the proposed debate between Lincoln and Douglas, but now a man rose in the audience whose word always carried weight. It was Mr. Tompkins, the planter.

"Mr. Chairman," he began, in even, modulated tones, "I am, indeed, surprised that men of intelligence should give vent to such expressions and such feelings as we have heard this evening—men who know the law, and claim to be law abiding citizens. Are we savages or border ruffians, that we must be swayed and controlled by mob law? Have we not a Constitution and Constitutional privileges? Have we not statute laws to protect us against wrongs which others may inflict? Then why resort to mob law? Why disgrace our fair State and put the blush of shame on all good citizens by attacking, like outlaws, a stranger among us? Our Constitution gives to all freedom of speech, and we have no right to deny any man this Constitutional privilege."

Mr. Tompkin proceeded quietly but forcibly, pointing out to the malcontents the error of their plans. In conclusion, he said:

"I may be the only one in the house who opposes these views, but as one I say this, though I be alone. I will oppose with violence the attempt to injure Mr. Lincoln. You are not compelled to vote for him, even to hear him speak; but if Mr. Lincoln comes here, by Heaven! he shall speak."

"So say I, an' I swar if any sorry hound attempts the mobbin' business, he'll have to cross my carcass fust." The speaker was Uncle Dan, and as he spoke he drew up his tall figure by the side of Mr. Tompkins, holding his ominous-looking rifle in his hand.

Abner also rose and took his place at his father's side, but Oleah kept his seat. This was the first visible difference of opinion between the brothers.

Several who had been emboldened by Mr. Tompkins' words now declared that they thought it best not to oppose Mr. Lincoln's speaking there, as it would increase his popularity in other localities.

One or two of the more fiery replied, maintaining that their case was beyond the remedy of civil law; that mob law was the only law which should be meted out to scoundrels and Abolition thieves, and if some of the citizens intended to espouse the cause of Abe Lincoln, and fight for him, now was as good as any to settle the matter. A riot seemed inevitable, but a laughable event now happened, changing anger into mirth.

Mr. Diggs, fearing that his legal knowledge would be called into question, now rose and said:

"I wish to make one other statement, in order to put myself right before the people. I knew the Constitutional law referred to by Mr. Tompkins, giving every man freedom of speech, and I can give you the book and the page—"

"Oh, you need not," said a wag in the audience. "Answer this question instead: Are you Crazy Joe's mud man, and why did you leave before he came back to exhibit you?"

"Oh, stop that nonsense! I came here to talk sense, not to hear of a fool's ravings," cried the indignant Mr. Diggs.

But everybody had heard the story of the mud man, and hostile feelings now gave way to laughter. The laugh was kept up until Mr. Diggs became enraged and left the assembly, swearing that they were "all a pack of fools."

A compromise was effected. Mr. Lincoln and Mr Douglas were to be permitted to speak in a grove near the village, but not in the village itself. The next day Mr. Tompkins and Abner, and a few others, with the aid of their negroes, erected a speaker's stand, and arranged seats for an audience of over two thousand persons. There were still low murmurs of discontent, but the most bitter malcontents had been overawed by the firm stand taken by Mr. Tompkins. Many others had caught his spirit, and defied the hostile threats of the opponents of free speech.

The occasion had been so thoroughly advertised by the meeting and the threats and opposition of those who wanted to prevent it, that the whole country for miles around turned out. People on foot, on horseback, in carriages and in wagons, came until thousands were assembled on the spot, many prompted by curiosity to see the bold Abolitionist who dared invade the sacred soil of Virginia and propound his infamous doctrine.

About ten o'clock two carriages rolled in from the nearest railroad station, bearing the two disputants, with friends of each in attendance. There was an eager craning of necks, and a hushed whisper went through that vast audience as the two opponents for the highest political honors of the country descended from the carriage.

"Who are they?" "Where are they?" "Is that big,

two-hundred-and-fifty-pounder Douglas?" "Is that short, stout-built man with big burnsides Lincoln?" and a hundred other questions of a like character were asked.

A few preliminaries were arranged. Mr. George Washington Tompkins was chosen chairman, and took his place on the stand. Two New York reporters were present with note-books and pencils.

The first speaker introduced was Mr. Stephen A. Douglas. His speech—eloquent, patriotic and straightforward—generously concluded with an exhortation to the audience to listen calmly, without any expression of bitterness, to his opponent, who chanced to differ from him on the great question of the day. When Mr. Douglas took his seat, Mr. Tompkins rose and introduced Mr. Abraham Lincoln, a tall man, wearing short, dark whiskers on his chin, and with hair slightly streaked with gray.

A subdued hiss from many lips was heard as the great "Abolition candidate" arose.

After a smile as of compassion upon his audience, Mr. Lincoln began speaking. He talked mildly and candidly, yet freely, notwithstanding the feeling evinced by some of his hearers. Those deep, rich tones rang through the surrounding grove as he clearly and forcibly expounded the principles of the Republican party, showing them to have been either misunderstood or misrepresented by his opponent. Many who had come to prevent the hated Abolitionist from speaking now listened with interest. This was not such iniquitous doctrine after all. Every point made by Mr. Douglas was successfully met, and his own argument arrayed against him. Mr. Lincoln spoke for two hours, and at the conclusion of his address his bitter enemies were forced to admit that he was a man of immense power. His oratory was so grandly sublime in effect that when he took his seat an outbreak of applause, which could not be suppressed, could not be restrained, burst from the spell-bound audience.

Mr. Tompkins went to the meeting a Douglas man, but he left with the full determination to vote for Abraham Lincoln at the coming Fall election, as did Uncle Dan and many others. This was truly a transition period, as the whole world was to learn in a few short months. The Whig party was dwindling away, and slavery was withered and scorched before the fiery eloquence of Lincoln, Sumner, and other similar orators. Freedom was dawning, but it was to be ushered in with fire, and sword, and death.

Mr. Tompkins and his sons were late in coming home that evening. Abner and Oleah sat side by side in the family carriage, yet neither spoke. Hitherto, every event had been fully discussed; every feeling shared by the brothers; but a silence that was almost coolness now sealed their lips. A thousand conflicting thoughts swept through their minds.

Abner was convicted, converted, by the new doctrine to which he had listened, and the melodious voice of the orator was still ringing in his ears as the carriage rolled homeward. He still seemed to see the tall, rugged form and plain face, lit up with something rarer than beauty by his eloquent pleading for four millions of enslaved human beings.

Oleah was in a gloomy mood. He had listened with angry impatience to the exposition of views so different from his own, and that his father should have presided over the meeting, and stood openly side by side with the Abolitionist, stung his Southern prejudices and vexed him to the soul.

The trio were driven home in silence, and parted for the night, without any reference to the events of the day.

At the table the next morning the discussion of the day before was first alluded to. Mr. and Mrs. Tompkins, Abner and Oleah, sat for some moments in silence—a silence both painful and awkward, and, in this family circle, unusual; but Irene entered the breakfast room, bright and unconscious, eager to know all that had passed at Snagtown the day before.

"We heard an excellent speech," said Abner.

"Yes; Douglas did well," put in Oleah.

"I mean Mr. Lincoln," said Abner. "Douglas' speech was good, but his position was entirely demolished by Mr. Lincoln's eloquent reasoning."

"You don't call the harangue of that contemptible old demagogue reasoning, do you?" asked Oleah, astonished and indignant.

"I certainly do," replied Abner. "His reasoning appeared to me clear, and his conclusions logical."

"And I," cried Oleah, laying down his knife and fork in his excitement, "I declare I never before heard so much sophistry, and not very plausible sophistry, either."

"You are prejudiced," said Abner, coolly.

"It is you who are prejudiced. Why he actually asserted we would be more prosperous if there was not a slave in the United States."

"Yes, and proved his assertion," said Abner.

"Oh, you let him pull the wool over your eyes." There was a sneer in his voice. "I tell you there was neither logic nor reason in what he said. No logical conclusions can be drawn from false premises; no assertions can stand unsupported by proof."

"What did he assert that he did not prove?" asked Abner.

"What did he prove that he asserted?"

"You evade my question by asking another."

"Precisely the same plan Mr. Lincoln adopted," replied Oleah.

"You are prejudiced against Mr. Lincoln, Oleah. Now, tell me what he said that any fair-minded man in the world can not agree to?"

"He said that slavery should not wither and blight another inch of territory if he could help it."

"What objection can even a believer in slavery have to that? We have an immense scope of country where slavery is permitted; then why extend it to Territories where it is unpopular?"

"But can you not see what lies in the background?" said Oleah, bitterly. "Mr. Lincoln lifted the curtain high enough for one who was not blinded by his eloquence to see what was behind it. I would not fear to wager everything I own that Mr. Lincoln, if elected, will set free every slave in the United States, before he has been in the presidential chair a twelvemonth."

"Did he not say that such emancipation would be unwise policy?"

"He said so, but his tone and manner belied his words."

"Confess now, Oleah, that you are a little prejudiced against Mr. Lincoln," said the father, good-humoredly.

"You may call it prejudice or what you like, father," Oleah answered, his flushed face showing how deep was his feeling; "but if Mr. Lincoln is elected you will not have a nigger when his term is over, if he should be permitted to take his seat."

"Why, my son, you can't think he would not be permitted to take his seat?"

"That is a question, father. Each State has its rights. Southern people have rights, and rather than be cheated of them they may resort to force."

"Now, Oleah," said Abner, "you don't for a moment suppose that if Mr. Lincoln should be chosen President by the voters of the United States, that any considerable body of intelligent people could be found who would be unfair enough, or foolhardy enough, to attempt to prevent him from taking his seat?"

"I certainly do," answered Oleah, with an air of conviction.

"You are a Democrat; do you not hold with us Democrats that the majority should rule?"

"That has nothing to do with it," said Oleah, hotly. "The North and the East outnumber the South, and they have formed a combination for her ruin, and the impoverishment of her people. They have nothing at stake in Lincoln's election; we have everything. They have nothing to lose—we, all. Our interests conflict. They see an opulent and growing South, and have set their inventive Yankee genius at work to compass its ruin. Our cotton fields, our rice fields, our sugar crops, our tobacco crops, are the production of slave labor, and the abundant wealth of the South excites the emulation of the cold and envious North. If they can deprive us of this slave labor, they will have killed the goose that lays our golden eggs, and may surpass us in wealth and power. This they have determined to do. They have tried it by legislation, and so far have failed. They outnumber us in votes, because there every worthless fellow's vote counts as much as that of a Governor or a man who owns a thousand slaves. How can they accomplish our ruin? By electing as president a man whose every breath is poison to slavery; a man who may, at any time, under the fancied exigencies of the moment, declare all slaves free. Their plans are deep and shrewd, but there are heads in the South as wise as their's, and eyes that can see the danger in time to avert it."

"You are crazy, Oleah," said Abner; ' your very words are treason."

"If treason, then his mother is infected with the same disease, and, in the language of Patrick Henry, 'If this be treason, make the most of it,'" said Mrs. Tompkins, with a laugh, in which all joined.

"I am sure we ought to get at the truth of this question," said Mr. Tompkins; "we have both sides represented."

"Who will judge between us?" asked Mrs. Tompkins.

"All have taken sides except Irene. Which side are you on?" asked Oleah.

"I know nothing about either side," the girl answered, lightly; "so how can I choose?"

Mrs. Tompkins' love for her sunny land was next in her heart to her love for her husband, and forced her to espouse a cause which, to her, seemed patriotic. This was the only question on which she and her husband differed, and it was avoided by both as much as possible, yet sometimes, in spite of their precautions, it would creep into their family conversations.

"Irene is the proper one to act as judge," said Abner.

"Why?" Irene lifted her eyes in wonder.

"Because you know nothing about it."

"Do they make the best judges who know the least?"

"Frequently; and a juror who knows anything of the case he is to pass a verdict on is incompetent, so you are a competent juror, any way, Irene; and as one woman is equal to twelve men you can complete the entire panel."

"I beg pardon of the court," said Irene, rising from the table, "but I can not sit on this jury. I am prejudiced on both sides. I have friends on both sides, and I could not render an unbiased verdict."

"That's no excuse," said Abner.

"If it's not, the new piece of music you bought me is, so I leave you to your discussion, and hope you may effect a happy compromise." She was gone.

There was a moment's silence, and then the rippling music of her voice filled the halls and rooms of the great house.

"I wish the name she bears was rightfully hers, though I am glad she is not my sister," Abner said to himself. The same thought flashed through Oleah's mind, and, as usual, the mobile face betrayed his thoughts. Every one seemed always to understand his feelings.

Irene had just returned from school, an accomplished beauty and an acknowledged belle.

No wonder strange emotions stirred the hearts of the brothers, and that thoughts gained entrance in their breasts which might prove more disastrous than mere political differences.

CHAPTER VII.

THE ELECTION AND THE RESULT.

The election of 1860 was an exciting one. No means were spared to poll every possible vote. Lincoln was the Republican candidate, Douglas a Northern, and Breckinridge a Southern Democrat, and Bell the Whig and "Know-Nothing" candidate, and all four parties worked vigorously.

Mr. Tompkins and his sons reached Snagtown early in the morning. The village was already alive with the stir and excitement. The polls opened at sunrise, and men were soon crowding around them, quarreling, disputing, joking. The morning air was crisp and frosty, and the people were compelled to walk about briskly to keep from being chilled.

A dirty faced urchin, with a pumpkin under one arm and some turnips under the other, paused in front of the polls, and, stretching out his neck like a young rooster achieving his first crow, bawled out:

"Hurrah for Douglas!"

It was the first patriotic wave which had caused an undulation of his infantile breast.

There chanced to be another boy, more dirty than the first, sitting on a fence near by gnawing an apple-core. His "pa" was a Breckinridge man, and, regarding this outburst as a challenge, he threw away the apple-core and fell with fury upon him of the pumpkin and turnips. Coming head first into the stomach of the Douglasite, he sent boy, pumpkin, and turnips into the gutter.

The enraged young Douglasite scrambled to his feet, and, leaving his vegetables behind, started in hot pursuit of the now fleeing Breckinridgeite, while shouts and cheers went up from the many spectators.

Mr. Diggs came along, engaged in conversation with a farmer whom he was trying to persuade to vote for himself and Breckinridge, for Mr. Diggs was a candidate for the office of District Attorney. On occount of his small stature, the candidate was compelled to walk with upturned face, in order to watch the effect of his words upon the tall Virginian. The sidewalk being crowded, they had taken the middle of the street, and Mr. Diggs struck his toe with such force against the abandoned pumpkin that he was thrown down, and, falling on the pumpkin, he rolled with it into the gutter, which was half full of mud and water. Shouts and yells of laughter greeted Mr. Diggs as he scrambled to his feet and picked up the glasses which he had lost in his fall.

"By jingo, Diggs, ye look like Crazy Joe's mud man now!" cried some one from the crowd.

This was too much for the candidate, and, with something very much like an oath, he hurried away to change his clothes.

As the day advanced, the crowd increased, and as electioneering progressed, the crowd became very noisy.

There was Mr. Snag, a direct descendant of the founder of Snagtown, who claimed political honors. He was a candidate for County Judge. He had been one of the pioneers, had bought Indians, bears, wolves, panthers, and rattlesnakes, to establish this growing country. He had always been the workingman's friend, and was now ready to sacrifice himself on the official altar.

Mr. Snag had been a clothing merchant, noted for close dealings with his customers and oppression of his employes; but two or three months before he announced himself a candidate, a change came over him. His harshness of voice and manner grew subdued. He became not agreeable only, but accommodating and charitable. He attended church and the bar-rooms regularly, and was developing into a general favorite. He was welcomed in the most select circles, yet he was not exclusive. No man was too ragged, too dirty, or too drunk to cause Mr. Snag to be ashamed of his society. He was more than changed; he was completely metamorphosed.

On election day he was more affable than ever. He was at hand to lift up a drunken rowdy who had fallen over the pumpkin, and led him at once to the voting place, to poll his vote for himself and Breckinridge. But the pumpkin remained.

Later in the day, two rowdies, from the country, having imbibed too much of the electioneering beverage, got in a quarrel. One struck the other, and he fell by the pumpkin. A friend of the fallen man seized the pumpkin, and broke it into fragments over the other man's head, bringing him to the ground, of course. A general melee was averted only by the appearance of some good-natured candidate, who tried to restore peace, followed by a couple of constables, who at once arrested the malcontents.

In the afternoon Abner and Oleah went up to the polls. The two brothers had been silent during the forenoon, both seeming to avoid the political question which was agitating the Nation.

"Who are you going to vote for," Abner?" asked Mr. Diggs, strutting up to the young planter with a smile he thought becoming a District Attorney. "Is it Breckinridge, Douglas, or constitutional unionist Bell?"

"Neither," Abner answered.

"Who, then, is your man?" asked the inquisitive Mr. Diggs, thrusting his hands deep into his pockets, and tipping first on his heels then on his toes, as he looked up, with an engaging smile, into the face of the man before him.

"I shall vote for Abraham Lincoln," Abner answered firmly.

"Pshaw! you are joking," said Mr. Diggs, his little eyes twinkling idiotically behind his glasses.

"I was never more in earnest."

"Why, man, they'd hang you if you voted for Lincoln!"

"I shall risk it, at all events."

His brother's words brought a sharp pain to Oleah's heart. He stopped suddenly, and laid a detaining hand on Abner's arm.

"Abner, you surely do not intend to vote for that Abolitionist?" he said, with a ring of defiance in his voice.

"I do," was the firm reply.

"For heaven's sake, think what you are about. Do you want to ruin the country?" Entreaty and distress was melting his indignation.

"No, I want to save it," was the calm reply.

"How can it be that you will vote for an abolitionist?"

"Because his principles and mine are the same," said Abner, earnestly.

The brothers were nearer a quarrel than they had ever been in their lives. Oleah's feelings were wounded, and he turned away, leaving his brother to go his way alone.

But three votes were polled in Snagtown for Abraham Lincoln, and Abner Tompkins, his father, and Uncle Dan, were supposed to have cast them.

Late that evening Mr. Tompkins and his sons rode home. The trio were silent and thoughtful, but they little dreamed what that day's work would bring forth.

Great was the consternation of the Southern leaders when the result of the election became known. Reports were fluctuating from the first, yet soon began to show favorable returns for Lincoln. Betting was heavy in Snagtown. In a few days the leaders began to threaten a dissolution, and no sooner was it ascertained beyond a doubt that Mr. Lincoln was elected than they proceeded to put their menaces into execution. At this time secession was rife, the very air was full of it. Southern politicians alleged that Mr. Lincoln was a sectional candidate, pledged to the overthrow of slavery.

On the 20th of December, 1860, a convention in Charleston declared that "the union before existing between South Carolina and other States, under the name of the United States of America, was dissolved."

By the 1st of February, 1861, through the influence of the press and the devices of a few leaders, Mississippi, Florida, Alabama, Georgia, Louisiana, and Texas, following the example of South Carolina, had passed ordinances of secession, and their Senators and Representatives left their seats in the American Congress.

On the 4th of February, delegates from six of the seceded States met at Montgomery, Alabama, and formed a union under the title of the "Confederate States of America." For provisional President they elected Mr. Jefferson Davis, of Mississippi, who had been a Colonel of some note in the Mexican War, a member of Pierce's cabinet, and a prominent advocate of Southern rights in the United States Senate.

But we must now attend to the individuals in this history, whom other historians have neglected.

On the evening of the 23d of December, 1860, Mr. Tompkins and his family were assembled in the large, cheerful sitting-room. The fire-place was piled with blazing logs, and the light and warmth of the room seemed more pleasant, contrasted with the soughing winds and falling snow without.

No thought of the approaching holidays seemed to have entered the minds of any of the group. The brothers were silent and sat apart. The cloud, so small as to be scarcely discernable, was growing larger and overshadowing each. It had first been visible on election day, when they parted on the way to the polls. Though no allusion had ever been made to this conversation, their brotherly union had been shaken. They drove, rode, and hunted together as usual, but there was one question they could never approach without disagreeing, and disagreement was apt to produce disagreeable feelings.

There was a ring at the bell, and the girl who answered the summons ushered in Uncle Dan, closely followed by Crazy Joe.

"Good evenin' to ye all," said the old man, as he entered the cozy sitting room. "How do you all do?"

"Pretty well, Uncle Dan. How are you and Joe this evening?" returned Mr. Tompkins, rising and grasping the hard, rough hand of the old hunter.

"We ar' both purty well," said Uncle Dan, shaking hands with all present. "I tell ye what's a fact, it's gettin' cold out, an' no mistake, snowing just like blazes."

Joe, who was in no talkative mood, took a seat in a corner, and fixed his gaze on the fire.

"I thought from the way the wind whistled it had grown colder. Come, Maggie, fix Uncle Dan and Joe some supper," said the planter.

"Ya-as, fur I'm hungry as a wolf," returned the old man, with the familiarity of a frequent and welcome guest.

"Are you hungry, Joe?" asked Mrs. Tompkins.

"I am, but it is written that man shall not live by bread alone, but by every word of God.'

"I'll put that ar' fellur agin any preacher in the settlement for quotin' Scriptur. He jest seems to know the whole thing by heart."

"Have you heard any news recently?" Mr. Tompkins asked.

"News! Don't talk about news! Jist wait till I've had some supper, an' I'll give ye a little mess o' news that'll make ye hair stand on ye head."

After the mountaineer had partaken of a warm meal, and returned to the comfortable sitting-room, Mr. Tompkins asked

"What is that remarkable news, Uncle Dan?"

"Wall, I kin tell it now," he answered, resuming his seat, "but I sw'ar it war too much for a empty stomach. About two hours ago the news first come to Snagtown, an' now the whole place is wild. The convention, which met at Charleston, South Carliny, three days ago, passed ordernances o' secession, and declar' the State out o' the Union."

"Oh, pshaw! it must be a mistake," said Mr. Tompkins.

"Mistake? Not by a jug full. It ar' a actual fact. The news came in as straight as a crow flies. There war rumors o' it before, but now it's sartin."

"Great heaven! that means civil war."

"It means war, but it wont be civil, not by a jug full.

They ar' already talkin' about musterin' men and gettin' ready to fight. Thar's to be a grand muster and speakin' at Snagtown next Saturday. They say that Mississippi, Florida, Alabama, Georgia, Louisiana, and Texas ar' sure to foller South Carliny, in a few weeks, and maybe all them slave States, even Virginia and Missouri."

"Have the people gone crazy?" cried Mr. Tompkins.

"It's no more than might be expected," said Oleah. "The North has set her foot on the South, and if she feels like withdrawing from the partnership, she certainly has a right to do so."

"Partnership?" put in Abner, with an astonished look.

"It is merely a confederation of States, formed by a compact, and, if one wishes to withdraw, she has the right," answered Oleah.

"Our Government is formed by the people, and not by the States," said Abner.

"Then, why is it not called the United People, and not the United States? Each State is a separate corporation, capable of suing and being sued, contracting and dissolving contracts. They were originally colonies, but when they freed themselves from Great Britain, for protection and safety, they united. Who can doubt that South Carolina has not the right, when she has become capable of taking care of herself, to withdraw from others?"

"There is a great difference between corporations and governments," said Abner. "Our Constitution does not say, 'We, the United States,' 'As the people of the United States, in order to form a more perfect union.' When they belonged to England, they were considered as a whole and not as a part. In the Declaration of Independence, declaring the Colonies free and independent States, does so in the name and by the authority of the good people whom they represented, and not of the States."

"All that sounds very well, Abner," said Oleah, bitterly, "but words will have no effect on an oppressed and downtrodden people. The South will be free—"

"Yes, if they have to enslave one-half of humanity to do so," interrupted Abner.

"That's just the point Abolitionists are driving to, though

few are as honest as you to admit. The slaves make the South wealthy and powerful. The North is jealous and wants to deprive us of the means of wealth. There is but one remedy left us—the same remedy adopted by the Colonies when oppressed by Great Britain—withdraw, rebel."

"You are too hasty," said Abner, more coolly. "You have no assurance that when Abraham Lincoln does take his seat, the 4th of March next, he will abolish slavery. Wait and see."

"Wait and see?" cried Oleah. "Wait until he has withdrawn every gun and armed vessel from the South? Wait until he has overrun the whole country with armed soldiers? Wait until he has bound us hand and foot? Then what can we do? No! Now is the time for action."

"I don't believe Lincoln will free the negroes," said Abner.

"I will stake my life as the wager," said Oleah, "that before his term of office expires, he declares *every negro in the United States a free American citizen*, war or no war. Mark my words and see if I am not a true prophet."

"Come, come, boys, we have had political discussion enough for the present," said Mr. Tompkins.

"Ya-as," said Uncle Dan, "we don't want the civil war to commence to-night; least of all places, heah. One thing sure about it, you youngsters had better let us old folks talk 'bout these things, we can do it without gettin' so red in the face. The whole country is in a bad fix, an' ef it comes to a smash up, I swar I don't want to see it begin between brothers."

CHAPTER VIII.

MR. DIGGS IN A NEW FIELD.

Mr. Diggs was defeated for the office of county attorney by a large majority, but he was young and buoyant, and after a few days of repining began to revive.

A new excitement took possession of him. Strange talk

came to his ears, and his little round eyes glistened with delight from behind his glasses, and his little round lips parted with smiles of pleasure. War on a gigantic scale—a new Nation, with new men at its head—was the all-absorbing topic. The Union was shattered, and a new Nation was rising out of the ruins and fragments of the old.

Mr. Diggs concluded to espouse the cause of the new Nation. He would raise a company of volunteers to fight its battles; he would be captain. From captain he would be promoted for his bravery to colonel, from colonel to brigadier-general, or commander-in-chief. Mr. Diggs' fertile imagination planned a glorious future for himself. Other men had risen from obscurity to renown, and why not he?

He strutted about with his hands thrust deep into his pockets, reveling already in his future greatness. The new and powerful Nation was his all-absorbing theme. When he met any one he would say:

"Well, what's the news, and what's the prospect of war?"

The prospect was very good, every one thought.

One day, talking with a young man about his own age, but cooler and less blood-thirsty, Mr. Diggs said they were too slow about fighting. Since the surrender of Twiggs in Texas no other event had transpired, and such indifference was monstrous.

"Don't be in a hurry, Diggs," said his friend. "Let them have time for consideration."

"There's no need of consideration. I am ready now. I will go, like Marion, to avenge my country's wrongs," said Diggs.

"This is war against our own countrymen," said his friend, "and I don't think there is any place in either rank for me."

"There is a place for me," said Diggs, strutting about with his hands in his pockets and expectorating profusely. "My country needs me, and I reckon there's a place for me."

"Will you take a colonelcy to commence with?" his friend asked, with a smile.

"I don't expect a colonelcy at first," said Diggs. "I

want to start at the foot of the ladder, as captain, and gradually rise until I am commander-in-chief."

"You would make such a noble-looking general!" said a bystander, surveying the fat little fellow.

"You can talk, Howard Jones, but I—hem! hem!—have always had a taste for military life."

"You would make such a fine-looking commander," said Jones. "Mounted on a tall charger you would yourself strike terror to the enemy."

"I can prove that all generals were small men," said Diggs, strutting about.

"Of course they were; but you—you would kill all your enemies. They would die with laughter when they saw a general on a horse seventeen hands high, looking like a bug on a log."

"Oh, talk sense, Jones."

"On a big war-horse you would look very much like a bug on a log," said Jones. "But wouldn't it be grand for Crazy's Joe's mud man to turn out a general?"

"Can't you talk sense, or are you a fool?" roared the exasperated Diggs; and, unable longer to endure the ridicule of his companions, he turned abruptly around and left the crowd gathered about him.

The Winter of 1860-61 passed away; but little had been done in Snagtown save mustering and speech-making. Those in favor of open rebellion were in the minority in the neighborhood, but those in favor of neutrality in the majority; but those in favor of standing for the Stars and Stripes the smallest class of all.

Patrick Henry Diggs was in a dilemma. His ambition pointed him to the battle-field, that his great abilities, which no one seemed to appreciate, might be shown to the world. The idea of a new Nation dazzled him and showed a path as splendor for his willing feet to follow. But he felt reluctant to draw his sword against the flag of Washington and Marion. He was sure, however, that these turbulent times meant something great for himself. He never lost an opportunity to muster in the ranks of the Home Guards or to make a speech.

The eastern part of Virginia seceded on April 17, 1861,

but the northwestern portion, about Snagtown, was at peace, save from the mustering of Home Guards to protect home and families from the incursions of either army.

Oleah Tompkins was an avowed secessionist, attended the Meetings of the Knights of the Golden Circle, and was already sworn to support the Southern cause. Secret meetings were taking place all over the country, and night meetings held three or four times a week.

Mr. Diggs joined one of these secret organizations, and met with them one night in an old school-house which stood on the side of an abandoned road, about four miles from Snagtown in the direction of the Twin Mountains. About forty in all had assembled there, among them Howard Jones and Seth Williams, two men who seemed, Mr. Diggs thought, to live only to annoy him.

Mr. Diggs had come to the meeting with the intention of making one of his most patriotic speeches; but when he discovered his old enemies, their eyes sparkling with mischief, his heart sank within him.

Nearly all present were armed with shot-guns, rifles and pistols, and a guard was placed about the school-house. Preliminary matters settled, Howard Jones rose and addressed the chairman of the meeting, stating that, as they had with them the distinguished attorney, Patrick Henry Diggs, who was in sympathy with the cause, he would like to hear from him.

Despite the stirring times, everybody present was eagerly expectant of fun. Cries for Diggs were heard all over the house. Mr. Diggs' opinion of Jones rose rapidly.

"Mr. Speaker," began Mr. Diggs, rising and gazing about through his glasses, "in the language of one of old

"'I come not here to talk. You know too well
The story of our thralldom.—'"

Here he made a gesture with both hands, which Jones declared looked like a turtle trying to crawl up hill.

"'We are slaves.'"

A solemn pause.

"'The bright sun rises to his course, and lights
A race of slaves; he sets, and his last beam
Falls on a slave.
Friends, Romans, countrymen—'"

"I say," interrupted Seth Williams, in an audible whisper, nudging the orator, "s'pose you leave Rome, and come down to our present age. Give us something about the new Confederacy."

"That's just what I am coming to," said Mr. Diggs, "and I hope you will not interrupt me again." After a short pause he resumed :

"It is no common cause which brings us here to-night. Tyrants and traitors are abroad in the land. A gigantic foe is invading the fair soil of Virginia, and we are here to protect our firesides All law writers, from Blackstone down, agree that all men should protect their homes. Now, fellow-citizens, remember our forefathers all fought, and bled, and died for this glorious Union." [Applause.]

"Touch lightly on that," whispered Jones.

"I repeat" said Mr. Diggs, "that Washington was the greatest man that ever lived." And now, grown eloquent and excited, he mounted a bench and whipped his left hand under the tails of his coat, while he waved his right in vehement gesture.

All the efforts of Seth Williams and Howard Jones to keep him on the track were unavailing. He commenced to speak about the Stars and Stripes.

"Oh, thunder! go back to Rome if you can't make a better secession speech," said Jones.

The truth was that Mr. Diggs, like a great many others at this time, hardly knew which side he was on. When he swore to preserve the Union at all hazards, his astonished friends pulled him down.

A call was made for volunteers, and Mr. Diggs was the first to enroll his name. Though calling themselves a Home Guard, these volunteers were really enrolled in the army of the Southern Confederacy. Oleah Tompkins was among the first to thus espouse the Southern cause.

The clouds of war grew darker and darker every hour. At any moment the storm might burst in all its fury. Snagtown was in a constant state of excitement as the crisis approached. Her more timid citizens trembled with dread.

Henry Smith, a farmer's son, a young man of limited education, but of strong common sense, stood in the street one bright morning, engaged in conversation with Seth Williams.

"Come, now, Harry," said Williams, persuasively, "you had better come in with us. The time has come, or will soon come, when our homes will have to be defended. We shall be overrun with soldierly hirelings, who will rob and burn and murder as they go. Our families will need protection, and this duty devolves on us."

"But, Seth, some say the Home Guard will be marched South into the Confederate army."

"Oh, nothing of the kind," said Williams. "Our only object is to protect our homes from the soldiers of both sides, and to meddle with neither unless they invade our State."

"I think we are justified in protecting our own interests; but, though I despise Abraham Lincoln, I cannot raise my hand against the old Stars and Stripes."

"Oh, there is no danger that you will be forced into the Confederate army. We are only organizing a Home Guard now; if we raise troops for the South, that will be another thing."

"When do you meet again?" asked Harry.

"To-morrow night; we go into camp next week in real earnest."

"Where?"

"On Wolf Creek, about three or four miles away, between here and the Twin Mountains."

"Where do you meet to-morrow night?"

"At the school-house on the road between here and Twin Mountains."

"I will be there," said Harry.

As Williams walked away, a young man who had been observing the two with keen interest, approached Harry and said:

"I can tell what you and Seth Williams were talking about."

"I will give you three guesses, Abner," said Harry, laughing.

"He was trying to persuade you to enlist in the Home Guards."

"That was just it," replied Harry.

"Don't do it, Harry, or you will repent it. I tell you the name Home Guard is only a cover, and every one who enlists will be in the Confederate army in three months. Unless you mean to take up arms against your country, keep clear of the Home Guard."

"I don't want to fight in Lincoln's army, nor do I want to enter the confederate ranks, so I thought the Home Guards would be the place for me."

"Don't you enlist," said Abner Tompkins, "or you will repent it."

As Harry walked away, Mr. Diggs came along, his short legs, in rapid motion, resembling the thick spokes of a wheelbarrow, and his head inclined backward at an angle of forty-five degrees, and his glasses, as usual, on his nose, and his little fat hands thrust deep into his pockets.

"Hold on, Diggs!" said Abner. "I want to speak to you."

"Hem, hem, hem!" began Mr. Diggs. "Good morning, Mr. Tompkins. Well—hem—I am—that is, I am—hem—glad to see you. I was just going to have my man drive me out to your house. Have a little important business with—that is with one member of your family, he—he he!"

"Diggs, I hear that you have enlisted in the Confederate army; is it so?" asked Abner, abruptly.

"Well, sir, I expect—that is, I apprehend, my dear sir, that—you—perhaps are correctly informed."

"Why, Diggs, what in the world do you mean?" asked Abner.

"Oh, our country is too large; should be divided. We intend to build up a vast Southern empire. The North has always trampled on our rights, and it is time for us to resist."

"But how do you intend to resist? By overthrowing the best government the world has ever known? Build up a

Southern empire! Is not the grand old republic established by Washington good enough for you? The North is not trampling on your rights. Your wrongs are imaginary And as to our country being to large, can a nation like ours grow too powerful? Think, Diggs, before you act, or, like Calhoun, you may expect Washington to come to you in sleep, and place the black spot on your hand which Arnold wears in the other world. Think Diggs! Don't raise your hand against your country without well considering the matter.''

Diggs, for a few minutes, was silent, and then he said:

"I think you are right, Abner. I will not prove a traitor to my country. I shall ask to have my name taken off the roll to-morrow night."

"Do so, or you will surely repent it as you live. If you want military honors, seek them in the ranks of your country. There is a call for seventy-five thousand volunteers."

"You are right, you are right. I will go and volunteer. Where shall I go?"

"We are raising a company at the junction, about twenty miles from here."

"I will go day after to-morrow, but I am in a hurry now. I am going to your house on business. The fact is—I don't mind telling the facts to you—I am going on purpose to see Miss Irene. He, he, he! I am determined to see how I stand there, he, he, he!"

Abner started back in amazement, but Mr. Diggs hurried away, without observing his movement.

The consummate fool!" muttered Abner. " The idiot! To think of our Irene!"

Mr. Diggs hurried off with an air of much importance, and ordered Mose to make ready the carriage, and drive him to the Tompkins mansion.

Mose was not as quick of movement as he had been fifty years before, but he managed to have the equipage in readiness by four o'clock in the afternoon.

At Mr. Tompkins' door Mr. Diggs alighted, to be informed by Miss Irene's maid that her mistress was calling with Mrs. Tompkins, and would not return for an hour.

"I will wait," said Mr. Diggs. "I must—hem, hem—must see Miss Irene."

After a few moments of waiting Mr. Diggs became tired of sitting in the house and sauntered out to the piazza, and there met the ladies on their return.

"Miss Irene,—hem, hem, hem," he began advancing. "I am delighted to see you, I—hem—that is—hem—I came on purpose to see you, and—and talk with you, and bid you good-by before I leave for the field of glory. I have joined the Confederate army—hem—no, I mean to say I am going to join the Union army in a day or two. That is, I don't know exactly which army I shall join yet—and I come to bid you adieu."

Irene looked a little puzzled and felt not a little annoyed at this address. There was something she did not like about Mr. Diggs' manner.

"Will you come in?" she said, "and I will see you presently."

Mr. Diggs according re-entered the house, and Irene went up to her room to change her dress. She manage to detain herself until tea was announced and then invited Mr. Diggs to the dining-room.

After tea the little fellow followed her back to the parlor, and she resigned herself to be bored for an hour or more by him, but did not yet suspect the real cause of his visit.

"Hem—hem," began Mr. Diggs, "Miss Irene, these are troublous times."

"They are indeed," answered Irene, from her seat opposite the loquacious Mr. Diggs.

"We don't know one minute what will happen the next."

"No, we do not," said Irene, who really did not imagine what was to happen on this occasion.

"Hem, hem! two large armies are raising."

"So I am informed," said Irene.

"And they mean destruction to each other."

"I fear some damage will be done."

"Hem, hem! Sumter has fallen."

"So I have heard."

"Deuce take it!" thought Mr. Diggs aside, "she is as

cool as an iceberg, and I am getting flurried. What had I better say or do next." Then a short pause.

"Some of your friends will doubtless take part in the coming struggle," he finally said.

"I fear they will be rash enough to do so," she replied.

"And some may go to return no more,"—voice and eyes were growing pathetic.

"Alas! such is too often the fate of war."

"I have concluded to enter the army."

"A great many young men are now talking of going into the army."

"I feel that my country needs my services."

"You are patriotic."

Mr. Diggs felt flattered.

"You are—hem—hem, very kind, Miss Irene, to attribute patriotism to me. Patriotism, true patriotism is one of man's most noble attributes."

"I agree with you."

"But, Miss Irene, it is hard to go, even to our country's aid, and leave behind friends dearer to us than life."

"Mercy!" mentally ejaculated Irene, "does the little fool mean to propose?" Then, still without any encouraging warmth in her tone, she asked, "When do you expect to leave Snagtown?"

"In two or three days at most, and I feel—hem—pardon me, Miss Irene." He rose and drew his chair nearer her's.

"He really means it!" thought Irene, her eyes bright, half with mischief, half with annoyance.

"I have something—hem, hem, hem!—I wish to say to you. I—I—that is—hem—I cannot leave for the field of danger until I—have—hem, hem! until I have revealed to you my feelings."

Mr. Diggs paused, and tried to look sentimental; but a more sheepish, simple-looking specimen of humanity Irene was sure she had never before beheld.

The farce had been carried too far, and she said coldly:

"Your manner and words are quite incomprehensible, Mr. Diggs."

"I will make myself plain," said Mr. Diggs, swallowing

something in his throat, and taking hope. "You shall understand me. I say I cannot leave for the field of battle, cannot face the cannon's mouth, in this suspense—"

"Then don't go, Mr. Diggs," interrupted Irene, with difficulty restraining her merriment, all her pity put to flight by his affectation and conceit.

"I should almost feel inclined to turn a deaf ear to the 'obstreperous trump of fame,' and 'only list to love and thine,' should you command me to stay."

"Sir, you are growing more and more incomprehensible, Let us leave this subject."

"Not yet, oh no, not yet! Wait until you have heard all. I love you, Irene, dearest, and—and—ah! come to my arms and say you will be mine!"

Down he went on one knee, with upturned face and outstretched arms. Poor Irene felt an almost irresistible impulse to laugh, and for a moment dared not speak.

He mistook her silence and again began to plead.

"Speak, O brightest sylph, fairer than the angels, sweeter than—hem, hem!—than the honey in the honey-comb!"

"For mercy's sake, stand up, Mr. Diggs!" said Irene.

"Not until you say you will be mine!" and his arms expanded, like an opened double gate.

"Then Mr. Diggs, I fear you will never reach the field of glory, for the war will be over before you rise from your knees," said Irene.

"Oh! ah! Hem, hem! You cannot be so cruel,"—still kneeling, and leaning further forward, as though to compel her to his embrace.

"Mr. Diggs, you can never be to me more than a friend. Pray, do not pursue the subject further."

"Miss Irene, dear, dear Miss Irene, you utterly wreck my life! I care not a straw for it now!" whinned little Mr. Diggs, turning, still on his knees, towards Irene who had crossed the room, the most pitiful of faces.

No answer.

"You are—hem, hem!—very cruel, Miss Irene," he rose and awkwardly took his seat.

"I regret to have given you pain," said Irene graciously, as, at Mr. Diggs' request, she rang for his carriage, "but I am sure you will soon forget it, and will see that you had mistaken your feelings."

As Mr. Diggs was in the act of getting into his carriage the sound of horse's feet came to his ear, and a moment later Oleah Tompkins galloped up to the side of the old rockaway.

"Halloo, Diggs! are you just leaving?" asked Oleah.

"Yes—hem, hem!—I am going home," said Diggs.

"Well, be on hand to-morrow night without fail, now. We want every member of the company there, as we shall go into camp in a day or two."

"Well,—hem, hem, hem!—Oleah, I have almost concluded not to go. I can not—hem, hem!—take up arms against the flag of Washington."

"Oh, that's abolitionist nonsense! What care you for a flag that will not protect you?"

"That's so," said Diggs.

"Then why should we consent to bow our necks to tyrant's heels simply because the great and good Washington fought under a rag with certain stripes and certain stars upon it?"

"That is so. Hem, hem, hem! 'They first have breathed treason.'"

"Yes, they stole our property. The interests of the North and South are directly opposite. They want to ruin us, and we must protect ourselves while we can. We can not live in peace with the North; the next best thing is to separate."

"That's so,—hem, hem!—that's so," said Mr. Diggs.

"Then why refuse to enter the Confederate army? The South is your country, and if you want military renown seek it in the ranks of your country. If they call you a rebel be proud of the name. Washington and Marion were rebels."

Mr. Diggs was completely won back to the Southern cause; and, assuring Oleah he would be with them the next night, drove away.

CHAPTER IX.

THE CHASM OPENS.

The storm clouds were gathering dark about the Tompkins mansion. The heads of the household were silent on the question, each knowing the different feelings and sympathies of the other. Their sons were also silent, but there was a sullenness in their silence that foretold the coming strife. There was one member of the once happy household who could not comprehend the trouble, whose very gentleness kept her in ignorance of the threatened danger.

Yet neither love nor loving care could keep her from knowing that trouble was brewing. She could not but notice the coldness gradually growing between the two brothers. Brothers whose affection she once thought no earthly power could lessen, were growing daily colder and more and more estranged. Every morning each mounted his horse, and rode away alone, and it was always late in the night when they come home, never together. Gloomy and silent, the morning meal was hurried through, the pleasant conversation that had always accompanied it, was heard no more, if we except the efforts of Irene, who strove with all her power to infuse some of the old-time harmony and brightness into the altered family.

It was the evening of Mr. Diggs' visit to the Tompkins mansion, one of those clear bright evenings when the curtains of night seems reluctant to fall, and the fluttering folds seem held apart to reveal the beauty of the dying day. Irene sat by the window, gazing up at the dark blue vault, and listening to the far-off song of a whip-poor-will upon the lonely hillside. Nature to her had never seemed more calm or lovely. The moon, serenely bright, shed mellow light over the landscape, and the dark old forest on whose trees the early buds had swelled into green leaves, lay in a quiet repose. Only man, of all created things seemed unresting. Far down the road she heard the clatter of horses' hoofs. At all times now, day and night, she heard them.

Clatter, clatter, clatter—sleeping or waking, it was always the same, always this beat of hoofs. To her it seemed as if ten thousand dragoons were constantly galloping, galloping, galloping down the great road : somewhere their marshalled thousands must be gathering. Horsemen singly, horsemen in pairs, horsemen in groups, were galloping, galloping, until her ears ached with the awful din.

As she looked, a horseman came dashing down the hill ; he passed through the gate and down the avenue.

"That must be either Abner or Oleah," thought Irene. "Six months ago, they would have gone and returned together."

When he stepped on the piazza, the moon fell on his face and revealed the features of Abner Tompkins. He came rapidly up the steps and into the house. Staying only a few momemts in the room below, where his parents were, then came directly to Irene's door and knocked.

She bade him come in.

"Irene," he said in tremulous tones, "I have strange news for you. I must leave to-night for months perhaps, perhaps forever, my home, my parents—and you."

Irene sprang to his side eager and excited

"Why, Abner, what do you mean?"

"Is it such a surprise to you? I will try to speak calmly, but I have only a few moments to stay. I have a load on my heart that I must unburden to you."

"What is it?" she said, drawing a low stool to his feet and seating herself she took both his hands in her own. "Tell me what troubles you, let me share it with you. Who should share your troubles if not your sister?"

"Irene, what I have to say will shock you."

"No, no, it will not. If you have done anything wrong, I shall be sure it was not your fault—"

"No, you misunderstand me ; it is nothing I have done," he interrupted.

"Then what is this secret, brother?"

"*I am not your brother.*"

Irene had promised that his secret should not shock her, yet had a bombshell burst at her feet, she could not have been more astonished.

She sprang from the low stool, and stood with clasped hands, the color fading from her face, her slight form swaying as though she had received a blow.

Abner, alarmed, sprang from his chair, and caught her in his arms.

"Irene, Irene, don't take it so," he said, bending tenderly over the white face.

"*Not my brother?* Why you must be mad!" she gasped.

"Irene, I am not your brother, but I love you a thousand times more fondly than a brother could love. It was this I wanted to tell you before I leave you. What, Irene, weeping—weeping because I am not your brother! My darling, let me be nearer and dearer than a brother!"

"Abner, I can not realize it, I can not think!" she said, pressing her hands to her throbbing temples.

"Think of it when I am gone, Irene, for I must go. To-morrow's sun must find me miles from here. But through all the coming strife I shall cherish your image. I shall hope for your love if I return. Now, good-by, my love, my Irene!"

He caught her in his arms, but it was only a sisterly embrace that Irene returned. She could not yet believe that Abner was not her brother.

He went down stairs, she heard his mother's sobs, his father's broken voice; the door opened and closed, and from her window she saw him pass down the avenue, out of sight. Soon she heard a horse galloping down the road, and knew that Abner was riding swiftly away in the gathering darkness.

Completely overcome, and not daring to meet Mr. or Mrs. Tompkins till she had controlled herself, Irene, throwing a light shawl about her shoulders, went down stairs, stepped through an open window out on the broad piazza. The cool night air fanned her cheeks and revived her spirits. She walked through the grounds to a summer house covered with trailing vines whose fragrant flowers filled the air with sweetest odors.

"It can not be, it can not be," she murmured. "He was surely jesting. I an outcast or foundling or a oh! merciful Heaven! I can not endure the thought!" and her beautiful eyes filled with tears. The whip-poor-will's call still sounded from the distant hillside, and soon another sound broke the evening stillness—the tread of a man's feet on the graveled walk. Irene turned her head quickly, and saw Oleah standing in the doorway.

"I thought I should find you here, Irene," he said. "You always choose this arbor on moonlight evenings."

"You have been absent all day, Oleah. What fearful business is it that keeps both my brothers from my side!"

"Ah! Heaven be praised, Irene, darling Irene, that you know nothing of it!"

"Abner left to-night, perhaps never to return he said," she went on, wiping the tears from her face.

"I see you have been weeping, dear Irene. I have more news for you. I too have to bid you what may prove a long farewell. I leave to-night for our camp, and shall soon march to join the main army. But I can not leave you, Irene, without telling you of something I have long kept a secret."

Irene could not speak; sobs choked her voice. Then from Oleah's lips fell those same startling words:

"I am not your brother."

She sat motionless. Then it must be true. They could not both be mistaken, could not both possess the same hallucination. If anyone was mad, it was herself. But Oleah went on in his quick passionate way:

"You are not my sister, dearest Irene, and that you are not gives me only joy. When you were left at our house a tiny baby, I claimed you for my sister, and when I learned you could not be my sister, I said you should one day be my wife. I loved from the first time those bright eyes laughed into mine, and that love has grown with my growth and strengthened with my strength, until it has taken possession of my entire being. O, Irene, Irene, you can never know how deep is the love I have born you from early childhood. I could not leave this old home without telling you that I loved you with more than a brother's love."

He paused, and Irene remained silent.

"Speak, Irene! Will you not speak?"

She was still silent, her large dark eyes fixed and staring, her white lips motionless, her whole form rigid as a statue. She thought of Abner's parting words, and pain and terror filled her soul. Had she entered this happy home only to bring discord, to widen the breach between the two brothers?

"O Irene, Irene," he pleaded, "by the memory of our happy childhood I implore you, speak once more before I go. Say that you will love me, that you will pray for me—pray for my safe return, pray for my soul if I fall in battle!"

The marble statue found voice.

"I will pray for you, Oleah, to heaven day and night, for your safe return."

"But will you give me your love? O Irene, if you only knew how dear you are to me, you will surely learn to love me!"

"I have always given you a sister's warmest love, Oleah," she replied, "and this is all too new, too strange, for me to change so suddenly."

"But you promise you will change?" he asked eagerly.

"I can not promise yet," she said. "I do not know myself, and neither do you comprehend your own feelings."

"Irene, dearest, I have known myself for years. Try to love me, and pray for me," he said, and taking both her hands as she came to his side, "for now I must go." He stooped and pressed a kiss on those white lips, and Irene was alone. Soon she heard again the hoof beats of a flying horse, and knew that Oleah had left his home.

When he had returned to bid farewell to his home, Abner Tompkins, before entering the house, walked down the long gravel walk, through the avenue of grand old elms, until the outer gate was reached. Here he paused a moment, and gazed up at the moon riding through the dark blue, fathomless vault of heaven; then he turned his gaze upon the spacious pillared mansion, his pleasant home, that he was to leave that night, perhaps forever. It was the home of his childhood; beneath its roof dwelt those he loved; and feelings of sadness filled his heart as he realized the fact that he must leave it. On his right lay the great road, the road that, in his boyhood, he had imagined, led to far-off lands and fairy kingdoms; the road he had thought must be endless, and had desired to follow to its end. Across the road was the forest where he and his brother had so often wandered. Every spot seemed hallowed with sacred remembrances of childhood, and associated with every object and every thought was that brother from whom he was gradually drifting away. He stood beneath the old hickory tree, whose nuts they had gathered, and whose topmost branches they had climbed in their adventurous boyhood. To-night all were fading away. He was going to different scenes, to see strange faces, to meet hardships, danger, perhaps death; worse than all to draw his sword against that very brother whose life had so long been one with his.

"Oh, what a curse is civil war," said Abner, with a sigh, "dividing nations, people and kindred." And, leaning against the trunk of the giant old hickory, he stood for a moment lost in painful reverie.

The beat of a horse's hoofs aroused him, and he saw his brother approaching. To reach the house he was compelled to pass within a few feet of the hickory tree, and must inevitably discover Abner, who, however, made no effort to conceal himself. Standing in the shade of the tree as he was, Oleah did not see his brother until he was within a few feet of him, and then could not distinguish his features.

"Halloo, whom have we here?" he said, reining in his horse abruptly.

"Who is there? Speak quick, or it may be the worse for you," cried impetuous Oleah, not receiving an immediate answer.

"It is I, Oleah," said Abner, stepping from under the branches of the old tree.

The two brothers had grown more and more estranged, but as yet there had been no open rupture between them.

"Well, I might inquire what you are doing there?" said Oleah.

"And I might ask what *you* are doing here, and where

you are going, and a hundred other questions. If I were to tell you I was star-gazing you would not believe me."

"I don't know; I might," said Oleah. "You were sentimental at times when a boy, and the habit of looking at the moon and stars may have followed you into maturer years."

"I was just thinking," said Abner, "that this tree is very old, yet very hale."

"It is," answered Oleah; it was a full grown tree when I first remember seeing it."

"Yes, and we have often climbed its branches or swung beneath them."

"That is all true," said Oleah, restlessly "but why talk of that, above all other times, to-night?"

"It brings pleasant memories of our happy childhood. And why not to-night as well as any other time?" said Abner."

"I have reasons for not wishing to talk or to think of the past to-night," said Oleah. "I have enough to trouble me without bringing up recollections that are now anything but pleasant.'

"Recollections of childhood are always pleasant to me," said Abner, "and when storms of passion sway me, such thoughts calm the storm and soothe my turbulent mind once more to peace."

"Have you been in a rage to-night?" asked Oleah, with a smile.

"No."

"Then why are you conjuring recollections of the past?"

"I have not conjured them up; they come unbidden. This night, *above all others*, I would not drive the thoughts of our past away."

"And why?" asked Oleah, uneasily.

"Because this night we part, Oleah, perhaps forever."

Oleah, rash, hot-headed, fiery Oleah, had a tender heart in his bosom, and now he was trembling with emotion, although he made an effort to appear calm.

"How do you know that we are to part to-night?" he asked.

"We are both going from our home, and going in different directions. We are standing on opposite sides of a gulf momentarily growing wider."

A fearful suspicion crossed Oleah's mind. "Do you leave home to-night?"

"Yes."

"Where are you going?"

"To join the army of my country and the Union."

Oleah started back as if he had received a stunning blow in the face. Abner was aware that Oleah had enlisted in the Confederate army, but Oleah did not dream that his brother would enter the army of the North.

"Abner, Abner," he cried, hurriedly dismounting from his horse and coming to his brother's side, "for heaven's sake say that it is not true!"

"But it is true," said Abner sadly. "To-night we separate, you to fight for the cause of the South, I for the preservation of the Union."

"O Abner, O my brother, how can you be so blinded? It is a war between the North and South, the only object of the North being to give freedom to our slaves. You will see if the North *should* be successful, that every negro in the land will be freed."

"And you will see that the North has no such intentions. Mr. Lincoln, although a Republican, was born in a slave State, and he will not free the slaves. But, Oleah, it is useless for us to discuss these matters; we part to-night, and let us—"

"But should we meet," said Oleah, his hot blood mounting to his face, "it will be as enemies. You are my brother now, but when you don the hated uniform of an Abolition soldier you will be my enemy; for I have sworn by the eternal heavens to cut asunder every tie of friendship or kindred when I find them arrayed against our cause."

"Oleah," said Abner, "be not too rash in your vows. Do not make them just yet."

"I have already made them; and whoever confronts me with a blue coat and a Yankee musket is an enemy, whatever blood runs in his veins."

"I pray that we may never meet thus," said Abner. "Rather would I have you find among the slain the body of one you no longer own as a brother."

One of the stable men now appeared, leading Abner's horse. Oleah's hot passion was gone; his eyes were misty, his voice was choked. The brothers clasped hands in silence, and five minutes later Abner was galloping down the great road.

CHAPTER X.

THE BEGINNING OF SOLDIER LIFE.

A curious scene presented itself at the Junction. But before we attempt to describe the former, we will give the reader some idea of the latter. The Junction was the terminus of one railroad and the junction of two others. One of the railroads led to Washington, one to Pittsburg, and one to Baltimore. It was not a large town; a village of perhaps twelve or fifteen hundred inhabitants, blackened by the smoke of engines. The surrounding country was broken and rough, with hills rising upon hills, deep ravines, rocky gorges, and winding streams, lined with a luxuriant growth of pine and maple, while far away in the distance the gray peaks of mountains could be seen.

The Junction was about twenty miles north-east of Snagtown, there being no railroad to the latter place, though there was a hard beaten turnpike, with a daily mail-coach running between the two. Some of the houses about the Junction were of brick, but the majority of wood. There were neat little cottages, looking like fairy abodes, amid the green vines and blooming flowers of Spring-time, and there were cottages neither neat nor fairy-like in aspect; the log hovel, showing signs of decay and neglect. But the village, taken as a whole, was a very pretty place.

It was about the 1st of May. The President had called for eighty-two thousand more men, finding seventy-five thousand wholly inadequate to put down the rebellion. Virginia was at this period in a constant state of alarm. Sumter had fallen, Harper's Ferry and Norfolk Navy-yard were in the hands of the rebels, while a mob, in the city of Baltimore, had attacked Massachusetts and Pennsylvania troops on their way to the defense of Washington.

The Federal Government, on the other hand, was straining every nerve. It had collected about Washington, as speedily as possible, under General Scott, the veteran hero of Chippewa, Lundy's Lane, and the Mexican War, the volunteers who flocked to their country's defense in answer to the President's call. Volunteer companies were raising all over the country. In the extreme Northern States, in the defense of the Federal Government; in the extreme Southern States, in defense of the Confederate Government, and in some of the Middle and Western States, companies were raised for both sides. In fact, there were men in some of the more Northern slave States, who mustered with the rebels and were actually in the Confederate service before they knew it.

In Virginia, as we have shown, both sides were represented. The Junction, on account of its railroad facilities, was an important point to guard, and about three hundred volunteers, under Colonel Holdfast, were here stationed. Of these raw recruits, there was but one company that was a complete organization, uniformed and armed at the expense of the Government. It was a company of mounted infantry, under command of Captain Wardle, armed with musket, uniformed in the Government blue, and furnished with horses in order to scout the country.

The Government found it impossible to turn out arms and clothing fast enough to supply the volunteers at once, and it was late in the Summer of 1861 before they were all equipped. Many armed themselves, as was the case with two hundred of those at the Junction. Their arms consisted of rifles, shot-guns, and such other weapons as they were able to furnish themselves with.

The Junction, as we have said, presented a curious scene. Five tall, white army tents had been erected for Captain Wardle's men, and there were a score or more enclosures, ambitious to be known as tents, made from Virginia wagon-covers, sail-cloth, oil-cloth, sheeting, and bed-ticking. They were of various sizes and shapes; some so small that four men would fill them; others large enough to hold twenty-five. Some of them were square, some round, like Indian wigwams, and others more like a circus canvas than anything we can compare them to.

The tents were a motley assemblage, and so, and to a greater extent, were the men therein sheltered. There was first the company of Captain Wardle, properly uniformed and armed, and intensely military in appearance and behavior. They were always drilling when not scouting the country; the raw recruits standing by, overwhelmed with admiration at their easy proficiency in the manual of arms, or the intricate and mysterious movements of the company drill.

It was early morning, and the smoke was ascending from half a hundred camp-fires. The scene was a constantly varying panorama of straw hats, linen coats, broadcloth coats, colored, flannel and white shirts. An orderly sergeant was trying to initiate a squad of raw recruits into some of the mysteries of drilling.

"Remember the position of a soldier," said the orderly. "Heels close together, head up, the eyes striking the ground twenty paces away. Now, shoulder arms! Great Moses! Tom Koontz, can't you learn how to handle a gun? Keep the barrel vertical. Do you call that vertical?"

"What d'ye mean by sayin' vartical?" asked Koontz.

The orderly explained for the hundredth time, that vertical meant straight up and down. He had them then count off by twos, beginning at the right, then he instructed them that at the order of "right face," number one was to take a half step obliquely to the right. and number two a step and a half to the left, bringing them in double file at right face. But when he gave the order, half of the men had forgotten their number. Confusion and dismay resulted, and the long suffering orderly sat down and swore until he was exhausted.

Camp-life was new to all, and its novelty kept all in a perpetual excitement. There was but little discipline. Officers ordered men and men ordered each other. Every one had suggestions to make, and those who knew the least offered the most of them.

"I tell you," said Sergeant Swords to Corporal Grimm, "that tent is not strong The center pole is too weak, and the guy ropes are rotten. It'll go down."

"I always knowed them boys didn't know how to fix a tent," said Corporal Grimm, plying his jaws vigorously on a huge piece of pig-tail tobacco.

"Yes, sir; they've got a good deal to learn yet," said Sergeant Swords, with a sigh.

"I do hate to see any one, who don't know anything about soldier life, pretend to know so much," said Corporal Grimm, who had had ten days' experience before he enlisted in his present company.

"So do I," said Sergeant Swords, who had seen at least six days' service. "They'll find yet they had better take some one else's advice what's had experience. Why, when I was with Captain Strong's men, and we marched forty miles to Goose Creek Bridge to keep the rebels from burnin' it, we fixed a tent up like that, and the first night after we encamped, there came up a rain-storm, and blowed the thing a quarter of a mile into a brush heap."

"Did I ever tell you what a hard time we had when I was under General Preston;" asked Corporal Grimm, by way of introduction to a story which should redound to his own greatness.

"No, I believe not," answered Sergeant Swords, with more courtesy than truthfulness, for he had heard the story at least a dozen times.

"Well, sir, them was tryin' times," said Corporal Grimm, shaking his head and masticating his quid with the air of a man who has suffered. "Why, sir, we marched eighty-five miles on foot, and all the rations we got was dried bacon, hams, and crackers. Oh, I just thought I would give anything for something substantial to eat, or a drink of coffee! The boys all run out of tobacco, too, an' we had an awful time." The thought of these hardships brought to his face an expression of extreme agony.

"Why didn't you press something to eat? You passed through a country where there was plenty, didn't you?" asked Sergeant Swords.

"Yes, but what could fifteen hundred men do at pressin? Why, they couldn't a got enough to feed one brigade, let alone our whole army," answered Corporal Grimm, who, as much service as he had seen, did not exactly know how many men it took to constitute a brigade.

"We soldiers have hard times," said Sergeant Swords, brushing some of the mud off his blue jean coat. "Wonder how soon we'll draw our clothing and arms?"

"Don't know, but hope soon. I'm tired of these farmer brown breeches. I want a blue coat with stripes on the sleeves."

At this moment there came a blast from the bugle.

"Roll call," said Sergeant Swords.

A general gathering of each company about the Captain's tent followed.

Abner Tompkins was First Lieutenant of the company of which Sergeant Swords and Corporal Grimm were members. He had been with the company now for over a week.

The morning drill was over, and the volunteers were lounging about the tents, on the grass; Abner was leaning with his arm across the saddle-bow of his faithful horse, that he was about to turn out to graze. The mind of the young lieutenant was full of fancies and memories. His sudden departure from home, his interview with Irene, the parting with his brother, all were fresh in his thoughts, and his eyes naturally wandered back toward the road that led to his home. A familiar sight met his view. Coming down the hill, attended by a member of his own company, who had been on picket guard, was his father's carriage driven by the family coachman.

Abner started. Why was he coming to the Junction? The carriage drove up to Abner's tent, and the guard, making what he meant for a military salute, said:

"Lieutenant, here is a man as says he wants to see you."

"All right, Barney, you can leave him here."

The guard turned, and hurried back to his post as though the Nation's safety depended on his speed.

The driver opened the carriage door, Mr. Tompkins alighted, and father and son met with a cordial hand-grasp. Abner led his father into the officers' tent which was at present deserted by its usual occupants.

"Have you seen Oleah since?" asked Abner.

"I have," was the reply.

"Where?"

"At his camp."

"Why, father, how dare you go there, when your sentiments are known to be directly opposed to their cause? It was very dangerous."

"Not very dangerous, since I have a son who is an officer in that army."

"What office does Oleah hold?"

"Second Lieutenant."

"I suppose Seth Williams and Howard Jones are there?"

"Yes, and Harry Smith."

"Harry Smith?"

"Yes."

"Why, he is no Confederate at heart."

"So are not a great many who are in their ranks."

"I have been daily expecting Diggs here," said Abner.

"Diggs, Henry Diggs?" asked Mr. Tompkins curiously.

"Yes; he promised me he would come here and join our company," said Abner.

"He is on the other side," replied Mr. Tompkins.

"What?"

"He is on the other side. He is a corporal in Oleah's company."

"Why, the contemptible little scamp! He promised me faithful he would come here and enlist."

"He is a man who cannot resist persuasion, and some one on the other side got the last persuade of him."

"True, Diggs has no mind of his own," said Abner.

"I have sometimes wished that my sons' minds were not quite so decidedly their own," said the planter with a sad smile and a doubtful shake of the head.

"Did you try to persuade Oleah to leave the Southern army?"

"No; he has conscientiously espoused the cause, and I would not have him do violence to his conscience. I talked to him mostly about you."

"About me?"

"Yes. I told him, as I now tell you, that if he had a principle which he thought right, he was right to maintain it; but while he fought in one army to remember always that he had a brother in the other, and, if by chance he should meet that brother in the struggle, to set brotherly love above party principle."

" What did he say ?"

" He promised that he would, and now I have come for your promise also."

" I make it freely, father. It has always been my intention to meet Oleah as a brother whenever we meet."

" This is now a sundered Nation," said Mr. Tompkins, "and its division has divided many families. It may be that brothers' swords shall drink brothers' blood, but, oh Abner, let it not be your fate to be a fraticide."

Mr. Tompkins lingered until late in the day, when he entered his carriage, and was driven towards his home.

That night the Colonel sent for Captain Wardle and told him that he had been informed of a body of rebels collecting on the headwaters of Wolf creek, not more than three or four miles from Snagtown, and instructed him to take sixty of his own company and fifty of the new recruits and proceed there the next day, starting early in the morning, to break up the rebel camp, and capture every person found there.

There was another motley and undisciplined body of men encamped on Wolf creek. Wolf creek was a clear rapid stream, whose fountain-head was in the Twin Mountains. It came dashing down their craggy sides in many small rivulets, which, at their base, united to form this beautiful stream that flowed through a dark, dense forest in the valley, passing at one place within a half a mile of Snagtown.

The camp, however, was three or four miles further up the stream, in what the military leaders considered a more advantageous location, on the main road that lead from Snagtown by the Twin Mountains to a village beyond.

The numbers of the Confederates were increasing daily. As soon as the volunteers went into camp, those in sympathy with the cause came in from all the country round, until between three or four thousand men had assembled, ill armed, undisciplined, confident, and full of enthusiasm. But one company had yet elected officers. Colonel Scrabble, an old Mexican soldier, was commander-in-chief of this force. Of the organized company, Oleah Tompkins was second lieutenant and Patrick Henry Diggs was corporal.

Mr. Diggs had experienced considerable disappointment when the company failed to elect him captain ; when a vote was taken for first lieutenant, he made a speech which secured him two votes; for second lieutenant, Oleah Tompkins was chosen. He was about to retire from the field and from the army, and had even applied for his discharge, when the captain appointed him corporal.

He did not like to accept a position so insignificant, but, when he reflected that there were a number of corporals who had risen to be generals, and that the prospect for his promotion was good, he became pacified, and very reluctantly assumed the office.

The spot where the Confederates were encamped had formerly been used for holding camp meetings ; it was a grove, surrounded on every side by a dense forest and the high road, which led past the place, approached it in so circuitous a manner that it could not be seen fifty rods either was.

The Confederates had chosen so secluded a spot that it was evident they wished their camp concealed. Wolf Creek bounded their camping ground on one side. The tents were fantastic affairs, and could vie even with those of the Junction in variety of shape and material, and showed quite as great a lack of skill in arrangement. The men were of almost every class, dress, and nation; but the dark, sharp-cut Southern feature predominated.

They were firey, quick-tempered men, whose rashness nearly always excelled their judgment. Most of them were dressed in the garb of Virginia farmers, without any appearance or pretense to uniform. Their arms were shot-guns, rifles, and ancient muskets—a few of them excellent, but the majority inferior. As a class, they were men who enjoyed fox chases, wolf hunts, and horse races, and the present phase of their life they appeared to regard as a frolic.

Camp fires were smoldering, and camp kettles hung suspended over them. As at the Junction, there was a great deal of talk about camp life, and suggestions by the score were indulged in. The sergeants walked about with much dignity, and our corporal had grown to feel the importance of his office; he had the drill manual constantly in his hands, and conned its pages with the uttermost diligence.

Corporal Diggs was a general in embryo, and his name was yet to ring through the trump of fame, until, among all nations it should become a household word; he felt within his soul the uprising of greatness, as he looked through his glasses with the air of one born to command. And to think that he was an officer already—a corporal, men under him, to whom his word was law! Truly, tne dream of his life was now beginning to be realized, his dearest desire was about to be fulfilled.

Corporal Diggs had, from his earliest boyhood, thirsted for military glory; he had poured over the pictures of famous generals represented as leading the dashing cavalry on their charge, amid blind smoke and flashing swords, or guiding the infantry by a wave of the hand, and had longed for an opportunity to do likewise. True, he was a mere corporal, but it took only a few sweeping strides from corporal to general. The soldiers did not seem at present to regard him with awe and admiration, but they had not yet seen him under fire; they did not know how cooly he could undergo so trying an ordeal. He longed for battle as the war horse that already sniffs the fray. Once in battle, he would so signalize himself by his coolness and daring as to be mentioned in the colonel's report, and would undoubtedly be at once promoted.

Corporal Diggs was full of fire and running over with enthusiasm. No man in all the camp seemed as busy as ne; his tireless, short legs stumped about from place to place continually, his head thrown back, his eyes shining brilliantly through his glasses, a rusty, naked sword in his right hand. Occasionally the official duty of Corporal Diggs brought him to a standstill and then he would thrust the point of his sword in the ground, and lean upon it. As the sword was a long one when standing upon end, it came near reaching the chin of the born warrior who carried it.

No one could appreciate the greatness of this great man. "Why did you leave before I showed you?" and other such frivolous phrases were constantly sounded in his ears.

The gallant soldier sometimes became highly indignant, b. he soothed himself with the reflection that all this would be changed after they had once witnessed his powers on the battle-field.

It was the middle of the afternoon. The recruits had exhausted all their means of amusement, and were lounging about under the shade of the trees, or cleaning their rusty guns.

"What shall we do to keep awake this evening?" said one fellow, lazily, reclining flat on his back under the broad branches of an old elm.

"Dunno," said another, who was almost asleep.

"Let's get up a scout," proposed a third.

"I'll tell you how we can have some fun," said Seth Williams, his eyes twinkling.

"How?" asked half a dozen at once.

"Get Corporal Diggs to make a speech."

"Good, good!" cried a number springing to their feet. The very thing."

It was finally decided to present to Corporal Diggs a written petition to address the members of his company on the question of the day, and enthuse them with his magnificent and stirring eloquence. The Sergeant himself circulated the petition, and had half a hundred names to it in less than fifteen minutes.

Corporal Diggs had just returned from inspecting the guard when the petition was presented to him.

"Well, yes—hem, hem!" began the soldier, orator, and general in embryo, "I have been thinking for some time that I ought to make the boys a speech. "They—hem, hem!—should have something of the kind occasionally to keep—to keep their spirits up."

"Well, come right along now," said the Sergeant pointing to where nearly a hundred had gathered around a large elm stump. "They're waiting for you."

Corporal Diggs felt that his star had risen, and with a face full of becoming gravity, which the occasion and his official position demanded, he went toward the place indicated, dragging his long sword after him, much in the same way a small boy does the stick he calls his horse.

The crowd received him with enthusiastic cheers, and Corporal Diggs mounted the stump.

"Hem, *hem*, HEM!" he began, clearing his throat by way of commencement. "Ladies and gentlemen"—a slight titter in the audience—"I mean fellow citizens, or, perhaps, fellow soldiers or comrades would be more suitable terms for addressing those who are to share my toils and dangers." [Cheers.] "'I come not here to talk,' as one of old said, for you know too well the story of our thralldom.' What would the gentlemen have? Is life so dear or peace so sweet that they must be bought with slavery and chains? There are those who cry 'Peace, peace!' but there is no peace! The next gale that sweeps down from the North will bring to our ears the clash of resounding arms. [Cheers.] But, my comrades, I—hem, hem!—feel it my imperative duty to tell you that the foe is near at hand, and battle, glorious battle, where 'flame and smoke, and shout and groan, and sabre stroke' fill the air." [Vehement cheering, and Seth Williams trying to kick the bottom out of a camp kettle.]

"Gentlemen of the jury—hem, hem!—No, fellow comrades, I mean, gird on the armor of determination, the helmet of courage, the shield of unity, the breast-plate of honesty, and with the sword of the right never fear to hew your way through the ranks of injustice." The orator paused for a moment for the cheering to subside that not a word of that sublime speech should be lost. All the soldiers in the camp, not on duty, had by this time gathered about the speaker.

"Gentlemen of the jury, or fellow soldiers, I should say, hem!" he resumed, "it may be that some day I shall have the honor of leading you to battle. Then, fellow citizens, I hope, nay, I verily believe, that not one in this camp will be found skulking or hiding. [Cheering, and cries of, "No, no!"] May that day come that we may all prove to the world that we have a principle, and that we can defend it. [Cheers and cries of, "Let her come!"] Gentlemen, hem! —comrades, liberty is in the very air, and the citizens of the South breathe it, and now that the tyrants of the North have seen fit to loose the war dogs, not one of the swords of Columbia's true sons shall be returned untarnished to its sheath. [Long continued cheering.] While this voice has power to speak, and this tongue power of proclaiming the truth, the wrongs of the South shall be told. [Cheers and cries of "You bet."] And while this eye has the power of sight to aim the gun, and this arm strength to wield the sword, they shall be used wholly for the South." [Cheers and cries of "Hurrah for Diggs."] Some scamp propounded the long unanswered question, "Why didn't you wait till I had shown you?" but the orator is unmoved by this attempt at ridicule. "Gentlemen of the jury, or, rather, fellow comrades, when I think of all our wrongs, I long for the day to come, when we may met the foe face to face. Yes, face to face, with bristling steel between, and canopies of smoke rolling above and mixing with the clouds of the heavens. Then shall they feel the arm of vengeance. Oh, ye boasters of the North," growing very loud and eloquent, while his right hand, with fingers all apart, cleft the air, "if you would know with whom you have to deal, come on! [Cheers and cheers of "Come on!"] Cowards, boasters, how I long to meet you where the canon roars—the glad thunders of war. [Cheering, and one young recruit trying to stand on his head.] I tell you that we can now say with the poet :

>"'Hark, hark, the trump of war awakes
>And vengeance from the vigil breaks,
>The dreadful cry of carnage sounds,
>It seems that hell's let loose her hounds.'

"My brave comrades, remember Marion and Washington of old, and be like them, ready to lay down your life for your country. [Wild cheering.] I am ready to die in defense of the land that gave me—"

Bang, bang, bang! went three muskets about two hundred yards up the creek.

"Oh, Lordy!" yelled Corporal Diggs, and he performed a leap which a frog might have envied, alighting from the stump on his hands and knees on the ground.

Bang, bang, CRASH! went half a hundred guns in the same direction, and the air seemed alive with whistling balls.

"What is that?" cried Seth Williams.

"To arms! We are attacked!" shouted Colonel Scrabble.

"Run for your lives," cried the four pickets who now came in sight, setting the example.

As the pickets had seen the enemy, and the Colonel had not, the men considered that the former knew more of their number. As for the gallant Corporal Diggs, after one ineffectual attempt to spring on a tall horse, he ran rapidly away to the woods as fast as his short legs would carry him, which Seth Williams afterward declared was faster than any horse could. It was in vain that the officers attempted to rally their men. The blue-coated soldiers of Captain Wardle, after the first fire, came galloping into view out of the woods, and, dismounting, fell into line of battle just in the edge of the cleared space where Corporal Diggs, not two minutes before, had been entertaining the entire camp with his eloquence. They poured another volley into the camp, which awoke the echoes of the forest and seemed to the terrified recruits to shake the Twin Mountains to their very center. They then charged down on the enemy.

"Oh, Lordy, Lordy, have mercy on my soul!" gasped Corporal Diggs as, impelled by the roar of fire-arms in his rear, the whistling of bullets among the trees, and the thunder of plunging horses on every side, he went over the ground at a rate of speed which almost took away his breath. He ran as he never did before. He crushed through underbrush, tore through thorns, dodged under limbs, and leaped logs, in a manner that would have astonished any one who took into consideration the shortness of his legs. He was leading the entire force, as, in his speech a few minutes before, he had said he would. He was the first to start, and as yet was ahead of any footman.

Many of the horses, about four hundred in number, which had been picketed about the camp, had broken loose during the firing and were running, plunging, and snorting through the thick woods, much to the terror of poor Diggs, who imagined a Union soldier on every horse, and supposed that there could not be less than fifty thousand of them.

On, on, and on he ran, for about three miles, when, coming up to a steep bank of the creek, he found it impossible to check his headlong speed, and tumbled head first into it.

Down into the mud and water he went, sticking his head so deep into the latter, that it was with some difficulty he extricated himself. When he washed the mud out of his eyes, he espied a drift a few feet away, and going to it managed to conceal himself amid the brush and logs.

"Oh! Lordy! Lordy! have mercy on me! Oh, I know I shall be killed!"

"Thump, thump! crash, crash! splash!" It was simply one of the frightened horses that had broken away from the camp, but it put Corporal Diggs in extreme terror as he supposed it to be a regiment of Union cavalry.

"Oh, I ought never to have engaged in this unholy cause! I thought I was in error. I'll leave the Southern army sure, if ever I get out of this."

For hours Corporal Diggs was kept in a state of perpetual terror by fleeing men and horses.

CHAPTER XI.

MR. TOMPKINS' PERIL.

Since the rebellion had assumed such proportions, and men, who had made war with pen and tongue had taken up the sword, Mr. Tompkins had been careful not to allude to the merits of either cause in his family. He had been made to feel the bitterness of the strife that, in dividing the Nation, had divided his home. He felt most keenly a parent's agony at having his two sons in hostile armies. That, at any hour or moment, they might meet in opposing ranks, was a horrible possibility, which, do what he would, he could not banish from his mind. He knew, too, that the companion of his life held views antagonistic to his own on the question of the war. So he was reticent on questions on which every one else was eagerly expressing opinions; but in his heart, he was firmly convinced of the justice of the Union cause. Though Mrs. Tompkins, like her husband, was silent as to her belief, she was as firmly convinced that the cause of the South was just. How could she, with all her native pride and prejudices, look on the subject in any other light? Her sunny home, the home of her childhood, the pride of her maturer years, was to be the field of contest. One side must win. On one side were arrayed the cold, calculating strangers of the North; on the other the warm-hearted, generous people of the South; but what endeared to her, more than any other circumstance, the Southern cause, was that it was based on principles which she believed just and right.

Americans, more than any other Nation on earth, fight from principle. Other Nations blindly follow king or emperor, regardless of right or wrong, but the American fights from principle approved by his judgment and based upon his earnest convictions.

Mr. Tompkins did not reflect on the dangers that might arise to himself from visiting two hostile armies. It was the day after his visit to the Junction that he chanced to be at Snagtown. He found the village in a state of excitement in consequence of "a large army of United States soldiers" having passed on their way to Wolf Creek. The villagers, unaccustomed to the sight of large bodies of men, put the number of Captain Wardle's command at several thousand, when in reality it did not exceed, including his own company and the others with him, one hundred and fifty.

"Where were they going?" inquired Mr. Tompkins of the village grocer.

"Dunno," was the reply.

"Which way did they go?"

"Towards the Twin Mountains."

"There is no question as to where they was goin'," said the blacksmith. "They was takin' a bee line for the camp on Wolf Creek, and they're going to gobble up our boys along there; but although they outnumber them twenty to one, they'll find the boys game."

"Where did these troops come from?" asked Mr. Tompkins.

"From the Junction."

Mr. Tompkins very well knew that the entire force at the Junction did not number over four hundred men.

While the loungers and others were attempting to estimate the number of the troops, and discussing the probable result of their visit to Wolf Creek, a volley of musketry saluted their astonished ears.

"There, they are at it!" said the blacksmith, smoking his pipe more vigorously.

The volley was quickly followed by another, another, and another. After this, for a quarter of an hour, an occasional shot was heard, but no more regular firing. Various were the conjectures as to the result of the battle. A frightened farmer, who had been near the camp at the time of the attack, came galloping in, declaring that the ground was strewn with dead bodies; that the Confederates were killed to a man, and other reports almost as wild, increasing the excitement and alarm of the villagers.

To say that Mr. Tompkins did not share the general anxiety would be to say he he was not human. He knew that his youngest son might be lying in the woods either dead or dying. And Abner—had he accompanied the troops sent to the Junction? A thousand conflicting emotions stirred the heart of the planter, and a double care weighed on his mind; His first impulse was to go at once to the scene of the conflict; but a moment's reflection showed him that such a course would be not only dangerous, but foolish. He resolved to return home and await the development of facts in regard to the attack at Wolf Creek.

Mr. Tompkins found his wife awaiting him on the piazza, and he knew by the troubled look on her face that she had learned of the attack. He said nothing about it, for a single glance from each explained all.

"You look wearied, husband," said the wife as he sank into a chair at her side.

"I am wearied," he replied, the troubled look deepening on his face.

A moment's silence ensued. Mrs. Tompkins was the first to break it.

"There has been trouble at the camp on Wolf Creek. I heard the firing."

"Yes," said the husband, "a body of Union troops passed through Snagtown to-day to attack the camp there.

There has been some sharp firing, but nothing definite has been heard of the affair."

An hour or so later there came a clatter of hoofs down the road, and a dozen horsemen paused in front of the gate, opening into the avenue that led to the house. Mr. Tompkins sent to ascertain what they wanted. The leader inquired if Mr. Tompkins lived there, and being answered in the affirmative, he said, with an oath :

"Well, tell him to come out here."

The speaker was a thick-set, low-browed man, dressed in homespun gray, and armed with a sword and revolver. His companions, as coarse as himself, were armed with rifles ; each wore the broad-brimmed black hat then common in the South.

"Does yer want ter see my master?" asked the negro, his black face turning almost white, and his frame shaking with apprehension.

For answer, the leader snatched a holster from his saddle so vehemently that the darkey needed no other inducement to return with all speed to the house.

"What is the matter, Pompey?" asked Mr. Tompkins, as the boy stood breathless before him.

"Oh, gracious, mars, don't know, 'cept they be's a band o' brigantines as wants to see you down at the gate."

Mr. Tompkins smiled at Pompey's terror, and rose to go, but Mrs. Tompkins, who did not like the angry gesticulations of the strangers at the gate, accompanied her husband.

"Is your name Tompkins" asked the ferocious-looking leader, as the planter and his wife paused just inside the gate.

"It is, sir. Whom have I the honor of addressing?" returned Mr. Tompkins.

"I am Sergeant Strong of the Independent Mounted Volunteers of Jeff. Davis, and I have come here to hang you, sir."

Mrs. Tompkins gave a scream and clung to her husband.

"The men are only joking, Camille ; can't you see they are only joking?" said Mr. Tompkins, to soothe his terrified wife.

"You'll find out that we're not joking," said the leader of

the band, dismounting and fastening his horse to an ornamental tree on the lawn. Six of his men followed his example, leading their horses inside the gate, and hitching them to the fence or trees.

"Men what do you mean?" said Mr. Tompkins, who took great pride in his shrubbery. "I do not allow horses to be tied near my trees."

"We'll tie you to one of your trees soon and see how you like it, with a dance in the air."

Mrs. Tompkins clung to her husband, half dead with terror, and Irene came hurrying from the house.

"Go back, Camille; go back with Irene, and wait for me in the house," said Mr. Tompkins. "This is nothing serious."

"Ye'll see, sir, if it ain't somethin' serious," said Sergeant Strong, unstrapping a rope from behind his saddle, and uncoiling it. "The law says spies shall suffer death, and we're going to make an example of you, sir."

"I am no spy," returned the planter.

"Don't suppose I saw ye hangin' 'round our camp, and then shootin' off after sojers at the Junction to come down and lick us! And they just come to-day an' cleaned us most all out, and you shall hang for it." As he spoke he threw one end of the rope over the projecting branch of a large maple tree.

"Those terrible men mean what they say," whispered Irene in Mrs. Tompkins' ear. She had comprehended all in a moment's time. "I will run for the overseer and the field hands."

She turned to fly, but her motive was interpreted, and one of the men seized her around the waist, saying: "No, my purty gal, ye' don't do nothin' o' the kind jist yit awhile."

In vain she struggled to free herself; she was powerless in the man's hands.

Mrs. Tompkins, completely overcome, had fainted.

"Now, boys, we are ready; bring him here," said Sergeant Strong.

Three or four men laid hands on the planter, but he felled them instantly. They did not expect such resistance from a man of his age, and were not prepared for it. It was not until Mr. Tompkins was stunned by a blow from the butt of a rifle that he was secured and bound; he was then led under the tree and the noose thrown over his neck. Mrs. Tompkins lay still and white on the greensward, and Irene was struggling with her captor and screaming for help. No one noticed the horseman who came dashing furiously down the hill.

"Up with him!" cried the Sergeant, and he seized the rope. At this moment the horseman thundered through the open gate, and just as Strong cried, "Now pull all!" the butt of a heavy pistol struck him on the head, and he fell like a beef under the hammer.

Then, with his hand still uplifted, he rode toward Irene's captor, but the fellow had released her and fled; the horseman fired a shot after the rapidly retreating figure. Then, turning on the remainder of the band, he asked in a voice of thunder, "What, in heaven's name, does this mean?"

Mr. Tompkins, for the first time, saw the horseman's face, and recognized his son, Oleah.

"Why, it's the Leftenant," stammered one of the men, his teeth chattering with fear.

"What does this mean, I say?" he again demanded.

"Why, Lieutenant," said one man, who had the rope in his hand when Oleah came up, "Strong said he was a spy, and he had set the sojers on us to-day, and ordered us to punish him; be we didn't intend to hang him."

Oleah's hot temper got the better of him, and he would have shot Sergeant Strong, who was still insensible, and the other ringleaders, on the spot, had not Irene and his father interfered. All danger being over, the servants came flocking to the scene, and Mrs. Tompkins was carried into the house. These men were a part of Oleah's own company. He ordered them to take the Sergeant, who was beginning to recover, and retire into the woods until he should join them. They obeyed and rode over the hill, quite crestfallen, conveying their wounded sergeant.

Oleah briefly told his father of the attack made on their camp. He said they were taken by surprise, their forces scattered through the woods, but he believed not one drop of blood had been shed, although Diggs was missing, as well as several others. It was thought they had been taken prisoners. Then he again mounted his horse and dashed off, to gather up his scattered forces.

CHAPTER XII.

FORAGING.

Captain Wardle's campaign had been a complete success. He had made twenty prisoners, he had secured most of the arms and the camp equipage, with one hundred and six horses. Vain search was made for the bodies of the dead who had been slain in the fight, none could be found; and from the marks of the bullets on the timber one would judge that no one had been touched, as no trees had been struck lower than twenty feet.

Camp-kettles, tents, rusty fire-locks, and weapons of nearly every description, were scattered about over the ground. The soldiers, the ununiformed especially, entertained themselves with the very exhilarating amusement of shattering against the trees these old fire-locks and such other weapons as could not be conveniently carried off. The plundering of the camp was an interesting occupation—interesting, even, to those who took no part in it. The ununiformed took the lead in this business. Perhaps they regarded it as their especial duty to be foremost now, since they had been in the rear during the attack.

Corporal Grimm and Sergeant Swords were both present, very busy, and trying to look very soldier-like, though their brown homespun suits and broad-brimmed hats gave them anything but a military appearance. Corporal Grimm kept his jaws in lively motion on a huge piece of pig-tail, while he kept up a lively conversation with Sergeant Swords and others immediately about him. Somehow the scene reminded him of his ten days' experience as a soldier with "General Preston," and he related that experience at length. The scene also vividly impressed Sergeant Swords with his experience under Captain Floyd, and he impelled to tell his comrades of that.

All were in excellent spirits. Captain Wardle congratulated the men on their coolness and gallant conduct, and the men congratulated Captain Wardle on his coolness and good generalship—all congratulating each other.

About three hours were spent on the late camping ground of the Confederates, and then the entire force, with their twenty prisoners and the plunder they could carry, started on their return to the Junction. Night overtook them about five miles after they had passed Snagtown, and, selecting a suitable place, they encamped. There was but one thing to dampen their ardor, but one thing had been overlooked. Their arms were in excellent condition, and they were all well mounted; but even riotous soldiers must eat, and this little fact had been overlooked. When night came they were tired and hungry, but there were rations only for about one-half of their force, and many went supperless to bed, with a fine prospect of having nothing to eat before noon the next day.

Captain Wardle felt most keenly his mistake in not bringing supplies, and spent most of the night in examining an old backless drill book to see how the thing could be remedied. Not finding anything in the tactics, he thrust it in his pocket and, throwing himself on his blanket, closed his eyes and in a few moments solved the problem. He then went to sleep, and it was not until his lieutenant had dragged him several feet from under his covering that he awoke next morning.

The sun was up, and so were the men, the latter hungry and ill-natured.

"Never mind! Tell the boys I've got this question fixed. They shall all have their breakfast. Tell the bugler to sound the roll-call."

The blast of the bugle called the men together, and the roll was soon called.

"Now," said Captain Wardle, who had been holding a conversation with Captain Gunn, "I think you are hungry—"

"You bet we are, Capen," put in a red-faced private.

"Shet up, sir, or I'll have you court-martialed and shot for contempt."

All became silent; the men looked grave and appeared willing to learn from the old, time-honored soldier, Captain Wardle.

"We haven't got enough in camp to feed more than about twenty-five men, so the rest o' ye will have to forage. Go in gangs of ten or fifteen and hunt your breakfast where yer can. The people all around here are secesh, and it will be a good thing to make them feed Union soldiers once in a while."

This announcement was received with applause, and the troops commenced dividing into small squads, the uniformed mixing promiscuously with the ununiformed, and waiting only for instructions where to join the main force, which now, consisting of twenty-five men and the prisoners, mounted their horses and rode off.

The eastern sun, like a blazing ball, was rising higher and higher in the sky as twelve men, among whom were Corporal Grimm and Sergeant Swords, galloped down a wooded road, keeping a sharp lookout for "bushwhackers." Six of these men wore the uniform and carried the arms of the United States Infantry, and six were dressed in citizens' attire and armed with rifles or double-barreled shot-guns. All rode at a furious pace, splashing through the mud and frightening the birds in the woods on either side.

A boy was riding down the road in the opposite direction. He was mounted on a thin, slow-moving mare, of an indistinct color, which might have been taken for a bay, yellow or sorrel. The boy was barefooted, had on a straw hat, rode on a folded sheepskin instead of a saddle, held an empty bag before him, and certainly did not look very warlike.

"Halt!" cried Sergeant Swords, drawing an old, rusty sword from its sheath and waving it in the air.

"Halt!" cried Corporal Grimm, drawing a many-barreled pistol, commonly known as a pepper-box, which he flourished in a threatening manner.

"Halt!" again cried both, "or we will fire."

The boy, being overawed by numbers, felt constrained to pull up the thin mare.

"Advance and give the countersign!" said Corporal Grimm.

"Shet up, Grimm! I command this squad," said Sergeant Swords.

Grimm chewed his pigtail in silence. In the meantime the boy seemed undecided whether to fly or to stand his ground, though his face betrayed a strong inclination in favor of the former proposition.

"Who comes there?" said Sergeant Swords, bringing his rusty sword to a salute.

"Who are ye talkin' to?" asked the boy, looking around to see if he could possibly be addressing any one else.

"I am talkin' to you, sir," said the Sergeant, sharply.

"What d' ye want?" asked the boy.

"Who comes there, I said?" answered the Sergeant more sharply.

"Me."

"Advance, then."

"Do what?"

"Come here."

The boy understood this. He had it delivered in just such a tone when he had been violating the domestic law. He advanced.

"What d' ye want?" he asked again.

"Where can we get our breakfast?"

"Dunno," he replied, wonderingly.

"Well, how fur is it to the next farm-house?"

"Taint more'n a mile."

"Who lives there?"

"Old Ruben Smith; but he ain't there now."

"Where is he?"

"Dunno; says he's gone to the war, him and his two boys."

"Which army?"

"Dunno."

"Are they Union or secesh?"

"Lor bless ye, we're all secesh here."

"You are? Well, we are Union. We'll take ye prisoner, then," said Corporal Grimm.

"Oh, but I ain't secesh."

"Well, then, you are a good boy," said the Sergeant. "Where are ye going?"

"Gwine to Snagtown to git the mail and buy some sugar and coffee."

"Well, you may go on," said the grim soldier, winking at the Corporal; the boy trotted on, looking curiously back at the men and their blue uniforms and big guns.

The cavalcade now galloped on towards the house of Ruben Smith. The steep gable roof soon loomed up in the distance, and after dashing down the lane, around a pasture, through a small wood, they pulled up in front of the house.

"Dismount!" commanded the Sergeant. The men were on the ground in an instant. "Now hitch where you can, and two of you stay on guard while the rest are eating."

"Who are ye, and what do ye want," demanded a sharp-visaged, ill-natured looking woman, coming out on the porch as the soldiers entered the yard.

"We are Union soldiers, and we want our breakfast," said Corporal Grimm, as the Sergeant was busy giving orders to the men.

"You low, nigger-lovin', aberlition thieves, I wouldn't give ye a bite if ye were starvin'," said the woman.

"Mother, don't talk that way to them," said a pretty, red cheeked girl of about fifteen, standing by her side.

"We want breakfast for twelve," said Sergeant Swords, now coming forward.

"Well, sir, ye won't git it here. Go to some nigger shanty and let them cook for ye."

"Oh, no, my good woman, we want you to get our breakfast. You are a good lookin' woman, and I know you can get up a good meal."

"If I was to cook for ye scamps, I'd pizen the last one o' ye," she fairly shrieked.

"We shall have you eat with us, my good lady, and we can eat anything you do," said Sergeant Swords, good-humoredly. The young girl was all the while persuading her mother to be more calm.

"Come now, I'll help you. I'll kindle the fire and carry the wood and draw the water," said the corporal.

"Come in my house an' I'll pour bilin' hot water in yer face, and scald yer eyes out!"

"Don't talk so, mother," urged the pretty daughter.

At this moment the kitchen door opened, and a negro girl peeped out.

"Say, kinky head, stir up the kitchen fire and get us some breakfast right soon," said Corporal Grimm. The black face withdrew, and the two non-commissioned officers entered the house to see that their bidding was performed.

While the latter were discussing the possibility of bushwhackers being in the neighborhood, they were suddenly startled by a loud cackling of hens and screaming of chickens; at the same instant a flock came rushing around the house with half a dozen soldiers in close pursuit.

"Good idea, boys! We will have chickens for breakfast," said Corporal Grimm.

A dozen or more chickens were caught and killed and carried to the cook. The soldiers politely inquired of the lady of the house if they could be of any further assistance, and then most of them returned to the front yard, where their arms were stacked or strewn promiscuously about. Three of them, with Corporal Grimm, remained to pick the chickens and prepare them for the cook, while there very amiable hostess was sullenly grinding away at a large coffee mill. The negro girl and the rosy-cheeked daughter of the house were both very busy hurrying up the fire, putting on the kettles of water, making biscuits, and attending to the various culinary duties.

"Where is your husband?" asked Corporal Grimm.

"None of your business," was the quick reply.

"Where are your sons?" asked Grimm.

"In Jeff Davis' army, to shoot just such thieves as you are."

"How long have they been in Jeff Davis' army?"

"Ever since the war commenced."

"How old is this hen I am picking?"

"I hope she is old enough and tough enough to choke ye to death," said the women, giving the coffee mill a furious rap.

"Your husband must be a very happy man," said Corporal Grimm.

"If he was here, you wouldn't be very happy," she replied, testily.

"No, I am happier with his amiable spouse."

"There, I hope that'll pizen ye," she said, emptying the ground coffee into a coffee-pot, and pouring boiling water over it.

"Make it strong enough to bear up an iron wedge," said Corporal Grimm; then, addressing his men:

"Watch the old vixen, for she may pizen us if she gets a chance."

The men needed no second bidding, and as the cooking progressed, they watched more keenly. They were all very hungry, yet none wanted to be poisoned.

Breakfast being prepared, the reluctant hostess was compelled to eat with the soldiers, who, being thus convinced that none of the viands were poisoned, did full justice to the really excellent meal.

CHAPTER XIII.

UNCLE DAN MEANS BUSINESS.

Colonel Scrabble found his forces, when the attacking party had retired, somewhat scattered. With Lieutenant Whimple he had sought safety in a hollow tree, whence, after waiting four hours, he issued orders to the lieutenant to go forth and see if the Federal troops had retreated. The lieutenant took a circuitous route, walking on tiptoe, lest he should disturb the slumbers of the dead, until he reached the camp, which the Union soldiers had just left.

Lieutenant Whimple then started to return, meeting on his way Captain Fogg. One by one they picked up men, behind logs, in tree-tops, and thick cluster of bushes, until they arrived twenty in number at the colonel's head-quarters, in the hollow tree. Here a council of war was held, and it was decided to send runners through the woods to notify their scattered forces that the enemy was gone; by night one hundred and fifty men had assembled around the hollow tree. They talked, in low determined tones, and all swore to avenge their lost comrades.

Lieutenant Whimple and a score of resolute men were still scouring the woods in search of fugitives. They had approached very near the bank of the creek when the foremost man started back, saying:

"My God! Just look at that!"

"Where?" asked a dozen voices, peeping through the underbush, expecting to behold a masked battery at the least. The sun was low in the Western horizon, and our soldiers could not see the object at first.

"There," said the first speaker, "sittin' right on the bank of the creek, is the devil come out to sun himself."

They could now describe an object that might be a huge mud turtle, or might be almost any thing a lively fancy could suggest. A closer examination, however, showed it to be a little man somewhat larger than an apple dumpling, but so plastered from his head to his heels with mud that one could hardly tell whether he was black or white.

The men drew nearer the strange object and finally rushed from their concealment. The poor fellow went down on his knees and threw up his hands imploringly. He was covered with the very blackest of Virginia mud, except great, white rings around the eyes and mouth, which gave a a most horrible expression to the features.

"Oh! have mercy, mercy—hem, hem!—have mercy!" he gasped, clasping his hands and closing his eyes, "and I will quit this unholy cause."

"Why, hallo, Corporal Diggs?" cried Lieutenant Whimple. At sound of that familiar voice, Mr. Diggs bounded to his feet, smeared as he was, threw his arms round the speaker's neck and wept for joy.

"Oh! Whimple, Whimple, Whimple! I never expected to behold your face again. Oh! my dear, dear Whimple, you're not killed, are you? Tell me that you are not dead!"

Whimple assured him that not only was he alive but in good health; after allowing the corporal time to recover, they picked up a few more men in the woods, also about forty horses, and returned.

Lieutenant Tompkins, who had been out in search of scattered men, now returned with the sergeant's squad, the Sergeant's head bandaged.

A hundred curious eyes were turned toward Whimple's squad as they came in; but it was not so much the numbers of the squad that attracted their attention, as the mud covered object that walked in their midst, in regard to which various conjectures were hazarded.

About three hundred and seventy-five men were gathered around the Colonel's head-quarters, the hollow tree, before nightfall. Something must be done, all agreed. There were several men in the country, the Colonel said, who must either take the oath of allegiance to the Southern cause or suffer death for their disloyalty. Several names were mentioned, among them that of Dan Martin.

"The hunter of Twin Mountains?" asked Oleah Tompkins.

"Yes," said Lieutenant Whimple, who had suggested the name.

"He is an old friend of mine," said Oleah.

"Well, but, Lieutenant Tompkins, we can't afford to screen all your friends," said the Colonel.

"Of course, no one can blame you for saving your father, but you can't expect all your Abolition friends will be left unmolested. Lieutenant Whimple, take twenty men and wait on old Dan Martin to-morrow."

When morning came, nearly all the horses were needed for the work of collecting the balance of the scattered forces, foraging for provisions and for arms and horses.

Corporal Diggs was second in command of Whipple's force, and, as he mounted his tall horse, he heard Seth Williams making audible comments on his appearance.

The mounted force galloped away toward the foot of Twin Mountains, where Uncle Dan lived, a distance of about ten miles from the camp.

It was near the middle of the forenoon when Uncle Dan, who was sitting in his door-yard, saw a cavalcade approaching. Crazy Joe was in the house drawing a map of Egypt, showing by lines how far the famine had extended.

Uncle Dan's fierce mastiff and his hounds seemed to scent

coming danger, the latter sending up mournful howls and the former uttering low, fierce howls of anger.

"By hokey, I don't like the looks o' that," said the old man, as he observed the armed band approaching his lonely cabin. "Seems like they ain't honest. They're secesh, sure as gun's made o' iron, for there is Jake Whimple leading 'em, and right here, too. Guess it won't do any harm to keep old 'Broken Ribs' handy, in case they should be ugly."

As the old man concluded he entered the house, and, taking his rifle from the rack over the door, leaned it against the wall while he took his seat in the door-way, his gun within easy reach. He had also placed a large navy revolver by his side.

The horsemen had now caught sight of him, and, with exultant yells, galloped up the slight elevation from the creek toward the cabin.

"Say, I reckin you'd better stop now and let a fellow know what ye want," cried Uncle Dan, snatching his rifle, and bringing it to a poise.

The cavalcade halted, the men looking apprehensively at the unerring rifle and then at one another. Finally, by common consent, all eyes were turned on Lieutenant Whimple.

"What do ye want, Jake Whimple?" demanded Uncle Dan in sharp, imperative tones.

"We have come to administer the oath of allegiance to you," said Whimple, riding a little nearer, his comrades following close behind.

"Then stop," cried the old hunter, "or I will make it hot for you, for I wont take no oath of allegiance from any one to the Southern Confederacy, 'specially such a sorry cuss as you."

"Then I shall take you a prisoner and bring you to camp," said Lieutenant Whimple, trying to throw some sternness in his voice.

"I'll drop some o' you fellars afore ye do that. Now jist advance one step further and see if I don't."

Although they were fifty yards away, they could distinctly hear the ominous click of that rifle which never failed.

"I've lost something down here," muttered Corporal Diggs, striving in vain to keep his teeth from chattering, "and I believe I'll go back and see if I can't find it."

The Corporal wheeled his big horse around, and galloped down the hill for about one hundred yards, and, dismounting, set about examining very intently the ground behind a large oak tree.

"Whoa, January," he said shivering, perhaps from cold, as the themometer was only 65° above in the shade.

"If you don't come along peaceably with us we shall have to use force," said Lieutenant Whimple, in a tone of as much severity as he could command.

The old man sprang to his feet and brought his gun to his face, "Now, turn about and git from here, or I'll drop some of ye where ye stand," he shouted.

Lieutenant Whimple spurred his horse, which reared, and wheeled and as he turned he fired his pistol at the hunter. The ball passed high over the old man's house, missing its aim by ten feet.

"Shoot the old rascal!" he frantically cried, as he saw the fatal rifle aimed at himself. The discharge of the pistol had frightened the horses; they had broken ranks and were now rearing and plunging in every direction.

"Crack!" went Uncle Dan's rifle, and a bullet went through the Lieutenant's hat, knocking it from his head.

With a wild cry, the Lieutenant threw up his hands, and fell forward on his horse's neck, believing, as did the others, that he was killed. The horse tore down the hill, followed by the entire company.

Uncle Dan's blood was up and snatching his revolver he fired three more shots at the retreating cavalcade. At the last shot he saw the dust arise from the back of one man's coat and heard a wild cry.

"Take me by force," said Uncle Dan, "May be," and re-entering the house he reloaded his weapons, to be ready for another assault.

Corporal Diggs was still searching for the treasure he had lost, when he heard the shots, and, looking from behind the tree, he saw the whole troop come tearing down the hill, retreating, as it seemed to him, in the midst of a storm of shot fired from a six pounder.

The Corporal made a spring for his saddle (as he afterward declared), to rally his men, seeing that the Lieutenant was wounded, but he could only succeed in grasping the horn of his saddle. Thus clinging, he managed to slip one foot into the stirrup, when the flying horsemen thundered by. The Corporal's long-legged horse gave one snort and started at headlong speed.

"Whoa, January! whoa, January! *whoa January!*" frantically cried the Corporal, clinging to the side of the tall horse, able neither to get on or off, while the excited beast seemed to be trying to outstrip the wind.

"Whoa, January," cried the Corporal, trying to stop his flying steed," but unable to touch the bridle.

Whoa, January," his arms and legs extended, and his short coat-tail flying, made him look like a spider on a circular saw. "Whoa January! Oh Lordy, won't no one stop this horse? I'll—hem, hem—be killed against a tree! Help, help! Whoa January."

January by this time had passed the foremost horse in the fleeing cavalcade, and his rider presented such a ludicrous appearance that the men, badly frightened as they were, roared with laughter.

Lieutenant Whimple, after swaying for some time in the saddle, plunged off in a helpless heap on the side of the road. Three or four of the men paused to pick him up. The man who had been wouuded in the back, fainted and fell from his horse, when another halt was made.

But on thundered January, his rider still clinging to his side and crying vigorously for help. The creek was reached, and January, by one tremendous leap, cleared the ford. The stirrup broke, so did Corporal Diggs' hold. There was a great splash, and those nearest saw a pair of short legs disappear beneath the surface of the water.

When the party came up, they beheld a mud-stained, water-soaked individual crawling up the opposite bank, sputtering and groaning, and swearing he would quit such an unholy cause.

The Lieutenant soon recovered, though he acted for

hours like a man dazed. The severely wounded private was carried to the nearest house, where he was left and medical aid sent for. Corporal Diggs rode behind one of the soldiers until they came upon the fractious January nibbling the fresh grass in a piece of bottom-land. He then mounted his own steed and took command of the company, which he led straight back to camp.

No sooner had the Confederates left Uncle Dan's residence than the latter packed up his few valuables, and, telling Crazy Joe to go to Mr. Tompkins, turned loose his dogs and set out through the woods to the Junction. Uncle Dan surmised the rebels would return in force and burn his dwelling to the earth.

CHAPTER XIV.

MRS. JUNIPER ENTERTAINS.

Mrs. Julia Juniper was a wealthy widow, of easy conscience and uncertain age. Courted and flattered alike for her charms and her wealth, for Mrs. Julia Juniper had both, she was the acknowledged belle of the country, the leader of the elite and the ruler of fashion. When Mrs. Julia Juniper gave a party it was sure to be successfully attended, and it needed only to be known that she was to be at a ball to ensure the presence of the very best society in the neighborhood.

The widow was a little above medium height, slender and graceful, with dark, sparkling eyes, clear white complexion, and black hair. She was vivacious as well as beautiful, and her sparkling wit was sufficient to enliven the dullest assemblage.

Mrs. Julia Juniper owned and possessed (as the lawyers say) a large plantation, and the granite mansion she had furnished with lavish elegance.

Two or three weeks have passed since the occurrences last

recorded, and many startling events have taken place. Colonel Holdfast, with his force at the Junction, had joined McClellan, and fought gallantly at Phillippi, on the 3d of June. Abner Tompkins had been promoted to a captaincy, and Sergeant Swords and Corporal Grimm wore uniforms. Uncle Dan Martin accompanied the army as guide and scout, and was of invaluable service, as he knew every inch of the ground over which they had to pass. Colonel Scrabble had been compelled to fall back with his force about forty or fifty miles south, where a large force was assembling near Rich Mountain. The colonel's regiment had been recruited, refitted, and furnished with arms by the Confederate States, and the colonel himself now held a commission. Owing to the fact that Lieutenant Whimple had been disabled, perhaps for life, by his fall from his horse in the race from Uncle Dan's cabin, Oleah Tompkins had been promoted to first lieutenant.

The regiment was now encamped in the neighborhood of Mrs. Julia Juniper, and Mrs. Juniper, a Southern lady with all a Southern lady's prejudices and passions, and intense likes and dislikes, loved her sunny South, and loved every one who was engaged defending it against the cold-blooded Northern invader, and, desirous of doing all she could to cheer the brave hearts of her country's defenders, resolved to give a reception in honor of the regiment. It was at the same time a first meeting and a farewell, for the colonel hourly expected orders to march further east and join the troops massing in the valley of the Shenandoah under Johnston and Beauregard.

It was the evening of the 9th of July, 1861, and the grand mansion of Mrs. Julia Juniper was ablaze with light and splendor. The drawing-rooms, parlors, reception rooms, and the spacious dining hall were lighted early in the evening, festooned with flags, and lavishly adorned with flowers. The piazza, the lawn, the conservatory, and even the garden, on this evening, were filled with a gay, laughing throng. Mrs. Julia Juniper had ordered all form and ceremony to be laid aside, and desired that her guests should consider her house their home. She met officer and private, as they entered, clasping the hand of each with a fervent "God save our sunny South." More than one young soldier, looking on that lovely face, resolved to fight till death for a cause so dear to her. Corporal Diggs was present, and as Mrs. Julia Juniper's hand clasped his, and he heard her say: "God bless, you, my dear friend and make your arm strong to defend our beloved country!" he felt proud that he had not deserted, as he declared he should, after the retreat from Twin Mountain. Mrs. Juniper was everywhere, shedding on all the light of her countenance, enlivening all conversation with the rich, warm tones of her voice or her merry, musical laugh.

At least two hundred officers, commissioned and non-commissioned, fell in love with the widow, and twice as many privates were willing to lie down and have their heads amputated for her sake. Many of our Southern soldier friends were present, among them Howard Jones and Seth Williams, both sergeants now. Corporal Diggs was in ecstacies of delight, but the presence of his old tormentor, Seth Williams, was a slight drawback at times to his happiness. Mrs. Juniper had introduced the corporal and Seth Williams to two charming young ladies, Miss Ada Temple and Miss Nannie Noddington, both of them bright, lively girls, fond of sport. Miss Temple made herself particularly agreeable to the little apple-dumpling of a corporal.

Mr. Corporal Diggs had on a neat little suit of gray, without shoulder straps, but with yellow braid enough on his coat sleeves to indicate his office and rank. His thick hair was parted exactly in the middle, his burnside whiskers were neatly trimmed, and his glasses were on his nose. He tried to appear witty, making him appear silly enough to enlist the sympathy of any one except Seth Williams.

Seth was bent on fun and mischief, and in Miss Nannie Noddington he found an able accomplice and ally.

Corporal Diggs was making an extraordinary endeavor to make himself agreeable to Miss Temple, who laughed at his witticisms in a coquettish way that was wholly irresistible, and Corporal Diggs became brilliant, drawing continually on his immense fund of knowledge, talking science, physics, and metaphysics, history, literature, and art, at last touching on the theme, sacred to love and lovers, poetry.

"Hem, hem, hem! Miss Temple, I presume—hem—you are very fond of poetry," he said, leaning back in his chair, his soleful eyes gleaming through his glasses.

"I am passionately fond of poetry, corporal," said the blonde beauty, with a winning smile.

"I—hem, hem!—before I entered the army, used to be passionately fond of poetry, but the multifarious duties of an officer during these exciting times will allow no thought of polite accomplishments.

"He is inflating now," whispered Seth Williams to Miss Noddington. "He will explode soon in a burst of poetical eloquence."

Mr. Diggs, as we have seen, had a peculiar stoppage in his speech, occasioned more by habit than by any defect in the organs of articulation.

"Yes, Miss Temple, I—hem, hem, hem!—admire, or rather I adore poetry. The deep sublimity of thought—hem, hem, hem!—given forth in all of poetical expression and—hem, hem!—as the poet says 'the eye in fine frenzy rolling.'"

"'That was in his 'Ode to an Expiring Calf,' was it not?" said Seth Williams, who was one of the group.

No one could repress a smile, and Miss Noddington was attacked by a convulsive cough.

"You always have a way of degrading the sublime to the ridiculous, Mr. Williams," said the little corporal, loftily.

"Who of the English poets do you like best, Corporal Diggs?" asked, Miss Temple, pretending not to notice Williams' sally and the consequent discomfiture of her companion.

"I—hem, hem!" said the little fellow, leaning forward and locking his hands, with all the dignity that he assumed when about to give one of his opinions. "I—hem—am rather partial to Scott. I don't know why, unless his wild poems rather suit my warlike nature. I like to read of Marmion, the Lady of the Lake, and the Vision of Don—Don —hem—Don—"

"Quixote," put in Seth Williams.

The bright black eyes of Miss Noddington twinkled, but Miss Temple feigned sympathy with the corporal, whose memory was evidently bad.

"But—hem, hem!—Miss Temple," he went on, heroic to the last, "that is a sublime as well as a truthful thought of Scott, who says,—hem, hem!—how does it begin? Oh yes:

> "O, woman, in our hours of ease
> Uncertain, coy, and hard to—"

"Squeeze," put in Seth Williams, who was really boiling over with mischief.

Miss Temple looked shocked, but Miss Noddington only buried her blushing face in her handkerchief.

The discomforted Corporal Diggs cast a furious glance at Seth Williams, who sat with a face as solemn as any judge on the bench.

"Mr. Williams, such talk is very unbecoming any gentleman," said he, rising and looking as furious, to use Seth Williams own words, "as an enraged potato bug."

"I beg the pardon of all the company," said Seth, whose face was gravity itself. "I wanted to find some word that would rhyme with ease, and spoke the first that came to my mind."

"The word, sir, is 'please,'" said Corporal Diggs, re-seating himself after entreaty from the ladies, who assured him that it was only a *lapsus linguæ* on the part of Sergeant Williams.

"Now, corporal, do go on and repeat the entire verse, for I do so admire Sir Walter Scott," pleaded Miss Temple, whose roguish blue eyes were sparkling almost as brightly as those of her friend, Nannie Noddington.

"Yes, Corporal Diggs," said the beautiful Nannie, "do go on and give us the entire stanza."

"Yes, the entire canto," put in Seth.

There was no refusing the appeal from those blue eyes of Miss Temple or the sparkling black eyes of Miss Noddington, so, after a few "hems" and a moment spent in bringing the poem to his memory, the corporal began again:

> "O, woman, in our hours of ease
> Uncertain, coy, and hard to please;
> Yet seem too oft, familiar with her face,
> We first endure, then pity, then embrace."

This time both ladies laughed outright, and even Seth Williams could not restrain a smile, while the corporal wondered what in the world could be the matter with them.

"Your version is no better than mine," said Seth Williams.

"Oh! Corporal Diggs, you are too cute, you made that mistake on purpose," laughed Miss Temple.

The corporal, hearing his witty blunder praised on all sides, concluded to pretend it was an intentional joke, originating from his own fertile brain; Miss Temple smiled on him, Miss Noddington declared him charmingly cute, and the corporal felt himself quit a hero.

After further favoring the company with choice selections, he launched out on history, which he brought down to the present time by allusions to his adventures since he had been in the army.

"Have you ever been in any engagement, corporal?" asked sweet Miss Temple.

"Yes, Miss Temple, I have been where bullets flew thicker—hem, hem!—than hail stones; replied Corporal Diggs.

"Where was it?" asked the blonde.

"Once at Wolf Creek."

"Were you not frightened?"

"I was as cool as I ever was in my life," replied Corporal Diggs, leaning back in his chair, and looking very brave.

"That was because you were so deep down in mud and water under the drift-wood," put in Seth Williams.

Corporal Diggs turned a look of wrath on his companion. "Who said I was in the mud and water?" he demanded, fiercely. "Who saw me in the mud and water?"

"No one, I don't suppose; but Lieutenant Whimple found you on the bank, looking very much as though you had just left the hands of Crazy Joe."

Before Corporal Diggs could reply, Miss Temple, rising, begged him to walk with her on the piazza.

As the two went away, Seth laughed for the first time during the evening, and told his companion the story of Crazy Joe's mud man.

The lawn had been converted into a dining-room, and long

rows of tables were spread there; Chinese lanterns hung from all the trees, and an army of black waiters was in attendance.

The dining hall had been cleared and fitted for dancing, and already the soft sound of music was heard there, and gay dancers were gliding gracefully through the waltz.

It was nearly two o'clock in the morning, when Oleah Tompkins tired of dancing walked into the conservatory, and from there into the garden. His thoughts naturally flew back to his home, to his parents, and to her he had learned to love with all the warmth and ardor of his Southern heart. A hand touched him on the shoulder. He turned and beheld standing behind him a mulatto, one who had played the leading violin in the orchestra. He was between forty and fifty years of age, a man of grave and somber countenance.

"Well, sir, what will you have?" demanded the lieutenant, turning sharply about.

"Is your name Tompkins?" asked the man.

"Yes. What is your business with me?"

"I was anxious to be sure," said the mulatto, "for I assure you, Lieutenant Tompkins, that I may sometime be able to give you some valuable information."

"If you have any information to give, why not give it now?" demanded the young officer.

"I have reasons that I can not give. To tell the reasons would be to give the information."

Oleah looked fixedly into the mulatto's face. There was something unusual about him, something that impressed the young lieutenant strangely, yet, what it was, he could not tell.

"What is your name?" he asked.

"They call me Yellow Steve."

"How long have you been in this State," asked Oleah, after a pause.

"About two years," was the answer.

"Have I ever known you before?"

"I don't think you ever saw me before."

"Well, have you ever seen me before?"

"No."

"Then what can you have to tell me that would interest me?"

"I can tell you something of the early history of her you call your sister, something that no one on earth but myself knows. You shall know it in the future."

The mulatto turned, pushed open the door of a Summer house near by, and disappeared.

"Stay!" cried Oleah. "By heavens, if you know anything of her, I will not wait, I will know it now."

He sprang through the door after the mulatto, but the Summer house was vacant. The strange musician had disappeared as suddenly as if he had sank into the earth. After searching vainly through the grounds Oleah returned to the house. The other musicians (all colored) knew the "yaller man who played first fiddle," but, as "he lived no where particularly, but about in spots," no one could tell where he would most likely be found.

It was late that night before Lieutenant Tompkins sought his tent, and sleep came not to his eyes until nearly daylight. When he did sleep, the strange mulatto was constantly before his eyes—his yellow skin, his yellow teeth, and yellow eyes all gleaming.

CHAPTER XV.

MR. DIGGS AGAIN IN TROUBLE.

McClellan, in the meanwhile, had been sweeping the Western portion of Virginia. On the 11th of July, he gained a victory over the unorganized or at most half organized Confederates under Colonel Pegram at Rich Mountain, which was at no great distance from the Widow Juniper's.

Colonel Scrabble then endeavored to reinforce General Garnett at Laurel Hill, but the latter was on his retreat toward the Shenandoah to join Johnston's army, when Scrabble and eight hundred men, three hundred of which were cavalry, came up with him.

The fight at Rich Mountain had taken place just two days after Mrs. Juniper's reception, and it was partly this reception that had delayed Scrabble, for, by forced marches, he might have reached Pegram before his defeat. While he and his officers were basking in the smiles of the ladies of West Virginia, General McClellan, under the excellent guidance of Uncle Dan, had slipped in between the two forces and defeated the larger. Having been thus reinforced and, seeing escape almost impossible, General Garnett resolved to make one more stand against the enemy. At Carrick's Ford, on Cheat river, is a small winding stream, flowing through the central part northward of what is now West Virginia. It has its foundation-head near Rich Mountain, and the towns of Philippi, Grafton, and Beverly are on its banks.

The main army, under General Garnett, took position near the road on a bluff eighty feet high, where he planted his cannon. Colonel Scrabble, with his eight hundred troops, was on a bluff covered with thick almost impenetrable forest trees.

Oleah Tompkins and many others of the company had on more than one occasion shown superior courage, and the raw troops, with very few exceptions, promised excellent behavior on this occasion.

Corporal Diggs was there; he had fastened January to a small tree, near a stump that would enable him to mount. Mr. Diggs was very cool on this occasion. He sat behind a tree, his gun across his lap, and although he felt some uneasiness, yet, when he looked about him and saw the many strong, armed men standing in front of him in double ranks, he felt almost brave. Occasionally a shudder would pass through his frame, especially when he heard that the Yankees were in sight.

The roar of cannon shook the air, and a ball, whizzing through the tree-tops, just over the heads of Colonel Scrabble's raw troops, scattering leaves and clipping branches in its course, shivered a tree to splinters in the rear.

"Steady, boys!" shouted the colonel. "Never mind that. Don't fire till you get the word." But a few of the more nervous did fire.

"Steady!" cried the captains as they heard the shots.

"Steady!" repeated the file-closers in trembling tones.

"Stop that firing, you fools! Wait for the word," cried the enraged colonel, galloping furiously up and down the line.

"Steady!" said Corporal Diggs, in a hoarse whisper, lying flat on the ground behind his tree, the branches of which still trembled from the passage of the ball.

Soon a long line of blue coats could be seen on the opposite side of the small stream; fire belched from their guns, and a shower of leaden hail fell among the regiment of Colonel Scrabble.

"Steady!" cried the colonel. "Wait for the word."

"Steady!" cried the captains and lieutenants.

"Oh! Lordy, I'll be killed, I know I shall," wailed poor Diggs, crouching close to the ground.

"Aim! Fire!" was the command given on the Confederate side, and their guns returned the leaden storm with effect. The whole line was engaged, and peal followed peal, shot followed shot, thunder-clap followed thunder-clap, while the white smoke rose in canopying folds above the woods. The dead and wounded lay on both sides of the stream. The trees were shattered by the flying balls. The engagement became general.

After the first two or three rounds, Corporal Diggs, finding himself as yet unhurt, ventured to peep around the tree. He observed a number of blue coats on the opposite side of the stream and saw a number lying motionless on the ground. Snatching his carbine, he fired, he knew not at whom, because he closed his eyes as his finger pressed the trigger. Then, as if convinced that his shot would turn the tide of battle, he sprang once more behind his tree—to reload.

Among the new officers most noted for their daring was Oleah Tompkins, who was everywhere the shots fell thickest, encouraging his men by word and act. Through the flash of guns and clouds of smoke he occasionally caught a glimpse of a familiar form in the enemy's lines. It was a Union captain, upon whose coolness and courage seemed to rest the fortunes of his entire regiment. There was no mistaking that form, he had known it since his earliest recollection. That brave young officer, in an enemy's ranks, had been his playmate in childhood, his companion in boyhood, his schoolmate, his college chum, his constant associate in manhood, and was still his brother. A mist swam before the young Confederate's eyes, as he thought a single chance shot might send that brother into eternity. Little thought had Oleah for himself. He saw his comrades fall about him and heard groan and cry ascend from the blood stained grass, the balls of the enemy whistled about, shattering the tender bark of the trees, but the lieutenant had no thought save of his playmate, companion and brother on the other side of the stream.

"Lieutenant Tompkins, you expose yourself needlessly," said Harry Smith, touching his officer on the sleeve. "The other officers do not stand constantly in front."

Oleah lowered the field-glass, through which he had been looking at the young captain in blue across the river, and with a sad smile turned toward the speaker.

"Harry," he said, "do you know who we are fighting, who those men are across the river?"

"No," said Harry, "only that they are enemies."

"Once they were neighbors, friends and brothers. That is the company commanded by my brother Abner and raised in and about our village. Every shot we fire, whose aim is true, drinks the blood of one who was once a friend."

"Once friends," said Harry, "but enemies now."

Harry, who at first could not brook to take up arms against the Stars and Stripes, had joined the Home Guards, under the belief that they were only to protect their homes. He found himself in the Confederate army as many others did, and determined to make the best of it.

Blood is thicker than water, and—in spite of the fierce hatred Oleah Tompkins had for the Northern armies—it was with a sinking heart that he entered into combat with Colonel Holdfast's regiment.

While McClellan's main body was pressing Garnett's army closely in front, and threatening each moment to cross the ford, a portion of two Indiana regiments crossed about three miles above the ford and came crashing down on the Confederate's right wing. In a few minutes the right flank of the rebels was turned and the Union soldiers, with wild cheers, dashed into the stream and pushed across to the opposite side. The whole rebel line began to waver. General Garnett, seeing the danger his army was in, rode gallantly forward, and strove to rally his panic-stricken men. It was in vain, and, in the midst of his useless efforts to turn the tide of battle, he was struck by a ball and fell dead to the earth. His fall completed the panic which had already begun.

Corporal Diggs, who had displayed a vast amount of coolness, as he lay crouched behind his tree shivering in every limb, was the first in his regiment to determine how the battle would go. No sooner had the right flank been struck by the Hoosier troops than, with far-seeing military judgment, he declared the day lost and, bounding to his feet, sprang toward his horse which was snorting and plunging in its endeavors to get away.

"Whoa, January, you old fool!" cried the corporal.

Whiz zip, went a musket ball past his ear, clipping a twig which fell at his feet, and causing January to prance and rear.

"Oh Lordy, I'll be killed, I know I shall! Whoa, January!" and his trembling fingers struggled to unloose the knot of his halter.

Harry Smith, who had fought with desperate bravery, was, with Lieutenant Tompkins, among the last to leave the field. As he was in the act of mounting his horse, he cast a glance down toward the ford, where the mass of Union troops were forming and beheld the Stars and Stripes streaming above the long line of blue coats. Harry turned pale for the first time during the fight. A shock, as of a galvanic battery, seemed to strike his frame.

"Oh! Heavens!" he thought, "why am I in these ranks, a rebel and a traitor, fighting against the best government this world has ever known?"

"Mount quickly, Harry, or we shall be taken," cried Oleah, who was already in the saddle.

Harry sprang into the saddle, and they galloped away after their now flying comrades, the enemy's cavalry pursuing them closely and firing an occasional shot into the retreating ranks, as they rushed and crowded down the road through the lanes and over the hills in the direction of Beverly.

Corporal Diggs finally succeeded in untying the halter-knot, that held January to his post, and after some trouble got into the saddle. The bullets were whistling around his ears, and January was plunging through the underbrush and out into the road, where he struck off in a western direction at a rapid rate. The corporal did not try to restrain him, and they were soon over the hill, three miles away from the battle ground.

"Oh Lordy, I know they are all killed!" murmured the little corporal, looking back as he galloped down the road. For an hour he rode on, in what direction he knew not, but away from both armies. His mind was full of wild fancies. He saw six men coming like the wind down a cross lane, and, although they were a mile or two in his rear, he knew by their dark clothes and bright flashing guns that they were Union cavalry.

"Oh Lordy! I shall be killed, I know," he thought, as he used whip and spur, crying: "Get up, January! Oh! for the Lord's sake, run!"

Corporal Diggs glanced back again, and saw the six dark horsemen in the lane, directly behind him, and coming on as fast as their horses could carry them. He thundered down the lane, which was bordered on either side by a hedge fence about five feet high. The ground for about one mile was level, and then came some hills, steep and abrupt as only Virginia hills are.

The corporal unbuckled his saber and threw it away, threw away his pistols, and everything that might in the least impede his flight. January flew over the mile stretch and dashed down the hills at a break-neck speed. Corporal Diggs, who was not an experienced rider, clung to his horse's mane, and several times came very near being unseated. The soldiers in his rear came nearer, and their shouts could be heard by the poor flying wretch, but when he descended the hill they were out of sight.

January, coming to a ditch at the side of the road, made a fearful leap, and Corporal Diggs, losing his seat, was plunged head-foremost into a hedge, which closed completely over him.

"Oh, Lordy, I know I shall be killed!" he groaned, as

he lay, bruised and bleeding, in the midst of the hedge. January never for a moment stopped his flight, and soon the six pursuers swept by. Immediately after this the corporal became unconscious.

Daylight had passed into night when Corporal Diggs recovered consciousness; lying in his thorny bed bleeding, sore at every joint, and with face and hands frightfully lacerated, it was needless to say that this brave soldier was very uncomfortable. His first thought, on regaining his senses, was to extricate himself from the thorns, and this was by no means an easy task. Thorns above, thorns below, thorns on all sides, made moving without additional laceration an impossibility. With great care and many a smothered imprecation, groan and prayer, he at last emerged on the meadow side of the hedge.

The sky was clear and dark, and studded with innumerable stars. Each silent watcher seemed twinkling with merriment as the tattered Confederate stood by the hedge, pondering which way to go. On the opposite side lay the broad, dark lane, leading he knew not where, and before him stretched the wide meadow. He choose the latter, and was in the act of starting on his journey, when the tramp of hoofs coming down the lane struck his ear, and he again crouched down under the shelter.

It proved to be a small body of Union cavalry, and their arms clanked ominously as they rode by. They passed on over the hill, and the corporal rose once more and scanned the broad, dark green meadow, whose waving grass was soaked with a heavy dew. But wet grass was nothing compared with Union cavalry just then, and he pushed boldy across the meadow, regardless of its dampness. The meadow was much wider than he had supposed; he traveled for a mile or more through the tall, damp grass before he came to a stone fence, on the opposite side of which he saw a thick wood.

After carefully reconnoitering the premises, Corporal Diggs scaled the stone fence and dropped down on the other side. He paused a few minutes to remove the thorns from his arms and legs, wrung some of the water out of his clothes, and then selecting one of many narrow paths, he walked down into the forest. He traveled for several hours, avoiding public roads, and at last came out in the rear of what seemed to be an extensive plantation. He found some stacks of new made hay, which offered quite a comfortable sleeping place, and in a few minutes, after he had crawled into one, he was asleep, and slept soundly until the sun was up. Then, stiff and sore and bruised, he crawled from his bed and look about him. The place has a familiar look. There was a magnificent stone mansion to his left, and those broad fields and numerous plantation houses he had seen before. *It was the plantation of Mrs. Julia Juniper*.

The corporal knew, that in the widow, he would find a warm and sympathizing friend, and he consequently made his way toward the house. It was certainly with no martial bearing that he presented himself at the door of the widow's mansion. He asked to see Mrs. Juniper, but was told by her maid, that it was too early for her mistress to be out of bed. She brought him to the kitchen fire to dry his stained and dew-soaked clothes.

The corporal dried his clothes, washed and bound up his wounds with such linen as the cook would furnish, and tried to make himself presentable. Seeing Mrs. Juniper's maid he desired her to inform her mistress that Corporal Diggs wished to see her as early as possible.

Mrs. Juniper, supposing that some important message had been sent by Colonel Scrabble, allowed herself to be hastily dressed, and sent to tell the corporal she would receive him. Diggs lost no time in obeying the summons. At sight of the lacetated and bandaged being who entered, Mrs. Juniper, who had risen to receive her guest, utter a scream, and sank back into her chair.

"Corporal Diggs," she cried, "what has happened?"

"We have met the foe," said Diggs, with a tragic tone and manner. "Hem, hem, hem!—yes, Mrs. Juniper, we have met the foe—" He paused, overcome with emotion.

"With what result?"

"I alone am left to tell the tale."

"Oh, heavens! Corporal Diggs, it can not, it can not be true!"

"Alas! lady, it is but too true. Our brave army *is* now

no more. I, wounded and hunted like a hare, have come to you for a few hours of peace and shelter."

Diggs endeavored to look the character of a wounded knight from Flodden Field.

"Pray, Corporal Diggs, tell me all; our cause is not, must not be lost. The South—but, pardon me, you are wounded, weak, and faint—"

Diggs had put one of his arms in a sling and had bound a bandage on his head.

Sarah, bring wine here at once. Ah! you must have been very closely engaged with the enemy from the number of your wounds."

The wine was brought, and Diggs, now refreshed, gave eager Mrs. Juniper a glowing account of the battle at Carrick's Ford. As the account given by history does not, in all respects, agree with that of Corporal Diggs, we will give his version of the conflict.

"Madam," said the little corporal, "yesterday occurred one of the most bloody battles that the world has ever known. Our regiment joined General Garnett, and we met the enemy at Carrick's Ford, some seven hundred thousand strong, headed by old Abe Lincoln himself. They had a hundred to our one, but we fought, oh, my dear Mrs. Juniper, we fought like lions, like whirlwinds, like raging hurricanes—hem, hem"—broke off Corporal Diggs, trying to think of some stronger term, "yes, my dear Mrs. Juniper, like cyclones—hem, hem! We piled the ground around us several feet deep with their dead, and Cheat river overflowed its banks with the blood, but—hem, hem! it was no use. They came on, and their cannon shot, musket shot, and grape shot mowed men down. I—hem, hem—I was last to fall, I fought the whole of them for some time alone, but, surrounded, wounded, faint and bleeding, I fell from my horse and was left on the field for dead. When I came to my senses I—hem, hem!—crawled away and came here, believing that, wounded and faint as I was, you would not refuse me rest and shelter, and—and—hem, hem—I am very weak from loss of blood, Mrs. Juniper."

"Poor fellow, I don't doubt that you are. Sarah, bring water and fresh linen. My own hands shall dress your wounds!"

"No, no, dear Mrs. Juniper, I would not permit a delicate lady to look upon the rude gashes of war. If you will permit me, I will retire and dress my wounds." He tried hard to convulse his features with pain.

"I will not allow that," said the widow. "These wounds were received in defending my country against the cruel Northern invader, and I shall dress them with my own hands."

"No; oh! no, dear lady, you can not know how a soldier, rough and used only to the roar of cannon and clash of steel, must shrink from inflicting on a lady such needless pain."

"Then I will have a surgeon brought," persisted kind-hearted Mrs. Juniper.

"Quite unnecessary, my dear lady, as they are only flesh wounds—what we soldiers call mere scratches."

Mrs. Juniper had his breakfast brought to the parlor and insisted on his reclining on the sofa. She asked a thousand questions, which Mr. Diggs answered in his extravagant manner. The day passed, and rumor after rumor, almost as wild and extravagant as Corporal Digg's report, came from the battle-field, confirming the defeat, at least, if not the utter annihilation, of the army.

As bodies of Union men were scouring the country, picking up stragglers from the Confederate army, who were fleeing in every direction, Mrs. Juniper suggested that Corporal Diggs had better have a bed prepared and sleep in the cellar, as her house might be entered and searched. The Corporal although asserting that, if armed, he would not be in the least afraid of half a hundred of the cowardly Yankees, consented, merely out of regard for the lady's feelings. Such scenes of carnage and bloodshed as must ensue, if an attempt should be made to capture him, would be too terrible for a delicate lady to witness. The corporal had no arms, all had been taken from him as he lay unconscious on the field, but Mrs. Juniper sent out among the hands and confiscated three guns, two old horse-pistols, and a long trooper's sword, which she had conveyed to the "brave soldier" in her cellar.

A horse had that morning been found with saddle and bridle on, looking hungrily at the barn and trying to make the acquaintance of the sleek, well-fed equines, who answered his neighs from its windows. The negro, who found the horse, had put him in the barn and given him all the oats and corn he desired, which was a considerable amount. The corporal, hearing of the horse, went to see him, and at once recognized in that tall, raw-boned creature his noble January. The meeting of knight and steed was of course very touching, as the wealthy, handsome widow was present to witness it.

As he walked back to the mansion he related many of the noble qualities of his horse, how he had fought over his master long after he lay insensible upon the battle-field. There was one little matter the "brave soldier" failed to explain, and that was, how, while insensible, the master knew what the horse was doing.

"What a brave man he must be," thought the widow as she sat in her boudoir after the corporal had retired to the cellar, where he put the guns and pistols at the extreme corner of the room, least they should accidentally go off and kill him. "What a brave man he is, who has fought so many men! On him alone now depends the success of our cause. He is the Alfred the Great, the Charles the Second, who must gather an army and strike when our foe least expects it. Brave, brave man!" And the widow dreamed that night that she saw Corporal Diggs lead a vast army against the enemy, and that victory crowned his attempts. She saw the glorious South an independent nation and honors heaped upon the man she had succored. He was seated on the throne of the new kingdom and became a wise and good ruler.

Waking, the widow actually wept with joy, for she would not believe that her vision was anything else than a direct revelation, and was sure that the fate of her beloved South hung upon the sword-point of the brave man, who was then sleeping in her cellar. True, he was small of stature, and, when mounted on January, did, as Seth Williams had said, look much like a bug on a log, but then he was brave, and many of the great military men were small.

The corporal spent three or four days in concealment at the widow's, and, although his thorn scratches were entirely healed, he still kept the bandage on his head and carried his arm in a sling. He had discovered that, wounded and suffering, he elicited more sympathy from the beautiful widow. They usually walked out at twilight, and spent an hour in the spacious ground.

Upon one occasion the widow told her dreams, and asked the brave man by her side what he thought of it.

"Think of it? Hem, hem! Why, my dear Mrs. Juniper—hem, hem, hem!—why, it will be fulfilled to the very letter. Yes, my dear lady—hem, hem!"—and Diggs turned his face aside in a reflective manner, and his little eyes glowed with meaning, "it is my design to gather another army and hurl back the tide of adversity. My dear Mrs. Juniper, the world yet knows not Corporal Diggs, but it shall, it shall," and he struck the end of a stout stick which he carried in his hand into the pebble-covered earth. "Oh, if these scratches would but heal, so that I once more could take the field and lead an army on to victory; then they should know—hem, hem, hem!—they would learn that the Cæsars are not dead."

"Oh! what a loss it would have been to our beloved South if you had been slain!" said the enraptured widow.

"Fear not—hem, hem, hem—my dear madam, I shall not be slain. I have my destiny to fulfill. And now—hem, hem!—my dear madam, my dear Mrs. Juniper, my dear Julia, let me call you by that sweet name, I have something of great importance to speak of."

An ambuscade could not have startled the widow more than this brave man's manner. She elevated her eyebrows, and her large dark eyes grew round with wonder as she said:

"Why—why, Corporal Diggs, what can it be! What can you mean?"

"Do you not comprehend me? Say, has love no sharper eyes? Oh, my dear, dear—Julia—" here Corporal Diggs' manner became demonstrative; he seemed to forget the severe wounds, and, starting from the garden seat, down he went on one knee, and drawing from the sling the arm that had been shattered by grapeshot, he clasped his hands as if in prayer. "Oh, my dear—hem, hem, hem!—my darling Julia, I love you! I have loved you ever since I first saw you, and I ask you—hem, hem!—to become mine. Accept this heart, which you have captured, and give me yours in return."

His speech delivered, the little corporal remained on his knee, with his eyes closed and his lips pursed, in his endeavor to appear absorbed and earnest.

"Mr. Diggs, your behavior is very unbecoming the brave soldier I took you to be," said the lady, after a moment's hesitation. "This is no time to talk of love."

At this rebuke Mr. Diggs rose from his knees, abashed and confused, and resumed his seat.

"We have enough, Corporal Diggs, to engage our minds for the present. While our beloved country is in peril we must forget all personal feelings. Let its dangers and its salvation be paramount."

"But when this cruel war is over, and peace returns once more, will you then consent to become my wife?" persisted the corporal. "I—I—love you, and I—I—I can't help it. Say you will be my wife!"

"It is growing rather late, Mr. Diggs, and the air is chilly. We will return to the house."

They accordingly rose, and Diggs, walking in sullen, abashed silence by the widow's side, entered the great stone mansion. Mrs. Juniper retired to her own room, and Corporal Diggs to the cellar.

Mrs. Julia Juniper had a tall, lantern-jawed, ill-disposed, and envious neighbor, who was a Union man for no other earthly reason than that all his neighbors were Confederates. He lived in a wretched little hovel, had a sickly wife, and eight children. He might have made a living on his little farm, but was too lazy to work, and continually engaged in petty lawsuits with his neighbors. Josiah Scraggs was a communist at heart, and he felt sure that, as he was such an excellent Union man and Mrs. Julia Juniper so decidely "secesh" in principles, that eventually her magnificent mansion and large plantation would be taken from the widow and given to him. He had confided his hopes to his sickly wife and dirty children, and all were anxious for the happy change. Josiah Scraggs was constantly reporting the conduct of his neighbors, especially of the widow Juniper, to any Union soldiers who might be in the neighborhood. He had been watching the mansion since the battle of Carrick's Ford, for he suspected that she was "harboring secesh soldiers." Sure enough, one evening he saw the widow and Corporal Diggs walking together in the garden, and away he went to the headquarters of Colonel Holdfast, who was about ten miles away, to give information that secesh soldiers were concealed in the widow's mansion.

He rode the old gray mare into the camp, and called for the colonel. Being shown to his tent, he quickly made the object of his visit known, magnifying many fold what he had seen, and leaving the colonel to infer that many more might be in the house.

Scraggs, having made his report, was dismissed by the colonel. He loitered outside the tent, waiting hungrily for the colonel to execute to him and his heirs and assign forever a title in fee simple to the vast plantation and magnificent stone mansion of Mrs. Julia Juniper. Instead, the colonel sent for Captain Abner Tompkins, and ordered him to take his company, with as many more men as he needed, and proceed at once to Mrs. Juniper's to take prisoners the rebel soldiers lying concealed there.

"My own company will be sufficient, I think, colonel," said Abner.

"All right, then," replied the former, and turned to his papers without having issued the deed to Scraggs.

As Abner was mustering his men, Scraggs re-entered the colonel's tent, and, reaching out a long, bony, finger, touched the officer on the shoulder. Colonel Holdfast looked up from his papers with a "Well, what now?"

"What do I get for reportin' on this ere secesh woman?"

"The consciousness, sir, of having done your duty," replied the colonel.

"Well, but don't I git no pay?" asked Scraggs, his face darkening with disappointment, the house and plantation of Mrs. Juniper vanishing from before his mental vision.

"None, sir; so good a Union man as you are surely would ask no compensation for doing his duty."

"Well, but ain't you a goin' to give me her farm and house?" asked Scraggs, the disappointment on his face deepening into agony.

"My dear sir," said the colonel, "I have no authority to give you any one's property. If you want a plantation you must purchase it of the owner."

"Well, but she harbors secesh."

"If her house becomes a nuisance in that way we shall be justified in burning it, but we can not take it from her and give it to any one else."

The colonel again turned to his papers, and Scraggs, his long-cherished hopes blasted, left the tent, mounted his old gray mare, and rode home.

Scraggs was only one of the many, on both sides, who reported their neighbors' deeds and misdeeds to reap reward therefrom.

As Mrs. Juniper sat in her room that evening, the tramp of hoofs came to her ears. She extinguished her light and, going to the window, looked out into the night. The pale rays of the moon fell upon a large body of cavalry dismounting at her gate, and, oh horrors! surrounding her house. Swift as the wind the widow flew down two flights of stairs to the cellar, where she acquainted the "brave soldier" of the fact, and implored him to be merciful, should they discover him, and not kill any more than was necessary in self-defense. Poor little Diggs sat cuddled up in one corner, his round face pale as death, looking anything in the world but dangerous.

Then came loud knocking at the front door.

"There," said the widow, "they are at the front door. I will try to send them away; but you are armed, and you are a brave man and there are not more than fifty; so, of course, you will not fear them."

The widow turned and left, while poor Diggs sat cowering and mentally ejaculating:

"Oh! Lordy, I'll be killed, I know I shall!"

Mrs. Juniper went herself to the door and opened it.

Captain Abner Tompkins stood there, sword in hand. Behind him were twenty or more of his men, all armed, while the others were scattered in different portions of the yard.

"What will you have, gentlemen?" asked the widow, holding the lamp above her head and looking fearlessly down into their faces.

"Pardon me, madam," said the young captain, bowing "but we have been informed that some rebels are quartering here, and have come for them."

"Your informant was both meddlesome and ignorant. There are no rebel *soldiers* in the house," was the widow's reply.

"I beg your pardon, madam," said Abner, entering unbidden, and followed by several of his men. "I have no cause to doubt, yet my orders are imperative, and I must search your house."

The widow had the tact to yield without more argument, and the search commenced. From her bedroom to the kitchen, all the house was thoroughly searched. The Captain laid his hand on the cellar door.

"Hold!" said the widow, laying her hand on his arm. "I told you there were no rebel soldiers here, and I told you the truth. There is, however, one of them in the cellar, but for humanity's sake I warn you not to encounter him. He is a host in himself, a perfect tornado, when roused. You will be all killed if you venture, for he is well armed."

The young captain smiled.

"You say he is a tornado; we are each a cyclone, and together we may raise a hurricane. But do not fear, madam, for, I assure you, we shall take him without the firing of a shot."

Opening the door, Captain Tompking boldly walked down the flight of stairs, leading to the cellar, a light in one hand and a drawn sword in the other—a number of his men following him. A sight met their view at the foot of the stairs, calculated rather to excite laughter than to strike terror to their hearts. A small man in gray uniform, rushing aimlessly about trying to scale the cellar wall, to hide beneath the boxes, to find some way—any way—of escape. His actions were more like that of a rat in a trap than a brave soldier.

Mrs. Juniper, left in the room above, faint with terror, sank upon the nearest chair and clasped her hands to her ears to shut out the sounds of conflict that must inevitably follow.

"Halloa, Diggs! what are you doing here?" cried Captain Tompkins, who could not restrain his laughter. Mr. Diggs had been performing leap after leap, in his vain endeavors to get away, ejaculating all the while:

"Oh, Lordy, Lordy! I know I shall be killed, I know I shall be killed!"

At the sound of a familiar voice, he looked around, and, discovering who his captors were, he sprang forward and threw his arms around the neck of the captain, crying:

"Oh! Abner, Abner, Abner, my dearest friend Abner, you will not let me be killed! Oh! say you will not let me be killed! Although I was persuaded into the rebel army, I am not a Confederate. I have always thought that it was wrong to fight under any but the flag of Washington and Marion. Oh! don't let them kill me! Oh, Abner, Abner, for Heaven's sake, say you will protect me. I have suffered death a thousand times since I entered this unholy cause."

Abner, still laughing, assured him that he should not be injured, that he should be treated as a prisoner of war.

Corporal Diggs, assuring men and officers that there was no stronger Union man living than he, that he was ready to enlist and fight until he died for the Union, followed the troops out of the house. The widow fixed a gaze of astonishment on the "brave soldier," upon "whom the fate of the South rested," and when she heard his imploring tones and his avowed determination to fight for the Union till he died, her proud lips curled with scorn, and, without a word, she passed from the room.

The corporal mounted January, and rode away in good spirits toward the Union camp.

CHAPTER XVI.

YELLOW STEVE.

Mr. Diggs fulfilled his determination to enlist in the Union army, insisting, the very day after his capture, on becoming a member of Abner's company. Abner told him that he had better consider the matter, but he declared he needed no further time; that now he was freed from error, and the pernicious influence of Seth Williams, who had persuaded him into espousing an unholy cause, and having wronged his beloved country by taking up arms against it, he wanted to atone by fighting for it. As the Union cause needed soldiers, Mr. Diggs, not corporal now, did not offer his services in vain. He was at once enrolled, and the same day the regiment started, by forced marches, to join the Union forces under Generals Scott and McDowell, where Mr. Patrick Henry Diggs was likely to see service in earnest.

On the 20th of July, the next after the day that Abner's regiment had joined the main army, and the day before the terrible battle of Manassas, or Bull Run, Abner Tompkins sat alone in his tent. It was late. The last picket had been stationed, the last order given, waiting for the morning to advance on the terrible foe, that lay sleeping over the hills only a few miles distant. It was but natural that his thoughts should wander back to his home. He drew out a small, many-folding locket, into which he gazed with looks of infinite tenderness. It represented the features of those whom his heart held most dear—his father's face, grave and most earnest, full of kindliness and honesty of purpose; his mother's face, beautiful and proud and tender; the third face on which the young officer gazed was young and fresh and fair. He seemed to look through the clear eyes into the pure, spotless soul. He gazed long and steadfastly, murmuring: "O Irene, Irene, shall we ever meet again?"

The next and last face was that of a young man—a dark, fearless face; firmness was in every lineament, determination in every line. Fearless, yet frank; proud, yet tender; the face was that of one who would be powerful for good or evil, who would scorn alike death and dishonor.

"War has severed the ties that bound us, my brother," spoke the captain. "Why can not political differences be settled without resort to arms? It is the ambitious and the great who stir up strife, and their humble followers fight their battles. They dwell in ease and safety, while my poor brother and I cross swords and shed each other's blood to uphold them in their greatness."

He closed the locket and placed it in his breast pocket, and the look of sadness deepened on his face. There came a gentle knock on the board that took the place of a door to the captain's tent.

"Come in," said Abner.

The board was set aside, and a pale, fair youth, about eighteen years of age, entered.

"Anything stirring yet, Willie?" asked the captain.

"Nothing, captain, except an occasional picket's shot," replied the boy. "But, if you please, there is a fellow out here who wants to see you."

"Who is he?" asked Abner.

"I don't know, captain. I never saw him before. He is a bright mulatto, and he says he must see you. He is dressed in citizen's clothes and unarmed."

"Let him come in, Willie."

The youthful soldier touched his cap lightly and withdrew, and a moment later a tall, yellow mulatto entered. He looked sharply about the tent, as though fearing that some secret foe might suddenly spring upon him.

"Have a seat," said Abner, pointing to the only unoccupied camp-stool that the tent afforded.

The mulatto took the proffered seat and fixed his bright, yellowish dark eyes on the young officer.

"Well, sir, what can I do for you?" asked the captain.

"Nothin'," replied the mulatto with a grin on his shriveled yellow face.

"Well, then, what can you do for me?"

"Nothin'," the grin broadening.

"Then, sir, what is your business here?" asked Abner, beginning to lose patience.

"I came to tell you that I was—here," said the mulatto, with provoking coolness.

"Well, what do you propose, now that you are here?" asked Abner, smiling in spite of himself.

"Your name is Tompkins—you are Captain Abner Tompkins?" said the mulatto.

"Yes."

"You have a brother Oleah, who is a captain in the Confederate army, that is right across the hill here?"

"Yes. What of him?"

"Oh, he is well," said the mulatto.

"What else have you to say?" asked Abner.

"Your father is George W. Tompkins, who lives on a plantation near Snagtown?"

"Yes. What of him?"

"Oh, he's well, too.

"Well, if you have anything to say, say it and be off," said Abner.

"Your sister as you call her, who was left at your door when a baby—"

"What of her?" cried Abner, eagerly. "Do you know anything of her?"

"Yes, she is well, too."

Abner, who had been started from his seat in his eagerness, sank back, and looked at his visitor in blank amazement. At length he said, sternly: "If you have nothing of importance to communicate, leave me. I have no time for pleasantry. From your manner I expected news—bad news—"

"And was disappointed," said the mulatto, with a smile.

"Who are you?" demanded Abner.

"I don't mind letting you know my name. I am called Yellow Steve—got no other name. I just come to say I shall be around, and if you should ever need me it is most likely you will find me right at hand. I am everywhere. Can come as near as possible being in three places at once."

"You must be a remarkable person," said Abner.

"I have a remarkable story to tell you at some time."

"Why not tell me now? I may fall in to-morrow's fight."

"Then I will tell your brother."

"But he may fall. Does it concern me?"

"It is the waif, the foundling, you call sister, my story concerns. Some time you shall have it—not now."

The man disappeared through the door as he spoke, and, though Abner rushed out after him, he was gone.

He inquired of Willie Thornbridge which way the man had gone, but Willie declared he had not seen him come out of the tent. He pursued his search and inquiries, but no one else had seen Yellow Steve at all.

Abner Tompkins, on the morning of the battle, was early astir, and, breakfast over, the bugle sounded boots and saddles. Abner kept his lines well dressed, and awaited the order to advance. The skirmish lines had already been thrown out, and the distant roar of guns could be heard.

Diggs declared that war was a cruel "institution," and that he was ready to retire at as early a date as possible.

"You present a nice figure on that horse," said Corporal Grimm. "Darned if a cannon-shot could afford to miss you."

"Yes," added Sergeant Swords, "you'll present as nice a mark for the sharpshooters up on that camel's back as if you were a squirrel in a tree."

"You'll come out all right yet, Henry," said Uncle Dan, the scout, riding up at this moment, with his trusty rifle on the pommel of his saddle.

"Do you think I'll be shot, Uncle Dan?" asked Diggs, shuddering in spite of himself.

"No, not if you do enough shooting yourself," replied the old man. "Ye must watch yer chance and pop it to them so fast they can't git a chance to pop back."

At this moment a pale, fair youth, mounted on a bright bay horse, came galloping up to Captain Tompkins. He was dressed in the uniform of a United States cavalryman, with a saber and carbine at his side, and pistols in his holsters. The sight of this youth, and the nearness of the coming battle, brought sad reflections to Abner's mind. Willie Thornbridge was just eighteen, the only comfort and support of his widowed mother. Abner remembered well the bright, sunny morning when Willie bade his mother farewell, and the mother, with tear-streaming eyes and aching heart, admonished Abner to take care of and protect him.

"What have you, Willie?" asked Abner, as the youth drew rein at his captain's side.

"Something the adjutant gave me," said Willie, handing a paper to Abner, who read and, carefully folding it, put it in the breast-pocket of his coat. At this moment the bugle sounded "forward."

"Fall in by my side, Willie," said Abner, and the boy

wheeled into line by his captain, with Uncle Dan on the other side of him.

"Forward!" came the order, and the vast columns of men were in motion, moving on toward those black lines of the foe that lay in the distance. The far off firing of skirmishers became more rapid.

"Are you afraid?" asked Abner of the boy soldier

"No. With you on one side and Uncle Dan on the other, I have no fear," and he smiled in such an assuring way that Abner could not doubt him.

Uncle Dan, as we have before said was an army scout, and not a regular soldier. However, he had volunteered on this occasion to accompany Abner's company. He was well mounted, his dress was half civil and half military, and his arms were his trusty rifle and a pair of holsters.

The vast columns were rapidly moving when Diggs exclaimed:

"Oh, Lordy! I feel very sick!"

"You will feel better soon," said Corporal Grimm, his file-leader.

"Ye'll have enough soon to take up yer attention," put in Sergeant Swords.

By nine o'clock the fight began in earnest. Colonel Holdfast's cavalry was at first held in reserve at the foot of the hill. When it was ordered to advance, just as the top of the hill was reached, January became frightened at the flashing guns, and, wheeling about, dashed down the hill with Diggs' saber dangling at his side.

The bugle rung out the fearful note—a wild dash, a moment's delirious excitement—and they were at the rebel's guns. The battery was captured with but little loss, and the guns turned on the retreating foe. The whole army now advanced, and a stubborn fight ensued, which resulted in the Confederate lines slowly falling back.

Cheer upon cheer arose along the Union lines, as the foe retreated and pursuit commenced. Mr. Diggs, who had viewed the battle afar off, seeing victory perched upon the banner of the Union forces, prevailed on January to join in the pursuit, and galloping up to his regiment, waved his sword high in the air, shouting:

"Hip, hip, huzzah, huzzah, huzzah! for the old Stars and Stripes, the flag of Washington and Marion! Charge everybody! I want to get among them! They shall know that Patrick Henry Diggs can fight."

The crest of the hill was reached, and the whole Confederate army suddenly burst into view, drawn up in a line of battle, a thunderclap shook the earth, and a huge volume of smoke seemed to enwrap it. Death and destruction was hurled among the advancing ranks. The ground was strewn at the first fire with dead and wounded. Out from these columns of smoke came the fearful Black Horse Regiment, bearing down like a dark storm on the already stunned Union lines.

Retreat was the only thing, and retreat became rout and panic. It was the arrival of General Johnston, who, having eluded Patterson, had come up with reinforcements that so suddenly turned the tide of battle, making defeat out of almost certain victory.

Abner saw his men and horses rolling in the dust from the deadly fire. A score of saddles were emptied at the first volley, and a score of riderless horses dashed back frightened, to spread panic in the rear. No bugle sounded the retreat, there was no need for any. It was vain to attempt to stem the current, for his men had lost all self-control.

As Uncle Dan wheeled his horse to follow the flying regiment, he saw Willie Thornbridge sink in his saddle. Reaching out his strong arm, he drew the slight boyish figure before him on his own horse.

"Are you hurt, Willie?" the old man asked.

The boy made no reply, but the uproar and confusion doubtless drowned the old man's words. He kept steadily on, bearing the slight burden, passing the infantry, the artillery, the baggage and ammunition trains, and on, until he reached the outskirts of the retreating army.

"Is he hurt?" asked Abner Tompkins, who had drawn up a portion of his shattered company.

"I don't know," said Uncle Dan, "he has not spoken during our entire ride. Can you get down, Willie?"

There was no answer. Captain Tompkins sprang from his horse and went to assist the boy. As the old man released his hold, the young soldier fell into the captain's arms and they saw he was dead.

Dead without a pang. Dead without a moment's preparation, without one word of endearment or farewell to his lonely and widowed mother.

Just behind Willie's left ear was a small, dark-red hole, from which the purple life-blood was still oozing. The small insignificant speck, as it seemed, had opened a door, through which his young soul had taken its everlasting flight.

Taking up the corpse, the cavalcade rode sadly on for a few miles, to where the tired Union army, or a portion of it, encamped for the night.

Mr. Diggs was in the very height of his patriotism and bravery, when the arrival of the re-enforcements so suddenly changed the tide of battle.

"Oh, Lordy! I'll be killed, I know I shall!" he shrieked, and January again turned and fled before the tempest. Taking a course to the left of that pursued by the regular army, Diggs soon found himself on the outskirts of the battle. As he looked over his shoulder, he beheld a powerful cavalryman in full uniform, mounted on a horse black as midnight, in hot pursuit of him.

"Oh, Lordy! he'll kill me, I know he will," yelled the miserable Diggs, as he urged January on at the top of his speed. Casting back occasional glances, he saw that the huge black horse was gradually gaining on him.

Things had really become serious, and Diggs was in momentary danger of the ponderous saber, which the cavalryman flourished threateningly in the air as he came on like the wind. They had been flying over a level piece of cleared land, but now a thick body of timber and brush loomed up before them. There was yet a chance. Once in the timber, Diggs might elude his dangerous pursuer. The Confederate cavalryman evidently uuderstood this, for, with a whack he sent his saber into the scabbard, and drew his pistol, without once slacking his speed.

"Oh, Lordy! I shall be killed this time sure," bawled Diggs. Again he glanced toward the cavalryman and saw him raise his deadly weapon. Diggs yelled, screamed, and implored, all the while urging January to greater speed. The wood was almost at hand.

"Bang!" went the pistol, and Diggs felt a sharp pain, as if a red-hot iron had been suddenly jerked across the top of his left shoulder.

"Oh, I am killed! I am killed!" he yelled, as January plunged into the thick underbrush.

The Confederate evidently believing he had killed the Yankee (having, indeed, the Yankee's own word for it), turned and dashed away.

January had not gone twenty yards in his mad race through the woods before he plunged into the mill-stream. Diggs' wound was not serious and the water was shallow, so he soon managed to crawl out on the opposite side, where he seated himself for a moment at the foot of a tree, gasping, spitting, and sneezing, the water running from his clothes in rivulets. "This soldier business don't suit me," he muttered, "and I know I shall be killed if I don't quit it. It is nothing but duckings, falls, being torn with thorns and shot with guns—"

A sharp firing in the woods roused him to a reality of his situation, and, mounting the dripping January, he galloped away to join his regiment.

CHAPTER XVII.

A SOLDIER'S TURKEY HUNT.

The armies of the North and the armies of the South had been concentrating for months prior to the battle of Bull Run, resulting in the defeat of the Northern troops and in heavy loss to both sides; after collision came recoil, as of mighty waves dashing against a rock bound coast. Predatory bands of disorganized soldiers from both sides roamed the country, and, in many instances, not plundering merely, but ruthlessly destroying what they could not seize.

Mr. Diggs had found his company the day after the battle, and narrated to his comrades his hair-breadth escape and the many heroic deeds which he had performed, among others, the deadly attack on the Confederate cavalryman, who had wounded him in the shoulder. He became quite a hero in Corporal Grimm's eyes, his experience at Bull Run reminding the corporal of incidents that had happened in his ten days' military service under General Preston, also recalling to the mind of Sergeant Swords details of his own service under Captain Strong, all of which was circumstantially narrated for the edification of Mr. Diggs, who again rejoiced that he had not carried out his rash threat of leaving the army. Laurels yet, he knew, must crown his brow. Already he had become a hero. True, when faced by danger and death and sorely tried, he acknowledged to himself that he wavered; but, in the quiet of camp, his patriotism returned and he again felt ready to meet the foe.

The day after the battle, the body of Willie Thornbridge was consigned to its last resting-place. There were but two mourners gathered over that little mound of earth—his captain and Uncle Dan, the scout, who felt, not only grief for the brave young life so early ended, but a deeper pain for the widowed mother at home, now childless.

Colonel Holdfast's regiment was falling back toward the Junction, its old head-quarters. Their movements were necessarily slow, as they were constantly recruiting, and they were compelled to be wary, for small parties of stragglers were occasionally picked up by independent companies of Confederates.

One evening Corporal Grimm suggested to Sergeant Swords that they form an independent foraging corps of half a dozen and make a raid on the turkeys of an old rebel, about a mile from the camp, that night. The sergeant acquiesced—we never knew a sergeant who would not acquisce in such a plan, even at the risk of being reduced to the ranks—and they were not long in finding plenty of volunteers. The corps must not exceed six, as the secret could not be so well kept among more, and a larger force could not be so well handled.

Our friend Diggs was easily persuaded to enter into the project. For the last two days he had been contemplating writing a book, to be entitled "Camp Life," narrating his own experiences. This freak, he thought, might afford a diverting incident.

Great caution and secrecy were necessary, for, if knowledge of their project reached head-quarters, it would have put an end to their sport. At dark, having provided themselves with a dark lantern, they passed the guard and wended their way over the long hill toward the barn-yard of the old rebel. The night was very dark with a rainy mist or fog, which made darkness and discomfort more intense.

"Now, boys," said Sergeant Swords, "this is an old rebel, and we have a perfect right to confiscate his turkeys; but let us be quiet about it, so as not to disturb the old man."

"Of course," said Corporal Grimm, "let him rest in peace, and dream sweet dreams of the coming glory of the Southern Confederacy."

They stole noiselessly over the damp ground, occasionally chuckling with delight at the thought of their coming feast. The long hill was passed over and the barn reached, where the unsuspecting rebel turkeys were roosting.

"This is delightful," thought Mr. Diggs, his short legs moving rapidly, in order to keep up with the rest of the company. "What an entertaining, amusing, and instructive chapter this will furnish for my book! This is one phase of soldier life. Night so black, so intensely black—hem—that one might write his name in chalk upon it. Dark, wild clouds and howling winds with thick banks of fog almost blocking the way, as six resolute, determined, dare-devil soldiers, of whom the modest writer was one— He, he, he!" chuckled Diggs to himself. "I'll make it capital."

His ruminations were brought to a close by arriving at the tall, dark barn, where Sergeant Swords called a halt and solemnly informed his command that the desired turkeys were inside.

"I say—hem, hem, hem!" began Mr. Diggs.

"Well, don't make so much noise about it!" whispered Corporal Grimm, clutching him by the arm, "or we will have the old rebel and his five hundred niggers on us in no time."

The door of the barn was locked, but this slight obstacle was soon overcome.

"Quick!" whispered Sergeant Swords, and the men glided in.

The loud barking of a dog from the house came to their ears, and the sound of angry voices. Tom Scott closed the large double door just as the nose of a ferocious dog came thump against them.

"Hist!" said the sergeant. "I believe we are discovered."

"What is it, old man?" came in shrill accents from the house.

"Some one's in the barn stealing hosses."

At this moment the turkeys, becoming alarmed at the very evident expressed intentions of the intruders, set up a loud "Quit, quit!"

"They're stealing the turkeys. It's some of them thievin' Aberlitionists," said the old woman.

"You bring the lantern, and I'll see," answered a deep voice, evidently that of the cross old rebel himself.

"We're in for it now, boys," said Sergeant Swords, turning on the light from his dark lantern. "Hunt holes somewhere."

Tom Scott had enough to do to hold the doors against the dog, which seemed determined to force an entrance. Corporal Grimm sprang into a meal chest, which he saw at the far end of the barn, and the lid closed down on him; two others found concealment behind a hay-mow, and Sergeant Swords and Mr. Diggs sprang up among the rafters, where the turkeys were roosting.

"Oh, Lordy! I shall be killed, I know I shall!" wailed poor Diggs, as he scrambled up.

The turkeys were now remonstrating loudly.

"Stop your chin music!" said the sergeant.

Tom Scott was still holding the doors when the old man and his wife came to them.

"Some one is in the barn," said the voice of the old man. "See here, the lock is broken off."

In a moment, in spite of Tom's efforts, the door was pushed open, and the bull dog, with loud, deep yelps, sprang in.

Tom kept well behind the door, and pulled it close

against him. The old woman held up a lantern, and the sergeant and our friend Diggs were both discovered by the man and the dog at the same time.

The dog announced his discovery by angry growls, and his master, a man about fifty years of age, by closely examining an old, ugly musket in his hand.

"Hulloa, you thieves; I've cotched you now?" he said, advancing.

"Good evening, sir," said Swords.

"What are you doing up there, you scamps?"

"Roosting," was the cool response.

"Shoot them!" said the old woman, holding up the lantern.

"Oh, no! don't, grandpa," said the sergeant.

"Oh, Lordy! I'll be killed!" wailed Diggs, trying to screen himself behind a turkey.

Click went the old musket.

"Quit, quit," peeped the turkeys.

"I second the motion," said Sergeant Swords.

"Shoot them, old man; shoot 'em dead," repeated the woman, whose eyes were blazing with fury at sight of the blue-coats.

"I intend to," he said, bringing his musket to his shoulder, which movement made Diggs fairly howl with fear.

"Hold on, grandpa; give a fellow a chance to say his prayers afore you pop him over," said Sergeant Swords. "If you don't turn away that old popgun you may hurt some of these turkeys. Besides, I've got a battalion of men here all around you, and I can raise the devil."

At this moment the dog, which had been prowling about, discovered Tom Scott behind the door, and renewed his attack upon him. Tom fired two shots from his revolver, one of which silenced the dog forever. The two men in the haymow now came rolling down, much like two huge balls, each snatching a turkey as he came.

Corporal Grimm sprang from the meal-chest, white as a snowball.

"Look there," old man; thar's a ghost!" cried the woman, pointing at Corporal Grimm. The old man leveled his musket and fired, but the shot flew wide of its mark, and Corporal Grimm advanced.

The old man and old woman took to their heels, and the next moment was heard the sound of many voices and the tramp of many feet.

"Secesh, by hokey!" cried Sergeant Swords, leaping from his perch with a gobbler's neck in each hand. "Git up and git!" and all made a rapid exit, leaving poor Diggs still perched on the rafters, bewildered and confused. In their haste they left the dark lantern in the barn with the slides open, by the side of the old woman's lantern, which she had dropped in her haste.

"Oh, Lordy, I shall be killed; I know I shall," wailed poor Diggs, frozen to his perch by his terror.

Bang! bang! bang! went a dozen shots, their blaze lighting up the intense darkness. It came from the new arrivals firing at the flying soldiers, who were rapidly retreating with their prizes. Tom Scott lost a thumb by a random shot, but he did not lose either of the two turkeys he had started with.

"Who were they, Seth?" Diggs heard a voice outside ask.

"I don't know; abolition soldiers, probably, stealing chickens," replied another voice.

Diggs thought he had heard both voices before, but in his terror he was not sure.

"Guess they got no chickens," said a third voice, and Diggs could hear the speaker ramming a load down his gun.

"Let's take a look in the barn," said the first speaker. Halloa! if they ain't left their lanterns burning; left in a hurry, I guess."

The blood fairly froze in the veins of our friend Diggs, as he heard several steps approaching the barn door. Flight was now impossible, if it had not been before.

Several men, dressed in the gray uniform of Confederates, appeared at the barn door.

"Halloa!" cried one, in the uniform of a lieutenant, "here is a dead dog. Can that be what those three shots were fired at which brought us here?"

"By Jove, Lieutenant Snapemup, there's a quee

rooster," and the speaker pointed to our friend Diggs, who sat trembling astride the rafter.

"Who are you and what are you doing up there?" cried Lieutenant Snapemup.

"Oh, Lordy, Lordy, Lordy!" groaned Diggs.

"Come down there, Stumpy," cried Diggs' old tormentor and former companion, Seth Williams, entering.

As Diggs showed no sign of an intention to obey his order, Seth adopted a summary method for bringing him down. Taking a musket from a soldier, he fired a shot which passed about a foot above the small, round head. With a howl of fear and desperation, Diggs, who verily believed he was killed, let go his hold and fell from the beam, head first into the open meal-chest that was just beneath him.

"Williams, what do you mean? You have killed him!" cried Lieutenant Snapemup.

"No, I have not touched him," replied Seth.

"Who is it?" asked Howard Jones entering the barn.

"A Yank," replied Williams, and, walking forward to the chest, where Diggs was floundering and sneezing in the meal, he seized him by the nape of the neck, pulled him out and deposited him on the floor, where he stood, white with meal, and his eyes and ears full.

"Who are you?" asked Seth, peering into the face of his victim, who stood digging his fists into his eyes.

"I—I—hem—that is—I don't know," stammered Diggs.

"Let me see," said Williams, giving him a shake so vigorous that the meal flew in white clouds from his hair and clothes. "I do. I know you. You are Patrick Henry Diggs, by all that's wonderful! Where have you been, corporal?"

"I—hem—I—I—that is to say, I don't know," gasped Diggs.

"You don't hey? Well, collect your ideas," replied Seth.

"Well, yes—hem—thas is to say—hem, hem—I have been a prisoner.

The men now crowded around Diggs, who, having collected his faculties, told them how he had been taken prisoner at Carrick's Ford, how he had tried again and again to escape, how he had joined the foraging party with the full intention of escaping; he told a moving story of the compulsion which had been used to force him to put on the uniform of a Union soldier.

Seth Williams told him that they were very glad they had found him, for they were going back to Snagtown, and he knew Crazy Joe would mourn if his mud man did not return with the rest. Diggs flew into a fury as of old; but the barn and premises having been explored, the word of command was given, and Mr. Diggs found himself again on the march, but this time with other matter for thought than a diverting chapter for his contemplated book.

CHAPTER XVIII.

MR. TOMPKINS RECEIVES STRANGE NEWS.

The war cloud grew darker day by day. The time had actually come when families were divided, and brother was arrayed against brother. But little business was done in the border and middle States. Men seemed to have suddenly gone mad. The once industrious farmer had deserted his farm, and the plow lay rusting in the weedy furrow. A majority of the able-bodied men were either in the Northern or Southern army. The wildest and most exaggerated rumors were flying over the land. Skirmishes were reported as tremendous battles, hundreds were magnified into thousands, and tens to hundreds. Men, who had always been peaceable and law abiding, seemed suddenly inspired with a mania for the murder, plunder and destruction of all who did not adhere to their opinions. Friends became enemies, neighbors looked upon each other with cold suspicion or expressed open hostility. All baser attributes of man's nature, kept in check by the strong arm of law in time of peace, were roused and brought to the surface.

The plantation of Mr. Tompkins had not been visited by

hostile forces since the visit of Oleah's company. But that event was sufficient to give him full knowledge of the seriously dangerous condition of the country. Mr. Tompkins was greatly changed. A careworn expression had settled on his face—a face haggard and livid—years older than when we first looked upon it, and hair whitening fast. The bloom had faded from Mrs. Tompkins' delicate dark face, and the happy smile from her lips.

The harmony of the household had been disturbed, never again to be restored. The peace which had lasted for years was broken, so were the ties of love, which had defined the ravages of time, and the thousand petty vexations of domestic life were sadly strained. Mr. Tompkins' political preference was cramped and choked by his family division. True, no open rupture had taken place between him and his wife, yet the very fact that both were silent upon the exciting topic of the day brought about that coolness which is sure to result when there is a forbidden topic between husband and wife. Mr. Tompkins spent the days in anxiety, and the nights brought no peace. He went to the village almost daily for the mail, and found the newspapers full of accounts of bloody battles, while from lip to lip passed horrible rumors.

When the defeat at Bull Run was rumored he waited to gather authentic news, with painfully complicated feelings—anxiety for the cause he could not openly avow, and for his sons, in either army, one always to be in the victorious army, and one in the ranks of the defeated. And this thought chased away the look of joy that for an instant lit up the face of Mrs. Tompkins when she learned the news.

Days passed, and weeks, but no news came of either son. All Mr. Tompkins knew was that armies were marching and counter-marching daily, and filling the country with alarm.

Communication north and south was cut off, and it was almost impossible for any letter to cross the line.

It was evening, three or four weeks after the battle of Bull Run. Mr. Tompkins had, as usual, been to Snagtown, and returned; the Summer sun was sinking, battling in golden glory, a thick, dark bank of clouds gathering in the northwest. Mr. Tompkins sat in a rustic seat on the lawn, beneath the spreading branches of a maple, which had of late become his favorite resort. As he sat, his eyes wandered off to the northwest, rather in listlessness than interest.

The sun went to rest behind the hill, and lightning flashed from the dark recesses of the clouds, and twilight, soft and gray, began to gather about the landscape.

A man entered the front yard and walked leisurely down the white gravelled walk toward the portion of the lawn where Mr. Tompkins was sitting. He was a man apparently near Mr. Tompkins' own age, but his form erect, and lithe, still seemed to retain his vitality and youthful vigor. His woolly, sun burned hair was streaked with gray; his yellow face was wrinkled, but his eyes were fired with energy. The rapid change of expression on his face was perhaps the most remarkable thing about this man—at one moment gentle, almost appealing, the next inspired with the fury of a demon. The mulatto carried himself with a boldness and a freedom not common with those of his color. Walking up to the planter and touching the brim of his weather-beaten hat, he said:

"Good evening, sir. Mr. Tompkins, I believe?"

"That's my name. What is your business with me?" returned the planter, sharply.

"I want to see you," replied the mulatto, coolly, taking, unbidden, a seat on the bench beneath the tree.

"To see me? Well, what for?"

"To talk with you," was the reply.

"What is it?" demanded the planter. "Have you a bad master, and do you want me to buy you?"

"No, sir, I am not for sale," replied the mulatto, his face glowing with a baleful light. "I am no slave, I am free, and free by my own exertions."

"Well, what is it you have to say to me?"

"Something, I think, you will be glad to hear."

The planter began to lose patience. "If you have any thing to say to me, say it at once."

"Well, to begin with, you have two sons, one in the Confederate and one in the Union army."

"What of them?"

"They are well."

"Thank you, thank you for the news," cried the planter, rising and grasping the old man's hand. "When did you see them last?"

"You are willing to talk to me now," said the mulatto, with a smile.

"Where did you see my boys last?" repeated Mr. Tompkins, eagerly, unheeding the interruption.

"Only a few days ago."

"Where?"

"In their camps. They both are moving back this way."

"How came you to see them both? Is one of them a prisoner?"

"No."

"You can not have been in both armies?"

"I have been."

"How did that happen?"

"How I go is a secret known only to myself, but I go wherever desire or duty call me, and armies, guards, and prisons, locked and bolted doors, are no impediment to me. I saw your sons, and they are well."

It had grown almost dark, yet the planter could see the eyes of his strange visitor gleam weirdly.

"Who are you?" he asked, the little superstition he had in his nature aroused.

"They call me Yellow Steve."

"Where do you live?"

"On the earth, in the air, almost on the air."

"By that you mean you live in no particular place?" said the planter.

"Yes. There was a time when I was human, when I had human desires and human feeling, but all that is changed. My soul has been tortured until what little reason I ever possessed has fled. There are times, sir, when I am not a human being."

"You are crazy," said the planter, with an incredulous smile.

"Have you ever read of Wagner, the Wehr-wolf?"

"Yes, in my boyhood I have read of that remarkable personage," replied the planter.

"You remember that periodically, he became a wolf, a

demon. Well, sir, I have passed through a similar experience. There are times when my human feelings, my human reason leave me." The mulatto's yellow face seemed to grow livid in the twilight.

The wind moaned wildly, and the clouds gathered in thick, rolling masses in the northwest.

"Have you any further business with me?" asked the planter uneasily.

"I am to tell you that I hold a key that will unlock one of the darkest secrets that has clouded your life, a secret that has ever been a puzzle and a torment to you. This dark war cloud will not roll of our land without sweeping many from the face of the earth, and I feel that I shall be among the number. I can not leave this earth without yielding up to you the key of this mystery."

"Where is the key, and what is the mystery?" asked Mr. Tompkins.

"I will arrange so that you shall receive the key after my death. The secret relates to the parentage of your foster child."

A loud clap of thunder shook, and, for one moment, a blaze of lightning enwrapped the earth. When Mr. Tompkins lifted his dazzled eyes, he was alone. The strange man had disappeared as suddenly as if he had melted into air.

CHAPTER XIX.

IRENE'S DILEMMA—THE BROTHERS MEET.

To Irene the varied and startling changes that had lately taken place, brought perplexity and grief. The political question, that she had heard discussed since her early childhood, until it had become to her as familiar as a household pet, and been deemed as harmless, had broken up the family, and now bade fair to destroy the Nation. Often in her childish innocence had she laughed to hear little Abner declare himself "Papa's Whig," little dreaming of the awful meaning lurking in these words, a meaning powerful for the destruction of homes and country.

A monster had been taken into the Tompkins' family and laughed over and caressed, and now it had arisen in its wrath to prove their destroyer. That monster was difference of political opinion. Irene, with her clear good senses saw the great mistake in the life of her foster parents. Their difference of opinion, kept alive by frequent discussion, and veiled by light and gentle jests, had at last thrown off all disguises, and stood forth a frightful reality, widening with alarming rapidity the chasm opened between them. It may be doubted, if it is safe for husband and wife to differ even in jest.

Irene had puzzled her brain in her endeavor to devise some plan, which might restore to the family the happy harmony of old, but, like many good men whose minds were engrossed with the same endeavor for the country's good, she failed.

The regiment of which Abner Tompkins was a member had returned to the Junction, and the regiment which Colonel Scrabble commanded was again in the neighborhood of Snagtown. Both Abner and Oleah had sent word to their parents that they would probably be able to visit home, while their companies were encamped in the neighborhood.

Colonel Scrabble, finding his position in the vicinity of Snagtown rather uncomfortably near the Junction, where Colonel Holdfast and two other regiments were quartered, fell back about twenty miles south, beyond the Twin Mountains. The good people about Snagtown felt greatly relieved at the departure of the colonel's forces, for they had been kept in a constant state of alarm, expecting battle every day.

It was the third day after the retirement of the Confederates that a single horseman, a cavalry officer, galloped down the long hill on the road leading from Snagtown to Mr. Tompkins' residence. He was a fearless looking young fellow, with blue eyes and dark brown hair, and he rode alone, though he wore the blue uniform of a Union captain.

Arriving at the front gate, he swung from the saddle, handing his reins to a negro boy, and walked quickly up the front walk, meeting his father on the lawn.

"Quite safe and sound, you see," he said in reply to Mr. Tompkins' eager, anxious eyes.

Father and son went together to the house, and, at the sound of the well-known voice, Mrs. Tompkins, with a cry of joy, rushed from her room to clasp her son in her arms. What though he wore the hated uniform of a Union soldier? He was still her son.

Irene's cheeks glowed with pleasure at sight of Abner, whom she had so long believed to be her brother. She gave him a sister's welcome, as it was.

During the evening, when alone with his father, Abner related the mysterious appearance and disappearance of Yellow Steve, and his strange words. Mr. Tompkins also had something singular to relate on that subject, and for half an hour they discussed this strange individual and his possible connection with Irene's history.

"He says he holds the key, which will unlock the mystery of her parentage," said Mr. Tompkins, "but how are we to get him to turn it?"

Abner said he would make it one of the duties of his life to search out this mysterious stranger.

"It will have to be managed carefully," said the father, "for should he be so inclined, this man, perhaps, might destroy the last trace of her parentage. My impression is that it was he who placed her, when a baby, at our door."

"What could have been his motive?" asked Abner.

"Motive? Any one of a thousand things might have been his motive. He might have done it with the hope of securing a reward for the recovery of the child, or he may thus have taken revenge for some real or fancied wrong, or he may have been hired by the parents."

"Come, Irene," said the young officer when tea was over. "I want to look around the old place once more."

They paused in the garden, where the air was sweet with the fragance of Summer flowers, and pulsating with the evening songs of birds.

"I never come out here now," said Irene. "It is so lonesome with you and Oleah so far away," and sat down upon a rustic seat.

As Abner gazed into the depths of those soft, gray eyes he

thought so much beauty had never before been concentrated in one being. Irene's goodness of heart he had learned to know long ago. He was he thought, almost on the eve of discovering her parentage, but he determined to win her, be it high or low.

"Irene," he said, "I am glad to be once more in this dear old home, to be once more with the parents I love; but the greatest happiness of all is to have you again by my side."

"O Abner," she answered, lifting her earnest, tearful eyes, "do not say to me again what you said to me that last night! It breaks my heart to give you pain, but I know that you are wrong, that you have mistaken your own feelings. I have loved you so long as a sister! Oh, how terribly all things have changed! Do not you change, Abner! Be my brother still!"

> "Let what is broken so remain,
> The gods are hard to reconcile,"

said Abner, looking sorrowfully into the pale, pleading face. "When change has come, nothing can bring back the old order of things. But I will wait, I will promise you not to speak again of my love, until you can answer me without tears in your eyes. Now, let me see you smile, Irene, once more before I go."

Irene could not sleep that night; her bed chamber was in the south wing of the house, and her window looked out upon a portion of the grounds directly shaded with trees and shrubbery. It was late when voices on the lawn below attracted her attention. The family, she knew, had been buried in sleep for hours, and it was something unusual for the slaves to select that portion of the grounds for midnight consultation. At last she arose and cautiously approached the window.

The night was beautiful, the moon shone brightly, even penetrating the dark shade of the trees, beneath one of which two figures were distinctly visible. The night was very still, and, though the men were at some distance from the house, she could hear distinctly every word they spoke.

The voice of one sounded familiar to Irene, and it took

only a second glance to show her that it was Crazy Joe, engaged in conversation with some stranger.

Crazy Joe had always made a strange impression on Irene. From her earliest recollection he had been either a resident or frequenter of the Tompkins' plantation. The poor lunatic had always shown the warmest attachment for her, and his strange wild talk, the mingling of early Scriptural and classical lessons, with ideas dwarfed by some sudden shock, had always had a strange fascination for her.

All her fear instantly vanished as she recognized Crazy Joe, for she knew that no harm could ever come to any one of them through him, but her curiosity to know who was his companion and what their topic of conversation, became almost painful in its intensity.

Crazy Joe had of late divided his time between the plantation and the cabin at the foot of Twin Mountains. Uncle Dan, when he entered the army, tried to induce Joe to desert the place altogether, but this he refused to do, always declaring he must have the house of his Uncle Esau ready at his coming.

Irene could discover that Joe's companion was a negro, a man past the middle age of life, of strong frame and strongly marked features. It was with a thrill of astonishment that she heard these words.

"When do you remember seeing your father last?"

"'Twas when my father dwelt in a distant land. I was much beloved of my father, for I was the sun of his old age."

"Oh, don't talk such nonsense! What was your father's name?"

"Jacob, my father was Jacob, the son of Isaac."

"No, he wasn't," replied the man. "Try and think if your father didn't have another name than Jacob."

The poor fellow for a moment puzzled his brain and then said slowly:

"No, it could not be otherwise. Joseph was the son of Jacob, and Jacob the son of Isaac, and Isaac the son of Abraham; so you see my father must have been Jacob. Joseph was sold into bondage and carried into Egypt, and I am Joseph, so my father must have been Jacob."

"Can't you recollect that your father had another name?"

"No, he never had any other name but Jacob, the son of Isaac."

"Your father's name was Henry," said the man. "Now don't you remember that his Christian name was Henry?"

The moonlight fell full on Joe's troubled face, and Irene thought she could discover a strange expression cross it, as though a stream of memory's sunshine had suddenly been let in on his long clouded mind, but a moment after it was passed, and he said:

"No, it must have been Jacob, and if Jacob is not my father, my father must be dead. The famine has been very sore in the land of Canaan."

"There has been no famine in the land where your father dwells," said the man, earnestly. "Your father never knew a famine, never knew want or care. He was a reckless, passionate man, but at times he was gentle and kind."

"My father, Jacob, was always good and kind," said Joe, thoughtfully.

"Your father's name was not Jacob," said the man, evidently annoyed and puzzled. "Your father's name was Henry—" Irene listened with strained attention to hear the last name, but the voice of the speaker was lowered, so that she failed to catch it. "Now," went on the stranger, "try and remember, while I tell you about your father and your home. Your father was a handsome man, with dark hair and eyes and heavy jet black whiskers. Do you not remember the home of your childhood—a large, brown stone mansion, surrounded with palmetto trees, and orange groves, and cane brakes? Do you not remember the vast fields of cotton and rice and sugar-cane, with negroes working in them, and your father riding about in his carriage with you by his side? Can't you remember your mother? Can't you remember the tiny boats she made for you to float on the lake?"

The mulatto paused, and looked eagerly at his companion, as though to catch a gleam of intelligence. Again that curious, puzzled look came over the face of Joe, and he seemed trying to pierce the gloom of forgetfulness with his blunted recollection. After a moment his face brightened, and he said:

"Yes, I remember the fields of cotton, and the carriage and my mother. I remember the great palmetto tree by the lake, where I floated my boats and made my flutter-mills."

"Well, listen now," said the black, still more earnestly. "Can you not remember what your name was when you played by the lake under the big palmetto tree by the lake?"

"I was not Joseph then."

"Can you not remember what your name was?"

"No."

"Would you remember if I was to tell you?"

"Yes."

Irene was leaning against the window-sill, holding the half-closed shutter in her hand. In her eagerness she pressed forward, pushing the shutter so far open that it slipped from her hold and swung crashing back against the house. She sprang back into the room to prevent discovery, and when next she glanced from her window, Crazy Joe was alone. His strange companion had disappeared, and Joe sat nodding under the tree more than half asleep.

It was nothing uncommon for Joe to pass the night under a tree, and Irene only watched to see him stretch down under a tree and compose himself to sleep, when she crept to her own bed, filled with wonder and curiosity. Crazy Joe's parentage, like her own, was shrouded in mystery, and perhaps it may have been their common misfortune that had awakened her sympathy and drawn her so strongly towards the lunatic.

It was late before Irene closed her eyes for sleep, and when she did, Joe's troubled eyes, Abner's eyes, sad and reproachful, and the gleaming eyes of the stranger haunted her dreams.

Early next morning she went out to where Crazy Joe was sitting on the grass, communing with himself. As she approached him she heard him say:

"Yes, yes, I remember the cotton fields and the palmetto tree by the lake, the boats I sailed there, but then something heavy strikes my brain."

She tried to persuade him to tell her who it was he was talking with on the night before, but the light of memory faded from his face, and his mind immediately averted to his father Jacob, who was soon to come down into Egypt.

It was about two weeks after Abner's visit that Oleah found himself at the head of a small scouting party in the neighborhood of his home.

Scouting parties were no novelty in and near the village of Snagtown, for this village lay about half way between the two hostile forces, and the scouts of both armies frequently entered it. These parties, not always made up of the most honorable men, kept the good citizens in the vicinity in a constant state of alarm. Hen roosts were robbed, apple orchards devastated, and melon patches stripped, vines and all.

Oleah's party, however, attempted no exploits of this kind, for his men knew that he would regard it as base and dastardly an act to filch from an unoffending citizen as to fly from an enemy.

Our friend Diggs was of the party, and when Oleah stationed his men in a grove, about a mile distant, and set out to visit his home, Mr. Diggs volunteered to accompany him. Oleah was annoyed, but, having no good excuse for refusal, submitted with what grace he could to the infliction. The short-legged soldier was now all smiles and satisfaction, being, in his own estimation, the favored of his captain.

"I tell you—hem, hem, hem!" said Diggs, as he kicked his heels into the flanks of his horse—not January, but a spiteful little mustang—to keep up with the fierce black charger on which the captain was mounted. "I tell you—hem, hem!—this reminds me more of the return of the knights of old after a battle, or a crusade, than any thing in my experience."

Diggs' conversation was not noted for brilliancy or point, but Oleah thought he never knew him to be so flat and pointless as on this occasion.

"I can't for the life of me, Diggs," he said, "see that we bear any possible likeness to knights or crusaders."

"Why, you see, they left their homes, and so did we. We are alike there."

Oleah made no answer. He was probably convinced.

Mr. Diggs went on triumphantly:

"They went off to fight, so did we; they came back clothed with victory and glory, so did we."

"I doubt whether either of us have achieved any victory to be boasted of. As to the glory, I lay claim to none, and you must have little, unless you acquired it in creek bottoms or turkey roosts."

It was Mr. Diggs' turn to be silent now. His face became almost livid with momentary rage, and the ill-assorted companions road on without speaking, until the Tompkins' mansion was reached.

The second son, in Confederate gray, was as gladly welcomed by his father as Abner in his loyal blue, while in the mother's eyes shone not only a mother's tender love, but the proud patriotism of a woman, who had given her son to the cause she believed holy and just.

"And here is friend Diggs, too," said the planter, taking the hand of the little Confederate with such cordiality that Mr. Diggs was in ecstacies of delight. "Have you been well?"

"Quite well, Mr. Tompkins—hem, hem!—have been quite well, except a few gun-shot wounds, received at Carrick's Ford. Hem, hem, hem!"

Mrs. Tompkins, too, welcomed him with gracious hospitality, and when Irene met him with friendly greeting, he felt more than rejoiced, that he had not given up a soldier's life. He had fought his battles and was now winning his just reward, and "sweet the treasure, sweet the pleasure, sweet the pleasure after pain."

"Hem, hem, hem!—my friends—hem, hem!—my dear friends, he, he, he!" chuckled the little fellow, looking as silly as it was possible for a man of his size, with glasses on, to look; "this gives me—hem, hem!—unbounded, I may say unlimited, satisfaction."

At this moment another character entered on the scene. It was Crazy Joe; he paused a moment, and a look of recognition lit up his features. He walked forward, and, placing his hand on Diggs' shoulder, angrily demanded:

"Why are you here, sir? Why did you not remain where

I left you? When I make a man out of clay, and stand him up, I want him to stay where I leave him, until I can show people the greatness of my handiwork."

It was impossible for those present to restrain their involuntary smiles, and Diggs, seeing this, lost his temper.

"Go away, fool," he cried; "take off your hands."

"Oh, Mr. Diggs, that is very unkind," said Irene.

"Yes," said Crazy Joe, sorrowfully, as he left the room, "it is very unkind for him to address such language to the man who made him."

In spite of themselves, those present could hardly restrain their laughter; but Mr. Diggs was easily pacified, and harmony was soon restored, and he related his hair-breadth escapes and miraculous victories.

Oleah had interesting adventures to relate, and the humorous mishaps of our friend Mr. Diggs, brought out the long, unheard of music of Irene's laughter. During the evening he told his father of his meeting of Yellow Steve at Mrs. Juniper's ball.

"Strange," said the father, "that he should have escaped us all. He knows something of Irene's history." Then he told Oleah what he himself had seen, and what Abner had told him of Yellow Steve's visit, the evening before the battle of Bull Run.

"I will fathom this mystery," exclaimed Oleah, "though it takes a lifetime to do it. He shall reveal all he knows, the next time we meet, if he does it at the point of my sword."

"Be not too rash, my son," said the father. "Never frighten a bird you wish to catch."

Then his mother and Irene came in, and with a loving imperiousness, as his brother had done, he made Irene come out with him, walked through the same paths and sat down at last on the same seat, with the same words trembling on his lips.

The sun had gone down, the moon was rising round and full in the East, and the whip-poor-wills were making night melodious with their song. Oleah was talking very earnestly to his fair companion; not only earnestly, but passionately.

"Irene, you comprehend what I told you before I left

my home to meet death and danger in the field, that the love I felt for you was deeper and stronger than a brother's. I love you—I love you more than all else on earth, more than life, and nothing shall keep you from me. You shall be mine—my wife."

"Oleah, believe me, let us keep the old love—I can give you no other. I can not give you what you want." Her voice died away. He saw the small, white fingers clasping and unclasping, and knew that she was resolutely keeping back her tears.

"This is something I can not understand," said Oleah, and his face clouded, "unless my brother has been before me."

Irene opened her white lips, but no words came.

"I understand now," exclaimed Oleah; "you can not choose between us; you know not which of us you prefer, or perhaps you prefer him." His eyes shone like burning coals, and his voice was hoarse with passion. "It is true, he must oppose me in every thing? When our country, our South, his birthplace and mine, is assailed by foes, he joins them. Is not that enough to turn all a brother's love to gall and bitterness? And now he would win you from me—my love, my love!"

"Oleah, do not so wrong your brother! I tell you truly that he does not know, he has no thought that he is opposing you," cried Irene, with an appealing look at the dark, angry face. "O, Oleah, for your mother's sake banish these evil thoughts. God made you brothers."

"Yes, and the devil made us enemies. It is coming at last—it has come! I have fought against it for the sake of our happy childhood, our parents, and the brothers' blood that flows in our veins, but it is useless. The fates have determined that we should hate each other, and the hatred of brothers is the hatred of devils. Irene," his voice softening, "I believe you love me though you will not speak," and Oleah seized her passionately in his embrace and rained kisses on her fair, pale face. "I must go now," he said, releasing her, "but you shall yet be mine, I swear it. Neither brother, nor father, nor mother, no power on earth shall prevent it."

Oleah went toward the house, and Irene stood motionless, where he had left her, till the trees hid him from her sight— her eyes widely strained, her face pale with terror, her lips white and bloodless. Those wild words Oleah had spoken in his passion, those fearful words, "*The hatred of brothers is the hatred of devils*," seemed burning into her brain.

And this was her work! This mischief she had done! She trembled like one guilty, and the love she would not own, and she could not master, seemed to her shuddering soul a crime.

So excited was her manner that it attracted the attention of others in the room. At this moment a negro boy entered the room, where Mr. and Mrs. Tompkins were sitting with Mr. Diggs, his face wearing a strangely puzzled look. He paused and looked around. Whether he was more frightened or puzzled it would have been difficult to tell.

"Well, Job, what is it?" asked Mr. Tompkins, noticing the negro's awkward manner.

"If you please, marster," he said, shaking his head, "Marster Abner—"

"What of him?" asked Mr. Tompkins, for the boy had paused.

"Why, he—he is comin'?"

Before any one could make reply, quick steps were heard on the graveled walk. Mr. Tompkins, motioning the servant aside, went himself to the door, and, as he opened it, heard Oleah's voice, imperious and harsh:

"You are my prisoner, sir!"

"Oleah, my son, this is a matter too serious for jesting," said the father.

I am not jesting. My first duty is to my country. He is an enemy to my country, and my country's enemies are mine. My men are within call," he continued, turning to Abner. "Do you surrender?"

"Most assuredly I shall not," replied Abner.

"Then, by heavens! you shall fare no better than any other Yankee spy. You are within our lines!"

He snatched his sword from its scabbard, and before Mr. Tompkins could interpose, there was a clash.

Again the door opened, and Mrs. Tompkins and Mr.

Diggs appeared; but the sight that met their eyes froze to terror the smile of welcome on the mother's lips, and sent Diggs, his radiant complacency all gone, shrinking back into the house, muttering, "Oh, Lordy, I know I shall be killed."

Clash, clash! clank, clank! the swords went, circling in the air, thrusting, crossing, clashing. Irene came flying down the path, and Mr. Tompkins sprang between and threw them apart.

"Hold!" he cried, "if you must have kindred blood, turn your swords first on me, and on your mother and sister. Abner, if your enemies are near, go. Let them not find you in your own father's house. Go at once!"

Without a word, Abner returned his sword to its scabbard and started to leave his home. His mother and Irene followed him to the gate, and, a moment later, his horse's feet were heard clattering up the hill toward Snagtown.

Oleah, soon after, left with Diggs, to join his men. Mr. Tompkins and his wife sat in silence in the silent house, while Irene, who believed herself the guilty cause of this new sorrow, crept up to her room to weep and pray.

CHAPTER XX.

WAR IN THE NEIGHBORHOOD.

It was a Sabbath morning in the latter part of October, clear and frosty. The sun had risen in a cloudless sky, the wind blew northward in rolling columns, the smoke from the village chimneys, and the leaves on the magnificent forest trees, which surrounded the village on the north, east, and south, had grown brown and sear, but the great plantations of the level valley on the west were still verdant. While on the west, faintly outlined in the distance, rose the Cumberland mountains.

An old man, with a basket on his arm, was walking down the broad sidewalk past the cottages, from which came the fragrant ordor of coffee, a sure indication that breakfast was preparing. The old man chanced to cast his eyes towards the eastern part of the town, and paused in amazement.

In a field of about twenty acres, as if they had risen by magic, were scores of snowy tents. Sentries were on duty, their burnished arms glittering in the sun, and hundreds of gray-coated soldiers were passing and repassing, white clouds of smoke from their camp-fires rose in the frosty air.

While the old man was looking beyond the streets and houses at the encampment on the hill, a neighbor, walking up the other side of the street, hailed him with:

"Rather sudden appearance ain't it?" pointing to the camp, over which the Confederate flag was floating.

"When did they come, Mr. Williams?" said the first old man.

"Last night," replied Mr. Williams, crossing over to where the other stood. "Can't you guess what's in the wind?"

"No," was the answer.

Mr. Williams, a corpulent, smooth-faced man of sixty, smiled.

"Why, you see, the boys are strong enough now to take the Junction, and they are on their way."

"How many are they?" asked the first old man, who was tall and thin, with long, gray beard. He spoke evidently with some concern.

"About three thousand in all, with five pieces of artillery."

The cannon and the ammunition wagons were plainly to be seen from the street.

"And so they are on their way to fight the Abolitionists at the Junction?" said the first old man thoughtfully.

"Yes, Mr. Jones, and your son, Hiram, is in that crowd and my son, Seth. They'll make it quite lively for old Colonel Holdfast," replied Mr. Williams.

"Yes, they will," said Mr. Jones, stroking his gray beard.

The sun rose higher in the heavens, and the frosty air grew warm and genial. By nine o'clock the forces were in motion, the long lines of cavalry and infantry proceeding slowly and cautiously towards the Junction.

The good citizens of Snagtown had recovered from the excitement, into which the appearance of the troops had thrown them, and the church bells were calling them to worship, when the boom of the cannon shook the hills.

All was instant excitement. The cannon shot came from the direction in which the troops had gone. It was followed by another and another, until the roar of artillery shook the hills and valleys for miles around, and then the rattle of grape and canister was borne to the ears of the villagers. Plainly a fight was going on. The firing lasted about half an hour, then it began to slacken, and at last, ceased, excepting an occasional dropping musket shot.

The villagers were gathered about in anxious groups, when a single horseman, dressed in gray, galloped furiously into the village. The men crowded eagerly about him to inquire how the battle had gone.

"There had been no battle," he said, "but their advance guard had met the advance guard of the Union troops, and a skirmish had ensued, a battery on either side having opened.

"We are falling back to more advantageous ground," he added, "and will be in the village in fifteen minutes."

The excitement, of course, redoubled. There was no service in the church, but the women and children were hurried away from the village, and the stern-faced who remained, locked and barred their homes and gathered, armed and resolute, in the streets. Stragglers from the army came in first, then followed the infantry and artillery. There was a long embankment on the north side of the village, where the earth had been partly washed and partly cut away. This embankment was nearly as high as a man's breast, and a fence ran along its top for a quarter of a mile to the east of the village. Behind this natural fortification the principal part of the infantry formed in lines. The artillery was placed in an orchard, where there was a dense growth of trees to mask it.

The advance of the Union forces came on slowly, and it was an hour after the entrance of the Confederates into the village before the deployed skirmishers came in sight. The crack of a rifle announced their approach, another and another burst on the air at once, and then the balls came rattling rapidly against the houses.

The engagement became general, and the roar of artillery and the rattle of musketry was deafening. The Sabbath morning, dawning so serene and calm, had been followed by a noon of bloodshed, terror and strife. The neat village cottages were shattered and balls had crashed through window lights and shutters. The little stone church had been struck by cannon shot and shell, and one building had caught fire and burned to the ground.

Finally the Confederate lines began to waver and give way, and the bugle sounded the retreat. They fell back, column behind column, in regular order, passing through the village, closely followed by the victorious troops.

No sooner had the last column left the village than the frightened inhabitants, who had been hiding in the woods at some distance away, began to peep forth upon the terrible scene.

Mr. Jones and Mr. Smith, returning, found occasionally, here and there, in the street a ghastly form. A man lay dead at the gate of Mr. Jones; some were even in the houses, while one was lying across the sidewalk in front of the church. Their houses had been struck with balls, but not near so badly shattered as might have been expected. Two or three cannon balls were lying in the street and fragments of exploded shells strewn on the ground.

The occasional dropping shots in the distance told that both armies were moving. Colonel Holdfast seemed determined to hold fast to Colonel Scramble this time.

The struggle we have described in this chapter is not recorded by most historians, and, if mentioned at all, is only considered a skirmish, yet the citizens of Snagtown thought it the most terrible battle of the war.

No one of the Tompkins family had left their home. During the night Irene had been awakened by the rumble of wheels and the tramp of hoofs, and, looking from her bedroom window down the broad road, saw long lines of dark, silent figures marching in the direction of Snagtown. For more than an hour those silent dark figures, with their bristling bayonets glittering in the cold moonlight, marched on and on past her window in seemingly never-ending procession—horsemen, artillery and baggage wagons rolling by.

Then the line was less solid and finally broken—an occasional group galloping by to join the army in advance. When daylight came not a soldier was to be seen on the hard beaten road.

Irene knew well what was the intention of the Confederates. She had recognized one form among those hosts that marched by in the moonlight, and, at sight of him, had crouched by in the window recess with a strange pain at her heart.

The whole family was aroused by the passing troops, and all rightly guessed their object. Through the long morning they sat watching on the veranda, Irene, pale and beautiful, leaning against one of the columns of the great porch running about the northeast side of the house, heard the first roar of the artillery, that ushered in the day's strife, and, during the long two hours that the battle raged, she stood motionless, except that her white lips moved in silent prayer. She saw the advance of the column in rapid retreat coming down the great road from Snagtown.

"Defeated!" she murmured. "O, Heaven, is he among the dead? Both may be slain!"

Little did she dream how close were the pursuers. One vast retreating mass of troops in gray poured down the hill, and, among the last of the Confederates, she saw the dark face of Oleah. His company was the last to descend the hill, and the rear was not half way from the summit when a line of blue coats appeared on the brow of the hill and quickly fell in line.

White puffs of smoke filled the air, and a rattling discharge of fire-arms followed.

Irene, forgetful of danger or too horrified to fly, stood motionless as a statue. She saw one or two of Oleah's company fall, and saw their captain wheel his horse and dash back among his panic-stricken troops. He reformed them almost instantly and returned the volley, driving back the advance of the Union troops, who immediately rallied and came on again to the conflict.

"Come, Irene, come in for Heaven's sake! You may be struck dead at any moment," cried Mrs. Tompkins, seizing the poor girl around the waist. "Come, come to the cellar; it is the only safe place."

"But, mother, see, he, they both, are there, in danger of being killed. I can not go until I see him safe."

But Mrs. Tompkins drew her away from the porch.

Contrary to the expectations of Mr. Tompkins and of the whole family, the house was not used as a fortification, and a running fight followed; then the bulk of the Union army swept on down the road in pursuit of the retreating Confederates.

Irene hastened from the house down the driveway. A dead horse lay on the hill, and two soldiers, one in blue and one in gray, lay motionless in the road, but their forms were stark and stiff, no earthly aid could reach them. As she turned away she heard a groan, and, hastening to the spot, she saw lying in a little hazel copse, which had before concealed him from her view, a Confederate soldier with a shattered leg, almost unconscious from loss of blood. One glance, and Irene recognized those pale haggard features. It was Henry Smith. She saw that he was badly wounded and flew back to the house for help.

The troops under Colonel Holdfast followed up the Confederates closely, harrassing them by repeated dashes on their rear guard, thus keeping up a continual skirmish. It so happened that Captain Abner Tompkins commanded the advance of Colonel Holdfast, while Captain Oleah Tompkins the rear guard of Colonel Scrabble. The men, under each, were from the immediate neighborhood of Snagtown, and, consequently, many in these hostile ranks were former acquaintances or friends. As the advance under Abner was approaching a farm-house, he threw out skirmishers, among whom was one Jim Moore, who had formerly lived in Snagtown. The house stood back from the road, surrounded by giant oaks, and the skirmishers, fifteen in number, led by Sergeant Swords, approached slowly and cautiously, warned by the crack of rifles behind the trees. The trees being plenty, each man concealed himself behind one of them, they commenced an Indian warfare. Jim Moore, who was behind a large oak, had been watching his chance to get a shot at a Confederate, behind a similar tree, about one hundred yards away. The Confederate was watching Jim the same time.

"I say," called out Jim, during a lull in the attack, "give a fellow a chance for a pop."

The Confederate thrust out his head for a brief second, and Jim blazed away; the bullet passed two inches over the reckless head.

"Too high!" cried the Confederate; now give me a chance.

Jim, not to be outdone, thrust out his head and shoulders, and a ball whizzed beneath his arm.

"Too low!" he cried; "but now, I'll bet a quart o' whiskey you and I have shot together before."

"Your voice is familiar," answered the man, reloading. "Who are you, any way?"

"Jim Moore, from Snagtown, and, if I aint mistaken, you are Seth Williams?"

"Right, old boy. We've shot ducks together many a time. How d' ye do?"

"Pretty well," said Jim. "How are yerself and all the rest of the boys?"

"Excellent. What are you fellows following us for?"

"To keep you out o' mischief."

"How many you got?"

"Not quite seventy thousand."

"You're lying, Jim."

"Well, I'll take that from an old friend, Seth, but don't repeat it too often, or I'll come over there and thrash you."

This dialogue attracted the attention of all the skirmishers, and not a shot for the last two minutes had been fired.

Re-inforcements now came up to the aid of the Union skirmishers, and the Confederates retired through the farmyard and across the pasture, into the woods beyond. A cackling and a squalling of hens told that they had made a raid, in passing, on the barn-yard fowls.

The Union soldiers ran forward and fired at the retreating rebels. The only reply was a chorus of voices, singing "Chich-a-my, chick-a-my, crany crow," followed by reckless yells and peals of laughter.

In the hurry and confusion of the pursuit, Abner became separated from his company, and eager to rejoin it, dashed down a woodland path. Both forces were now between Snagtown and Twin Mountains, in the forest, which spread out for miles on either side of Wolf and Briar creeks, and the constant popping of guns told that the sharpshooters were at work. Not a human being was to be seen on the forest path Captain Tompkins had taken, but he could hear shooting on all sides. Suddenly he came upon a man standing by the side of a dead horse. In his headlong gallop, Abner would have run over him, had not the msn seized the former's horse by the bit with an iron grasp and hurled it on its haunches.

A glance told Abner that it was a Confederate officer, and that he held a naked sword in his hand. In an instant he had drawn his own weapon and leaped from the saddle, to discover that he was confronted by his brother.

"So, we meet again," cried Oleah, his eyes flashing fire. "You are my prisoner, sir."

"Release my horse, and remember that we are brothers," returning his sword to its scabbard. "We shall find other foes to fight. Loose my horse and go."

"When I go you will go a prisoner with me. Brothers!" exclaimed Oleah, sneeringly. "In all things you oppose me. You are joined now with my enemies, fighting to rob me of country and home; you have tried to take from me more than my life—why not my life? Defend yourself."

Again the brothers' blades clashed together, but a tall, powerful form sprang from the thicket into the road and hurled them apart, as though they were children.

"Brothers seeking each other's blood?" cried the new comer in a ringing voice. "Shame! oh, shame! There are enemies enough for both your swords without drawing them on each other."

The new comer was the mysterious negro, Yellow Steve.

"I know you," cried Oleah; "you have something to tell me—"

"But it is not to slay your brother," interrupted Yellow Steve. "Shame on you both! Put up your swords, lest I take them from you and break them on my knee. You, Oleah, go, and go quickly. Your enemies are all around you."

"Hilloa!" cried another voice, "what does all this mean?" and Uncle Dan Martin, the scout, stepped out of the woods, with his rifle, ready cocked, in his hand.

Oleah, hearing others advancing, sprang into the bushes and made good his escape. Abner looked after him for a single moment, and when he turned to speak to Yellow Steve, that mysterious person had disappeared.

"Who was them uns?" asked Uncle Dan, hastening forward to where his bewildered captain stood.

"One was my brother Oleah, the other was that strange negro, who calls himself Yellow Steve."

"Where did he go?" asked the scout.

"I don't know," answered Abner. "His ways of appearing and disappearing are quite beyond my comprehension."

"I'll catch him," replied Uncle Dan. "I know the tricks of the fox and mink, and others, and I'll set a trap, which will get him yet."

"Will you?" cried a mocking voice some distance up the path, and looking up, they saw the mysterious black, standing by the trunk of a tree his arms folded on his breast, a look of defiance in his gleaming eyes. Almost simultaneously with the discovery came the crack of Uncle Dan's rifle. When the smoke had cleared away the black had again disappeared.

The place all about was searched, but no trace of him could be found.

"I believe he is the devil," said Uncle Dan. "I never missed a squirrel's head at that distance in my life."

"He is certainly a very extraordinary person," said Abner.

CHAPTER XXI.

CRAZY JOE'S MISTAKE.

Uncle Dan had long prided himself on his skill in woodcraft, and, to be thus outwitted in his old days, was more than he could endure. He plunged recklessly into the brush, which was so dense that no object could be seen a dozen feet away. He ran several narrow risks, coming two or three times almost into the rebel lines.

"To think that a nigger should get ahead of me that way! It's too much!" exclaimed the old man, as he leaned against a tree, and listened to the occasional shots which awoke the echoes of the forest. "But what do I want with him, if I should catch him? My business is to lead the army through the woods, and not to be following a strange nigger up and down."

A crushing in the underbrush told him that some one was advancing, and, a moment later, Corporal Grimm and Sergeant Swords with half a dozen soldiers came up to where the old man stood.

"Hilloa, old boy!" said Sergeant Swords. "Pausin' to view the land ahead?"

"No, I've been trying to git a pop at a nigger," replied Uncle Dan.

"What are niggers doing here?" said Corporal Grimm. "When dogs fight for a bone, the bone seldom fights."

"The bone is in these woods, but I'll be hanged if I know what it's here for. Let's be moving on."

"D'ye know the lay of the land?" asked Sergeant Swords.

"Every foot," said Uncle Dan.

The long line of Union skirmishers was moving slowly through the thick woods, and the line of Confederate skirmishers was retreating at the same pace to cover the rear of their army. The crack of rifles rang out frequently, but it was seldom with effect. It was evident that the Confederates were making for their stronghold beyond the Twin Mountains. The line of their retreat led by the foot of the mountains, where stood Uncle Dan's cabin.

With some anxiety Uncle Dan watched the movements of the retreating mass of soldiers. Among them was one short fat little fellow on foot, whose legs were too short to ably execute his prodigious exertions to keep pace with his companions; his little gray coat-tails were streaming in the air or whipping wildly against the trees. The officers, who were in the advance, amused themselves by popping away at the fleeing rebel with their revolvers. Still he flitted on among the trees, into the brush, out of the brush, over the logs, and under the lower branches of the trees, straining every nerve to keep up with his swifter companions. The soldiers were gaining on him rapidly, and it was painfully evident, that, when he reached open ground, one of these many loaded guns must bring him down. His companions, who were several rods in advance, suddenly turned abruptly to the left, which he, evidently too terrified to comprehend which way he was going, kept straight ahead.

Crack, crack! went the pistols of Grimm and Swords, and the bullets whizzed uncomfortably near our short friend's head.

"Oh, Lordy, Lordy, I know I shall he killed!" he cried in tones so wild and shrill that his fear could not be doubted. He reached the thicket bordering Wolf Creek and—crash, crash, bang!—he went through the thicket into the creek. The splash was plainly heard by his pursuers and, in spite of themselves, they could not repress a laugh.

In a moment they were at the bank and beheld a half drowned little man, sneezing and coughing as he struggled to the bank and clung to some pendant vines.

"Hem, hem, or Lordy!—achew—hem, hem!—oh Lordy, achew!" he murmured. "I'll—achew—quit this horrible soldier—achew—business. Oh! Lordy, I know I shall be killed! Achew! oh, Lordy. I want to quit this, I never was made to be a soldier."

"Helloa!" cried Uncle Dan. "Come out o' there, and tell us who ye are."

He looked up on the bank and, seeing the soldiers, with a cry plunged under the water. In a moment more he came up to breathe.

"Come out o' that and don't be playing mud-turtle," cried Uncle Dan. "Ef I ain't mistaken, ye are Patrick Henry Diggs, and yer lost."

It really was Diggs, and, with a yell of recognition and delight, he scrambled up the bank.

"O, Uncle Dan, Uncle Dan, Uncle Dan!" he cried, falling almost exhausted at his feet. "Save me, save me, save me!"

"Save ye from what?" said Uncle Dan.

"From being shot and drowned and killed. Oh, I solemnly swear that I will never have anything more to do with this soldier business. It is only run, run, from beginning to end, and then plunging head first into a muddy stream. Oh, I'll quit it, I'll quit it. Heaven forgive me, Uncle Dan!" he cried vehemently.

"This is sorry business, Diggs. What war ye doing?" said Uncle Dan seriously.

"Running for my life," answered Diggs.

"Get up, Diggs," said the old scout solemnly.

The little fellow arose, looking more like a school-boy who was going to be thrashed.

"Diggs," said the old man, and there was not the slightest tinge of jest in his tones, "what war ye doing with the rebels?"

"If you please, sir,—hem, hem—" began Diggs, greatly confused, turning pale as death and beginning to tremble, "I—I—was taken prisoner with these two gentlemen," pointing to Corporal Grimm and Sergeant Swords.

"No, you were not," said both at once. "We were never taken prisoners."

"Oh, I beg your pardon—hem, hem!—gentlemen, please hear me through, and I can explain all this to you. I was taken prisoner by the rebels one night, when I went out with these two gentlemen, and they—hem, hem!—I mean the rebels, kept me for a long time until they made me go with them to-day, and you found me with them."

"Do you mean to say that ye have been a prisoner all this time?" asked Sergeant Swords.

"Yes," said Diggs, after a moment's hesitation.

"Then what was ye doing with a gun in yer hand, when we come on ye and the others?" said Corporal Grimm.

"You are mistaken, it was some one else," said Diggs, becoming confused.

"No, I am not. We all saw you throw it away and run with the rest," said the Corporal.

"Well, it was one I had just picked up. I was tryin' to escape, when you came up, and I ran with the rest."

"But here ye are with the cartridge-box belted around you," said the Sergeant, "and you have the gray uniform on."

Diggs was too much confused to reply, and his eyes dropped under the searching glance of the soldiers.

"Diggs," said the old scout, with great earnestness in his tones, "I'm afraid it will go hard with you. You are a deserter and a spy. It's sorry business, Diggs."

"O, Uncle Dan, Uncle Dan, promise me you will not let me be hurt!" cried Diggs.

"Come along. You shall be treated as a prisoner of war, but I can't say what a court martial may do about your desertion."

"O, Uncle Dan, you wont let them shoot me, will you? Say you won't, and I'll do anything in the world you want me to do. I'll enlist in your army and fight on half rations."

"You've 'listed a little too much already," said Uncle Dan. "This tryin' to sarve two masters won't do."

"Oh, you surely would not let me be killed. Oh, promise me, you will not let them take me out and shoot me." Poor Diggs broke down and sobbed like a whipped schoolboy.

"Hush up blubberin'. Be a man, if ye've got any manhood about ye, and come along."

They now begin to retrace their steps back to where the main army had paused.

"But, Uncle Dan, you have known me from a child, and you knew my father before me. Say that you wont have me killed!" sobbed Diggs, as he walked along with a soldier on either side of him.

"That's beyond my control," replied Uncle Dan. "I'll turn ye over to the authorities, and I can't make promises."

Poor Diggs felt his heart sink within him, His very breathing became oppressive, and the soldiers who walked by his side seemed like giants of vengeance.

"Oh, what must I do, I know I shall be killed," thought Diggs. He reflected on his past life and commenced preparing for his exit from this world.

In his mind he opened a double-column ledger account of the good and the bad acts of his life. He tried to think how many times he had prayed. They were few. Only on occasions, like the present, when his danger was imminent. He remembered with horror, now, that when the danger was gone, he had always forgotton his good resolves, and mentally blamed himself for his weakness. The bad column ran up so rapidly that it seemed impossible for the accouut to be balanced.

"If I ever can get out of this," he mentally ejaculated, "I shall devote my life to the Lord's service. I will be a preacher; I would make a capital preacher; I was meant for a preacher, I know. If the good Lord will only get me out of this scrape, I will not go back on my word, sure!"

When Uncle Dan's party came up, they found Colonel Holdfast, Colonel Jones and Major Flem.ng holding a consultation under a large tree.

"Here is Uncle Dan, the scout, the very man we wanted," said Colonel Holdfast. "But who have you there? Did you find your prisoner in the home of the beaver and musk rat?"

Uncle Dan explained how they captured Diggs, and then the scout was instructed that he was to p.lot two of the regiments through the woods to Snagtown, while the other was to follow up the retreating enemy. Uncle Dan understood in a moment how matters stood. There was no danger from the retreating Confederates, but it was very important that fortifications be thrown up at Snagtown.

Poor Diggs spent the night following in the jail building with several other prisoners. He passed the weary hours in prayer, good resolutions and in the firm determination to be a preacher, if the Lord would get him out of this scrape.

"When the devil was sick, the devil a monk would be.
When the devil was well, the devil a monk was he."

Major Fleming, to whom was left the task of completing the rout of the Confederate forces, was a bold, energetic man. He pushed forward with no delay after the demoralized and retreating enemy. The science of war was yet new to both sides, and, while bravery and tact was displayed at an early day of the war, there was a lack of the veteran's skill.

The retreat was up Wolf Creek toward the mountains, through a rough, wild region. The advance of the Confederates came to where Uncle Dan's cabin stood. It so happened that Joe, who had so often been Uncle Dan's companion, was at the cabin, which he kept always ready for the old man's return. He stood in the door way and watched the advancing throng, his mild blue eyes wide with wonder.

"Do you come from the land of Canaan, and is the famine over where my father dwells?" he asked of the rough soldiers, who paused at the spring to drink.

"Come from Canaan? No; we come from h—l," replied one, with a laugh at his own wit.

"Have you seen my father?" asked Joe, in astonishment.

"No; but we have seen the devil," replied another, and he is close at our heels."

The poor idiot looked alarmed. He vaguely comprehended that some danger was advancing, and his eyes filled with tears.

"Oh, what shall I do?" he cried, in tones so plaintive, so pitiful, that they might have touched a heart of stone.

"Do? Run," said one of the soldiers, "run for your life, and hide among the rocks. There are plenty about here."

"No," said a third," "fight them. Here is a gun," handing him a musket. "Take this and shoot the first one you see."

Joe took the gun, but no dangerous light shone in his blue eyes.

"I will fight no one but the Philistines," he said, thoughtfully.

He was stunned and confused, and stood by the spring with the old musket in his hands, as group after group of armed soldiers hurried by.

"Hilloa, Joe, what are you doing?" said a familiar voice, and Howard Jones came towards him.

"I am here to assist Samson slay the Philistines," replied the poor lunatic.

"Put that down," said Howard, taking the gun from him and laying it on the rocks by the spring. "Now run. Go that way," pointing to the west, "and don't you take any guns in your hands. If any one says 'halt!' stop at once."

Howard Jones hurried on, hoping rather than believing, that Joe would follow his advice.

"Helloa, where are you going?" cried another soldier, as Joe started away.

"Fleeing from Sodom," replied Joe.

"Well, sir, don't you flee. Pick up that gun and fight the d———d Yankees. Shoot 'em as fast as they come out of the woods."

Joe, always obedient, took up the gun again and remained automaton-like, to obey the last speaker.

"For shame, Bryant!" exclaimed Seth Williams, who came up at that moment. "He is crazy. Would you have him expose his life that way, when he doesn't know what he is doing? Put the gun down, Joe, and go that way," said Seth, pointing to the west. "Go to Mr. Tompkins; he wants you."

Joe hastened to obey, and Seth hurried on.

There seemed to be some fatal attraction about that long line of moving men, with burnished arms and glittering bayonets, to poor Joe. He had not gone a dozen rods before he paused to look back at them. Tramp, tramp, tramp, they went, on and on, and he looked till his weak mind became all confused with wonder. As the dangerous reptile chains the bird it seeks to destroy, and draws it involuntarily to its death, so poor Joe felt involuntarily drawn towards that moving line of gray coats and glittering steel. Who were they? Where were they going? When would that long line end?

They kept passing, passing, passing, so many men, and so much alike, that poor Joe finally concluded it must be only one man, doomed for some misdeed to walk on, and on, and on forever, never advancing on his endless journey. Joe forgot Howard Jones and Seth Williams, and, pausing, gazed on in mute wonder.

But the main body had at length passed. Then the line became broken, and only straggling groups of horsemen and footmen went by; then these finally came at longer intervals, but in larger groups. Joe thought the end must be near.

The rear guard of the Confederates paused in front of Uncle Dan's cabin, to check the advance guard of Major Fleming.

"Halt!" cried the officer. "Deploy skirmishers and the advance."

"They're almost upon us, lieutenant," said a subordinate officer, riding in from the woods.

"Let 'em come," said the first speaker. "Take shelter behind trees or rocks, and make sure of every head that peeps out of the woods."

The men, about fifty in number, sprang to cover. The officer in command. chancing to look around, saw Crazy Joe, still spell-bound with wonder.

"Hey, fellow," he cried, "what are you doing there?"

"Nothing," said Joe.

"Well, then, come here and I'll give you something to do."

Joe obeyed. One look in his face was enough to betray the poor fellow's weakness.

The lieutenant knew that he was crazy, but, reckless of what the poor fellow's fate might be, he pointed to the musket Joe had laid on the rocks, and said:

"Pick that up, get behind those rocks, and when I say 'Fire!' shoot at the men you see coming from those trees."

Joe knew nothing else to do, but obey, little dreaming of the dread consequences that were to follow.

"What do you expect that crazy chap to do?" asked a soldier, as he rammed a ball down his rifle.

"He can shoot, and his bullet may strike a blue coat."

"Brace up and look more soldier-like," said one.

"Who greased yer hat?" asked another.

"When was yer hair cut?" put in a third.

"What ye got in the pockets of that great coat?" said another.

"Attention!" cried the lieutenant. "Here comes the enemy. Steady! Be sure of your aim, and fire only when you have it."

The Union skirmishers advanced cautiously, and the Confederates blazed away, taking care not to expose their own persons to the sharpshooters in the woods below and above. The fire from the woods became deadly, and the lieutenant ordered a retreat just as the Union forces in the woods, receiving re inforcements, made a charge.

"Run, run for your lives!" cried the lieutenant, setting the example.

A storm of leaden hail swept around Uncle Dan's low

cabin, rattling against the walls and shattering shade trees in front of it.

Joe's face was now white with terror. The dread monster had come. He saw the men about him take to flight, and, in his simplicity, he threw aside the unused gun and followed them. He had not gone far before he changed his course, running off to the left, down the creek bottom, where the grass was tall and dry. The Confederates kept straight on across the woods, making for the mountain pass.

A detachment of soldiers came up to the cabin, and, seeing Joe in flight, the others already out of range, levelled their guns upon him.

"Hold!" cried an officer, in the uniform of a United States captain, as he galloped up to the group.

He was too late, before the word was fairly uttered, a dozen rifle shots drowned it.

"Great God, you have hit him!" cried Captain Abner Tompkins, as, through the smoke of the muskets, he saw Joe throw up his hands, reel, and fall. "You have hit him, and he was a poor, crazy fellow."

In a moment Abner was beside the prostrate form. He sprang from his horse and raised Joe from the ground. A deadly pallor had overspread his face; his blue eyes were glazed and he was gasping for breath.

"Who is it? Is he hurt? cried Major Fleming, riding up to the spot, where the young captain was supporting the dying man on his knee.

"It is a poor fellow called Crazy Joe, and some of our men have shot him by mistake," said Abner, a moisture gathering in his eyes.

"He may not be badly hurt; perhaps he is only stunned," said the major.

But while they yet spoke, Joe breathed his last. Crazy Joe was dead; dead, without one ray of light piercing the dark cloud he had so vainly tried to lift; dead, with the dark mystery of his life unexplained; dead, not knowing who or what he was.

A musket ball had struck him in the back, passing out at the breast, and he lived but a few minutes after Abner had reached his side; he was past recognition then, and never spoke after he was shot.

Abner had the body conveyed to his father's house. The troops returned to Snagtown, having orders to pursue the enemy no further than the foot of Twin Mountains.

When Irene beheld the body of Crazy Joe, her resolution, which had borne her up under so many trials, gave way. She swooned, and, when she recovered, her grief so touched Mr. Tompkins that he had a costly burial outfit prepared for the poor dead boy. Abner obtained leave of absence to attend the funeral, and, early in the morning, he entered the home of his childhood, where he had so often played with the helpless being, who now lay there cold and lifeless. Irene met him in the hall, her eyes red with weeping.

"O, Abner," she cried, "it was such a cruel thing!"

"Yes, dear Irene, it was cruel, but it was a mistake, we were powerless to prevent," replied Abner, thinking it was the suddenness of his death that affected her.

"But, O, Abner, you do not understand me. I cannot tell you how strangely the death of this unfortunate being affects me. I loved Joe as we love those whose blood flows in our veins. I knew it all along, but never felt it so forcibly as now. 'Tis some great instinct, some higher power than human reason, that prompts me. Come, see how peaceful, how happy, how changed he looks."

He went with Irene into the darkened room. Joe's body was dressed in dark clothes with spotless linen, the hair trimmed and brushed, the eyelids closed over the troubled eyes. A look of intelligence had dawned in death on the face for years expressionless. There was a striking beauty in the face, with its perfect curve, its delicate, clear-cut features, and it seemed that there might have been a brain of power behind that lofty brow, on which he perceived the same deep scar that he had seen on his head when a boy. Abner was astonished. He had never thought Joe handsome with the old, pitiful look on his face, and his astonishment deepened, when, for the first time, he observed a striking resemblance between that face and the face of the girl who bent over it.

"It cannot be possible!" he thought. "Yet it might be; the birth of both was shrouded in mystery."

He did not give his thoughts expression, but he turned with deepening compassion from the white face of the dead to the face scarcely less white of the girl beside him.

CHAPTER XXII.

DIGGS GETS OUT OF HIS SCRAPE AGAIN.

Mr. Diggs' views, in the cold, dark prison, and through iron bars, of a soldier's life, were very gloomy. The first night of his incarceration, for hours, he tossed about unable to sleep.

"I am a failure," he moaned, "a miserable failure. I went into the army, intending to rise to be a general, and only got to be a corporal; then taken prisoner, lost my office, retaken by my own company and treated coolly. No chance of promotion, only kicks, cuffs, and bumps all through this cruel world. Others have risen to higher positions. There's Abner and Oleah, both captains. They were never taken prisoner, ducked in a creek, or thrown into a thorn bush; why should I? and now I am to be tried by a court-martial as a deserter, and I know I shall be killed."

"Shut up!" yelled half a dozen fellow prisoners. "Do you intend to sleep, or let any of us sleep to-night?"

"We're all going to be led out and shot to-morrow," whined Diggs.

"Well, is that any reason ye should be keeping' us awake all night?" replied one gruff fellow in an adjoining cell. The doors of all the cells were open.

Diggs was awed into silence by the tones of his companions, and, while wondering how these men could take their coming fate so coolly, fell asleep. He attributed his own emotions to the possession of finer sensibilities than those of his companions.

"What's to be done with us?" he asked next morning of the soldier who brought their breakfast.

"Don't know," was the reply, as that worthy set the breakfast on the stand and departed. Mr. Diggs did not have an excellent appetite.

"Say, messmate," said a mischievous prisoner, "don't eat too much, for these Yankees are cannibals, and, when they have fattened their prisoners, they eat 'em."

Poor Diggs pushed back his plate, sick at heart, and commenced pacing the hall in front of his cell. Seeing a soldier on guard duty outside, he went to the grating and called to him:

"Can I speak to you?"

"I reckon you can," was the answer.

"Do you know what's going to become of me?"

"I think, sir," said the soldier, gravely, "that you will be in h—l before morning."

"Oh! they do really intend to kill me," cried Diggs, and running back to his cell, he fell upon his knees and tried to pray.

"If ever I get out of this," he vowed, "I'll be a preacher. I was made for a preacher."

"Well, now, who cares if you are?" said a fellow prisoner, roughly, who was playing cards with three others at the table. "You needn't be disturbin' honest men, who hev no desire for sich things. Keep yer jaw and yer preachin' to yerself!"

"How can you be so wicked," said Diggs, "to carry on such unholy games, when you know that the judgment awaits you?"

"Oh, dry up!—I'll pass," said one.

"Remember, you wicked men, that you have souls to save!" cried Diggs, growing quite warm and earnest in this, his first exhortation.

"Oh, hush up yer nonsense!—Order him up, Bill," said another.

"You have souls," persisted Diggs.

"We've got no such thing!—I'll order you up and play it alone," replied the one called Bill.

"Remember, poor dying sinners, you have souls," Diggs went on.

"Remember, sir, you have a head," said one of the

players, "and if you don't keep it closed, you'll get it punched."

Abashed and crestfallen, Diggs again retired to a corner to pray, this time in silence, and to wonder at the perverseness and wickedness of this generation.

The day passed, the next, the next, and the next without any news from the outside world. Diggs asked the soldier, who brought their meals twice a day, at each visit, what was to be done to him, the soldier on each occasion answering that he did not know.

Diggs had grown despondent; his round, red face had become pale and attenuated, and his little gray eyes had lost even their silly twinkle. He thought of all the imprisoned heroes and martyred saints he had ever read of; finally he came to imagine himself a hero, and determined that, when he was released, he would write a book on prison life, relating his own experience. As an author, he certainly would achieve fame. If only he could have pen, ink and paper, he would at once begin the wonderful production, which was to astonish the world. Mr. Diggs thought, if he himself could not be a hero, he could portray heroes with life-like effect. He was half persuaded to become a novelist. He would be a preacher or lawyer, a novelist, any thing in the world but a soldier; he had had enough of that. As he had not yet been ordered out and shot, Mr. Diggs' hopes began to rise in his breast, and already, he felt half ashamed of the weakness he had displayed.

On the fifth day after his arrival at the prison, he was called to the door. It was not more than ten o'clock in the forenoon. Half a dozen soldiers, headed by a sergeant, were waiting outside the prison. He was ordered to come out, and once more stood in the open air. He was marched at once to Colonel Holdfast's head-quarters in the Courthouse at Snagtown. Colonel Holdfast, two other Colonels, Major Fleming, and another officer were sitting in the place, which was occupied by civil judges in times of peace. An awful silence seemed to pervade the court-room, as Mr. Diggs was marched in. A number of soldiers were lounging about on the seats, and several officers were conferring in whispers. What it meant Mr. Diggs was not long in conjecturing. It was the dreadful court-martial. His hopes sunk, his knees knocked together, and his head swam as he was placed before the terrible tribunal. The orderly placed a seat for him in front of the officers, and he rather fell into it than sat down.

"Is your name Patrick Henry Diggs?" said Colonel Holdfast.

"I—I believe it is," faintly gasped the terrified man.

"You are charged with having deserted from our army and gone over to the enemy. What have you to say to the charge?" asked the colonel.

There was no response. Diggs hung his head.

"What do you say, sir?" demanded the colonel, sharply.

"N—n—not guilty, your honor."

"Here is your name on our rolls as having enlisted in my own Company B, Abner Tompkins, captain. Is that true?"

"I—I—I reckon so."

Corporal Grimm and Sergeant Swords were called, and both testified that Diggs had been captured with other rebels in the late encounter; that, when taken, he was armed and fighting in the rebel cause. Uncle Dan Martin also testified that he had been present at the capture of Diggs, and that he was in arms for the Southern cause.

There was no jesting this time. Mr. Diggs found it all serious business. The officers were not long in arriving at a verdict. They retired into another room for a few moments' consultation, and returned with their verdict, which Colonel Holdfast read. It was simply the terrible word:

"Guilty!"

"Stand up, prisoner, that sentence may be passed," said the Colonel.

The prisoner did not move. He had fainted outright on hearing the verdict pronounced. The regimental surgeon was present and administered restoratives, and Diggs was held up by two strong soldiers.

"In view," began the colonel, "of the accumulative and convincing character of the evidence against you, proving you to be a spy, you are condemned to death."

"Oh, I knew, I always knew I should be killed!" interrupted Diggs, in a feeble voice.

"Therefore," went on the colonel, slowly and solemnly, hoping his words might have effect on the listeners and prevent other desertions, "you will be taken from here to your place of confinement, and there kept until this day week, when you will be taken therefrom, led to the field north of this town, at the hour of ten o'clock in the forenoon, and there shot until you are dead, and may the Lord have mercy on your soul."

The colonel sat down, and Diggs, again fainting, was carried back, almost insensible, to his prison.

When Abner heard of the trial and the decision of the court-martial, he endeavored to persuade the officers to reconsider the case, representing to them that Diggs was imbecile in mind and not actually responsible for his deeds. Irene, hearing with horror that the poor fellow was awaiting execution, which was hourly approaching, hastened to Snagtown to plead with the commanding officers in his behalf, and Uncle Dan used his influence, too, for poor Diggs' fate, but argument and entreaty were alike unavailing, the officers declaring that the case was plain, and justice must be done, and an example made.

Irene visited poor Diggs in prison and found him on the verge of despair. He had wept until his eyes were swollen. He would not eat or sleep, and his abject terror, his want of food and sleep had made him a pitiable-looking object. She remained only a few moments, but they were the only moments of comfort he had known since his sentence was passed, for Irene came to tell him it had been arranged that Captain Tompkins should go to Washington to intercede with the President on his behalf. Almost daily Mrs. Williams and Mrs. Jones, who had known Diggs from his babyhood, came to visit him. They both had sons in the rebel army, and so could sympathize with poor Diggs. These were the only faces from the outside world that he saw, except the guard, who were sometimes kind-hearted, allowing him all possible privileges, but often rough and surly, adding to his misery by coarse taunts and harsh treatment.

A man with a heart of stone might have felt compassion for Diggs. The little fellow's vanity and boasting were gone. He was humble and meek, and he seldom spoke.

Even his fellow prisoners treated him with consideration, and endeavored to cheer and encourage him. Captain Tompkins obtained leave of absence, went to the Junction, and took the first train for Washington. He knew that if he could see the President, a pardon would be obtained, but to secure an interview with the President, when the country was in such a condition as it was at that time, was no easy matter. Days and weeks might elapse and leave him still waiting for an opportunity. The village pastor found in Diggs a ready convert now, but while he professed to have found peace for his soul, he was by no means anxious to quit this world. Hour after hour dragged slowly by, until the day was gone, and no news from Captain Tompkins. The next day and the next came and passed, the doomed man waiting anxiously, hour by hour, the captain's return. He had heard of James Bird, the hero of Lake Erie, celebrated in song and story, how he had been condemned to death and pardoned, and how the messenger came bearing the pardon a few seconds too late, even while the smoke of the executioner's gun yet hung in the air, and feared that this fate would be his. It was now Wednesday, and the captain had not come and had sent no word. Diggs did nothing but pace his narrow cell—he was closely confined—bemoaning his fate and imploring every one, who came to see him, to save him from his horrible fate, from being cut off in the prime of life. Thursday dawned, and the captain did not come. Even if he did return, he might not bring the pardon. It was a day of agony to poor Diggs. To-morrow, that dread to-morrow, he must die. The minister remained with him most of the day, and Mrs. Jones and Mrs. Williams stayed with him several hours. Singing and prayers were frequently heard from the cell of the condemned man, who, most of the time, crouched in the corner with his face bowed in his hands.

The fatal morning dawned. Poor Diggs! despair had seized him. His most intimate friends would not have recognized that haggard, wild-looking face. The minister, at his request, came early to his cell, also the sympathizing old ladies, who had passed so many weary hours with him. But the morning hours now seemed to fly. No message or messenger came. The minister looked at his watch. It was only a few minutes before ten. All was silence, save an occasional sob from the prisoner or the old ladies. No one dared speak. The minister sat silently holding his watch, noting the swift flying moments, his lips moving in silent prayer for the soul of the man, who was soon to appear at the bar of God.

Ten o'clock came. There was a rattling of keys, a sliding of iron bolts and bars, and the jailer called the name of

"Patrick Henry Diggs!"

The minister and all, in the doomed man's cell, bowed for a moment in silence, then the good man lifted up his voice to that God, whom all the universe worships, in a prayer for a soul about to take flight.

Two soldiers entered and supported the prisoner beyond the prison walls, the minister following with the guard.

The dread place was reached. Sergeant Swords and Corporal Grimm had charge of the execution. At the farther extremity of the field was a fresh dug grave—a rude coffin beside it—and, standing in line beneath an oak tree, were twelve soldiers with muskets in their hands. The sight was too much for Diggs and he again fainted. The regimental surgeon administered restoratives, and the officers in charge advanced to prepare the prisoner for his fate.

The minister approached Sergeant Swords, asking permission, before this was done, to offer a last prayer. It was granted.

The prayer was long and earnest, appealing to the Ruler of the universe, in universal terms. The minister prayed for the prisoner, he prayed for his executioners ; he prayed for the officers who composed the court-martial ; he prayed for the soldiers, who were to execute the sentence ; he prayed for the army, for both armies, for all the armies in the world, for all the armies that had been, and for all that might be. Having completely finished up the army business, the preacher commenced on civilians, and prayed, and prayed, and prayed, until both soldiers and officers looked at him and at each other in amazement.

"Sergeant," whispered Corporal Grimm, "did you ever hear as long a prayer in your life?"

"No," was the whispered reply. "There! I'll be hanged if he ain't gone back to Moses!"

The prayer still went on, and on, and on; and the soldiers, tired of standing, kneeled; tired of kneeling, sat; tired of sitting, lay down—and still the prayer went on. It was long past high noon, before the faltering "Amen!" was pronounced.

"Ready, fall in!" came the sharp order.

The men rose from the grass and fell in line, and the sergeant led Diggs over to the coffin by the side of the grave; but Diggs, sobbing piteously, clung to him with such tenacity that it was difficult for the sergeant to free himself. He finally succeeded, forced him to kneel by his coffin, put the bandage over his eyes. Just as he stepped away, the clatter of hoofs were heard coming around the bend in the road.

"Attention!" said the sergeant. "Ready!"

A loud cry interrupted the order, and a horseman came dashing up the hill.

"Hold!" said Sergeant Swords. "There comes the captain."

On, on he came, waving a paper high over his head. The soldiers rested on their guns.

Abner Tompkins was among them in a minute, and declared the prisoner free by the authority of *Abraham Lincoln*.

When released, Diggs sprang to his feet and, in his joy, embraced the preacher, embraced the officers and would have embraced the soldiers, had not one threateningly pointed his bayonet at him.

As they returned to the village, all pleased with the happy result, Corporal Grimm, approaching the minister, said:

"I shall always hereafter be a believer in the saving power of prayer. Praying often and praying *long*, does the work."

CHAPTER XXIII.

THE ABDUCTION.

The Union forces stationed at Snagtown did not remain there many days after the event related in the last chapter. Diggs was paroled, and the regiments ordered into Winter quarters at the Junction. The retirement of the Union forces was followed by predatory incursions of the Confederates, who were encamped just across the Twin Mountains. Small parties on foraging expeditions frequently crossed the latter, and greatly harassed the citizens in and around Snagtown.

Since the last battle of Snagtown and the Confederate defeat, the peace and quiet of the Tompkins mansion was broken. Mrs. Tompkins openly and warmly avowed her principles, and Mr. Tompkins, old as he was, had almost decided to enlist in the ranks of the Union army and fight for his country.

Irene could range herself with neither party; her sympathies were too equally divided.

"To think," said Mrs. Tompkins to Irene, in her husband's presence, "that the Yankees, not content with killing poor, harmless Joe, should attempt to murder Diggs in cold blood!"

"How unfair it is," said Mr. Tompkins, "for you to charge the soldiers, who are fighting for our country, with what was purely a mistake in one case, and what, in the other, was the result of laws which have existed in all armies since military law was established."

"Don't say *our* country," said Mrs. Tompkins, bitterly. "They are fighting for your cold, frozen North, not for my sunny South, which they are trying to desolate and destroy. Sooner than see them victorious, I would willingly follow both my sons to the grave."

Before Mr. Tompkins could reply, Irene interrupted the discussion.

"Oh, father, mother, do not talk about this dreadful war It has brought us misery enough; let it not ruin our home. It is all wrong—wrong on both sides—and the world will one day say so. The Nation is a great family, and if members of that family are in arms against each other, is it any credit to either—can it matter which side is defeated? I know nothing about either side, but I know it is nothing to take pride or pleasure in. Rather let us pray for its ending, than rejoice or sorrow over triumph or defeat."

Mrs. Tompkins went sobbing from the room, and the planter went out and seated himself beneath his favorite maple, in his rustic chair. His face was clouded. A barrier was gradually rising between himself and his wife—the wife whose love had blessed his youth and his manhood, the wife whose estrangement he had never dreamed of, between whom and himself he had thought no obstacle, material or immaterial, could ever come.

To no one was this sad change more painful than Irene. Left alone in the great, silent room, her heart swelled with pain, her eyes grew dim. Clouds were rising thick and fast about her life; it seemed to her that no ray of light could ever pierce their darkness. She could not stay in the house, it seemed so cold and empty, and she went out, walking almost mechanically from the garden to the high road leading past the house.

The road was very pleasant this Autumn evening; great oaks grew on either side, their brown leaves rustling musically overhead. Irene followed it to the grave-yard, and, like one treading an accustomed path, made her way between the grass-grown graves and paused by the side of a new-made mound.

"Poor Joe!" she sighed. "Your life so sad, your death so terrible and swift. No home, no friends, no hope on earth! Then why should I mourn for you?"

As with soft fingers, the evening air touched her aching eyes, and the evening stillness fell like balm on her aching heart; but on the stillness suddenly fell the sound of horses' feet. She started from the grave. The tramp of hoofs was approaching. What could it mean? Alarmed, she turned to fly. She had caught a glimpse of a horseman in gray uniform, and she had taken but a few swift steps toward her home, when the horseman galloped down the forest path and drew rein at her side.

"Stop, Irene, it is I," said a familiar voice, and the rider sprang from the saddle and stood before her.

"Oleah!" she exclaimed, in joyous surprise. "How you did frighten me!"

"You should not be out at this hour alone," said Oleah. "Where are you going, Irene?"

"I am going home," she said.

"Well, you need be in no hurry to leave me. It is not often you see me Irene."

"Leave you? Cannot you come with me?" her lovely gray eyes full with entreaty.

"No," he answered, his head shaking sadly and his lips tremulous with emotion. "When last I was beneath the roof I met an enemy—"

"Oleah," she said sadly, "I wish that I had never been taken beneath that roof to bring discord between you and your only brother"

"A brother once," he cried bitterly; "a brother once, whom I loved—never loved as brother loved before. But now he has turned that love to hate. He is the enemy of my country, the enemy of my happiness, the destroyer of all my heart holds dear. Brother! Harp no longer on that word. I am not his brother, nor yours. Here, in the face of heaven, I tell you, you must choose. I will not have friendship, or your sisterly affection. Tell me you cannot love me, and I will leave you and my home forever. Tell me! I must and will know my fate now!"

"How hard you make it for me!" she cried. "Do you not see, can you not understand, that you ask impossibilities of me?"

"Irene," he said, in his low, deep, passionate tones, "you cannot say the words that will send me from you. My life is in danger here. Every moment that I stand by your side, holding your little, trembling hand in mine, increases my danger. We must go. I will never again leave you till you are my wife."

"Oh, heavens, Oleah! What is it that you mean?"

"I shall take you to my camp, and our chaplain shall marry us. Come, we have no time to lose."

"Oleah!" she cried, in such a tone, so firm and sharp, that he paused involuntarily. "Think what it is you would have me do. Think of the disgrace, the anxiety, the suffering, you would cause!"

"There cannot be disgrace for you, when your husband is by your side; and, as to the anxiety of my parents, theirs can be no greater than mine has been. My father cares not how much misery I and mine may undergo; need I care if a few gray hairs are added to his head? My love, my darling, listen! That old Yankee hunter, Dan Martin, is in the woods, his rifle is certain death five hundred yards away; and every moment I stand here, I do so at the peril of my life."

"Then, dear Oleah, go! Leave me, and go!"

"I came for you and I will not go alone."

"I can not, can not—"

He seized her in his arms and attempted to place her on his horse.

"Oh, let me go!" she cried. "I don't love you, no, not even as a sister! Now, let me go!"

Oleah uttered a sharp whistle and four horsemen, dressed in gray, galloped to his side and dismounted.

"Help me," said Oleah, briefly.

The next moment Irene was on the charger, her determined lover holding her before him. They dashed through the dark woods like the wind, the four cavalrymen following closely after.

Irene resisted and implored in vain. From the moment his strong arms closed round her, Oleah had spoken no word except to urge on his horse. Then she uttered shriek after shriek, which only died out in the great forest as the little cavalcade thundered on.

Mr. Tompkins was still sitting in his rustic seat, beneath his favorite maple, as the sun sank behind the Western hills. He was thinking, and his clouded brow told that his thoughts were far from pleasant. For twenty-five years he and his wife had lived together, and never before had the lightest word or deed disturbed their perfect harmony, but now the breach, that had divided brothers, yawned between husband and wife; he must either sacrifice his principles or lose the love of his wife.

The sun had set, and the planter felt the chill of the evening air. He rose with a sigh and was turning to go toward the house, when he observed a negro, hatless and breathless, running in at the front gate.

"What is the matter, Job?" he asked, as the black paused breathless in front of his master.

"Why, marster—oh! it am too awful to tell all at once, unless you are prepared for it," said the darkey.

"What is it? I am prepared for anything. Tell me, what is the matter?" demanded the planter.

"Oh, marster, I had been to town and was comin' home froo de woods. I went that way afoot, kase the seceshers might a kotch me, seein' as de road is full of 'em all the time. An' Jim Crow, one of Mr. Glaze's niggers, told—told me as how they jes' hung up a nigger whenever they could find him. Jim told me that over on tother side o' mountains they had de woods hangin' full of niggers. Well, you see, hearin' all dem stories I was afraid to go on hossback de roadway, when I went arter de mail, but goes afoot froo de woods."

"Well, go on now, and tell what it was you saw and what is the matter," said the planter growing impatient.

"Well, marster, I had been to de post-office and brought you these papers and dis letter," producing them, "and was on my way home froo de woods, when I hears an awful thumpin' and thunderin' o' hosses feet comin' down the wood path, that leads in the direction o' Twin Mountains. I think, may be, its seceshers comin' arter dis yer nigger an' I gits behind a big tree dat had jist been blown down not berry long ago, an' watches. I knowed it warn't no use for dis chile to 'tempt to run, kase dey would cotch 'im shua."

Job paused for breath, and the planter waited in silence, knowing that he would comprehend the meaning of Job sooner by letting him tell his story in his own way.

"Well, pretty soon I sees five seceshers on hossback, comin' just as fast as dere hosses could go froo de woods. An' de one what was afore de others had a woman, carrin her like she was a baby. Just as dey got in front ob me I see dat de woman was fighting an' tryin' to git away. She hollered, 'Oh! I won't go, I won't go!' an' den I recognize dat it was my Miss Irene, an' dat dey were carrin' her off. I knowed her dress, I knowed her har, an' all de time she scream I knowed it was her. Den I jist wait till dey git by an' run ebery step home."

"Oh, pshaw, Job, what an old idiot you are!" said the planter, with a laugh. "You had almost frightened me. It was not Miss Irene."

"Oh, marster, it war," persisted Job.

"I just left Miss Irene in the house."

"But, marster, you is mistaken. I tell you it war her. I know for shua!"

At this moment Irene's waiting-maid was crossing the lawn. Mr. Tompkins called to her:

"Maggie, is you mistress in her room?"

"No, sir, she went down the road about an hour ago."

The planter fell back in his chair, as though he had been struck a blow, and buried his face in his hands, while the terrified maid hastened into the house to spread the news.

Mrs. Tompkins hurried out on the lawn, where half a dozen blacks had already gathered about their master.

"Oh, what shall we do? what shall we do?" she cried, all her patriotic fervor swallowed up in terror. "Maggie run to her room and see if she is not there."

"No, missus, I have just been to see, an' she is gone."

"Oh, my poor Irene! In the power of the mountain guerillas! What must be done?"

"Be calm, Camille," said the planter, "we will immediately plan a pursuit and rescue her."

The overseer aroused the neighbors, but it was quite dark before they had gathered on the lawn in front of the mansion.

Twenty men, black and white, were chosen, and, with Mr. Tompkins at their head, they went down the road into the dark forest.

When morning dawned no trace of the missing girl had been found, and all the day passed in fruitless search.

The exhausted men were assembled in the road in front of Mr. Tompkins' house, arranging what should be done the next day, when down the hill came a troop of Union scouts, headed by no less a personage than Uncle Dan himself.

"Well, what's the matter here?" asked Uncle Dan in astonishment halting his party.

Mr. Tompkins told him what had happened.

"Thunder! Jehoshaphat! Ye don't say so?" were the frequent interjections of the old scout during the brief narration.

"Well, if that don't beat all creation, you may call me a skunk," said the old man at the conclusion. "We chaps are jist after sich sorry cusses, as them what carried off the gal; but we are tired out, hevin' been in the saddle ever since daylight and two scrimmages throwed in; so, ye see, we'll have to camp for the night; but we'll have that gal afore the sun circles this earth again."

"There is plenty room for all in the house, and you are welcome to it," said Mr. Tompkins.

"We'd ruther hev yer barn," said Uncle Dan. "We don't care about sleeping in houses, seein' we don't seldom git to sleep in one, besides we'd rather be near our hosses."

The efficient aid of the old scout having been secured, Mr. Tompkins' party dispersed, and the scouts, forty-one in number, were soon in the barn, their horses being stabled with quantities of corn and hay before them; then bright camp-fires were built in the barn-yard. The planter told them to take whatever they required, and soldiers seldom need a second hint of that kind. That night they fared sumptuously.

This scouting party was under the immediate command of Uncle Dan. They were all experienced scouts, their rifles were of the very best make, and each was considered a marksman. Uncle Dan placed a careful guard about the premises, and then, while all the men not on duty lay wrapped in their blankets sleeping quietly on the fresh, sweet hay, he sat by the side of a smouldering camp-fire, under a large oak tree, smoking a short black pipe and wrapped in thought.

A hand was laid on his shoulder. Supposing it to be one of his men, he glanced up at the person by his side. His astonishment can better be imagined than described, when he recognized the mysterious black, who had frustrated him in the woods during the retreat from Snagtown.

That copper-face, the grizzled hair, the marvelous, bright, eyes, were not to be mistaken. It was Yellow Steve.

Uncle Dan's astonishment for a moment held him dumb. How could that man have passed the line of pickets? Gaining his voice after a few moments, he said:

"Well, I must say you are a bold 'un. I would like to know how you passed the pickets?"

"Pickets, sir?" said the stranger, seating himself by the camp-fire opposite the old scout, "are very useful on ordinary occasions, but I have spent the most of my life in hiding, in avoiding guards, in running for my life, and consequently have become very expert in the business."

"Who are you, and what do you want?"

"I am called Yellow Steve. You are to start to-morrow in search of the young lady who was abducted?"

"How did you learn that? How did you learn that any lady was abducted?"

"That, sir, is a part of my profession. I learn things by means which ordinary mortals would never dream of. I came here to give you information that will lead to the discovery of the young lady you are in search of."

"What do you know of her?" asked the old scout.

"She is at the foot of the Twin Mountains, confined in the cabin you and Crazy Joe occupied for so many years. There is only ten men to guard her. She is there to-night. I saw her to-day when she saw me not. What is more, I know she will be there to-morrow. Then she is to be removed from there."

"Are you laying a trap to catch us?" asked the old man sternly.

"I am telling you heaven's own truth. Now I have performed my errand, I will go."

Before the old scout could reply, the mysterious messenger rose and stole silently away in the darkness. He waited to hear the picket challenge him, but no challenge came.

CHAPTER XXIV.

HE IS MY HUSBAND. OH, SPARE HIS LIFE.

Irene soon discovered that her cries and her struggles were quite useless. The strong arm of Oleah held her firmly in the saddle, and the powerful horse swept steadily on. Night was falling fast, and she observed that the country, through which she was passing, was entirely strange to her; but, judging from their course, they would pass the Twin Mountains before morning. Looking appealingly into the dark, determined face, she said:

"Even now it is not too late, Oleah; take me home."

"Can you not trust me, Irene?" he answered, with a look of tenderness veiling the fire of his black eyes. "You are mine already, because you love me. No, your lips have not said it, but your eyes have betrayed you. I am fulfilling an oath, the violation of which would be perjury and the eternal ruin of my soul."

"What can you mean?" she cried. "Oh, you are mad, mad!"

"I have been mad," he answered. "A fire has been raging in my breast, that had almost burned my life away. One word from you would end my torture. What is the reason that locks your lips!"

"Is it a proof of your love that you take me from my home to a soldiers' camp, bringing disgrace to me and grief to those to whom I owe more than life?"

"I am taking you to no soldiers' camp. No rude gaze shall fall on your sweet face, and no rude words reach your ear. You shall sleep safely to-night within four walls, your companion gentle and kind, and men with strong arms and brave hearts shall guard the door, each willing and ready to lay down his life for yours."

They rode on over hill and vale, crossed streams and passed through grand old forests.

It was near midnight when they crossed a small, rocky

stream and approached two log cabins that stood at the foot of the Twin Mountains. The moon had risen, and the Autumn night was calm and peaceful. The cry of night birds or the rustling of leaves, stirred by the light breezes, were the only sounds that broke the stillness. The tall mountain peaks in the distance looked like giant sentinels keeping guard over a sleeping world.

A man stood in front of the most comfortable looking of the two cabins, apparently waiting for Oleah and his party. He was dressed in the gray uniform, had a very red head, red whiskers, red eyelashes, red eyebrows, and red freckles on his face. This Irene noticed as he came forward to assist her to alight. The next thing she noticed, was his musket leaning against the cabin wall.

"Is every thing arranged, Jackson?" asked Oleah, as he sprang from the saddle.

"Every thing, captain; the cabin is as neat as a pin," and the red-headed soldier lifted his cap, blinking and nodding his head.

"Did you bring your wife?"

"Yes, sir; Mrs. Jackson is in the house, sir, and will wait on the young lady," again touching his cap, blinking and nodding his head.

"You will stay here to-night, Irene," said Oleah.

She knew that, for the present, she must yield; yet she determined to resist when the time should come. She found a neat, pleasant looking woman within the cabin, evidently a mountaineer's wife, and supper ready laid for her. But she was too much agitated to eat, only tasting a cup of fragrant coffee. She noticed that the cabin in which she was confined bore evidence in more places than one of bullet marks, and rightly conjectured that there had been a recent fight there, though she little dreamed that she was so near the spot where Crazy Joe had breathed his last, and that she was beneath the roof that had so long sheltered him and Uncle Dan Martin, the hunter. It was nearly morning when she threw herself on the bed Mrs. Jackson had so carefully prepared for her, and in spite of her strange surroundings, her anxiety, her dark forebodings, she slept soundly.

Morning came, and she ate Mrs. Jackson's carefully

prepared breakfast, assiduously waited on by that pleasant-voiced woman. Irene noticed that no man entered the room. Mr. Jackson came to the door occasionally, to bring wood or water for his wife, but never entered. From the sound of voices without, she knew that there must be a dozen or more men about the house, yet she saw none save the red-headed Mr. Jackson, who was evidently on his best behavior, and never approached the cabin door without removing his cap.

Though her comfort was carefully provided for, Irene saw that her every movement was watched and guarded. There was no possible chance of escape, surrounded by a guard so vigilant. About the middle of the afternoon, Oleah, who had evidently been away, returned, and with him came a man dressed in citizen's garb, with a meek face and frightened air, and the same four cavalrymen who had accompanied them the previous day. The man in citizen's garb, she was sure, must be a prisoner. Oleah approached the door with the meek-looking, timid stranger, and both entered. At a motion the four cavalrymen followed.

"Irene," began Oleah, "it is necessary, in these troublesome times, that I have the right to protect you. This is a clergyman. We will be married now."

"I will never marry you, Oleah," said Irene, firmly, her beautiful hazel eyes flashing fire on her determined lover.

Without another word, Oleah forcibly took her right hand in his, then he turned to the clergyman and said:

"You know your duty, sir; proceed."

"But, sir, if the young lady is unwilling—if she refuses——"

"She will not—does not," said Oleah.

"I do! I do! I do!" cried Irene, struggling to free her hand.

"Go on, sir!" said Oleah, sternly.

The four cavalrymen ranged themselves behind their master, and the poor clergyman cast about him one desperate glance, and then, in faltering tones, began the marriage ceremony. Oleah's responses came deep and low, but Irene's "No, no, never!" rang out loud and clear.

At a sign from the young captain, one of the tall cavalrymen quickly stepped behind her and forced her to bow assent.

The minister stopped, aghast.

"Go on, sir; go on!" thundered Oleah, his eyes gleaming.

The terrified clergyman concluded the ceremony, pronouncing them man and wife, and then, burying his face in his hands, burst into tears.

Immediately upon conclusion of the marriage ceremony, Oleah obtained a certificate of marriage from the minister, who was then allowed to depart under the escort of the faithful four, and Mrs. Jackson followed them from the room, leaving Oleah alone with his reluctant bride.

"Irene, my Irene," said Oleah, in his low, thrilling tones, "this was my only hope. In peaceful times I might have pressed my suit as others do—I might have wooed and waited; but to wait now was to lose you. Will not my wife forgive me?" he cried, imploringly.

"This is no marriage—I am not your wife!" said Irene, in a low, steady voice. "Leave me! You have forfeited even a brother's claim. No, no; I will not listen to you!" she cried desperately, as Oleah came a step nearer. "You will not leave me, then! You will force me to defend myself!" As she spoke she snatched a pistol from his belt and leveled the weapon at his heart.

Oleah folded his hands. "Fire if you wish," he said calmly. "Death at your hands is preferable to life without your love."

She lowered the pistol, the flush faded from her face, her eyes grew misty with tears.

"If to love you is a crime, deserving death, then, indeed, you shall be my executioner; for never did mortal love as I love you."

She hesitated a moment, then laid the revolver on the table, and sinking into a chair burst into tears.

"Heaven forgive you!" she sobbed, "for the misery you have caused!"

"It is your forgiveness I want, my darling," he said. "I will leave you now since you bid me. To-morrow you shall be returned to your home, and I will never come to you save at your bidding."

She did not lift her bowed head. There was a moment's stillness, broken only by her sobs. Then Oleah took the pistol from the table, returned it to his belt, and left the room.

It was scarcely daylight when Uncle Dan ordered every man to the saddle. The drowsy soldiers protested, declaring the music of the crowing cock made them the more sleepy, but their leader was inexorable. Every man must be prepared to mount in thirty minutes. Breakfast over, they filed out of the barnyard, while the darkness of the night still hovered in the shadows of the thick forest. Uncle Dan had not deemed it prudent to reveal the interview of the night before, and none of the men knew what direction they were to take or what was to be their destination.

When they had reached a clearing in the woods, the men were drawn up in a double circle, and the old scout rode in their midst, and, holding in his hand his broad-brimmed hat (he would not wear the regimental cap), he addressed them :

"Now, boys, we're gwine where there will likely be some powder burnt and some lead scattered about loose. The gal, you heerd about last night, is up near the Twin Mountains, and we've got to get back home to-night. But the whole place is alive with guerrillas and bushwhackers and you may bet there'll be some hurting done. I want every man to be prepared and not to be taken by surprise. Look out for a big bushwhack, and be prepared to shoot at half a second's notice. Keep yer guns in yer hand and yer fingers near the locks. That's all, come on!"

He led the way at a gallop, and the others followed, their horses' hoofs clattering on the frosty ground. The sun was just now rising over the eastern hills, and grass and leaves and bare brown twigs glittered resplendent in its rays. The country, over which they were passing, was rough and broken, with occasional bottom lands, covered with gigantic forest trees, and the morning air was clear and chilly, as they swept so swiftly through it, close after their veteran commander, who was a striking figure mounted on his powerful bay horse, with the broad brim of his hat turned back from his earnest bronze face. He kept the bridle-rein in the same hand that held his trusty rifle on the pommel of his saddle, leaving the other free for any emergency—the emergency most frequently arising now being the persistent flapping of his hat-brim. The sun was two hours high at least and was fast dissolving the crystal covering that glittered above the denuded vegetation, when they came to the creek that flowed by the mountain cabins. Just beyond the creek rose the Twin Mountains, not more than a mile away, and the cabins were within a few hundred yards. They had traveled sixteen miles or thereabout that morning, and men and horses were weary with the rough riding. The creek was thickly fringed with timber, yet retaining the leaves, which the florist had turned from green to brown and gold. Uncle Dan paused, before the creek was reached, and urged his men to use their utmost caution, the objects of their search were in two cabins just beyond the stream.

"One thing I want ye all to understand," he said, with great concern. "That gal, what the rebels took in, is in one of them cabins, and no shot must be fired into 'em for fear o' hurting her. Remember, not a hair o' her head must be touched."

They halted, and Uncle Dan, with twelve picked men, dismounted and proceeded ahead on foot, while the others remained under cover, until a signal should be given to surround the cabins.

It happened that the red-headed rebel, Jackson, had gone to the stream with two pails to bring water for his wife. A thin skim of ice overlaid the stream, which Mr. Jackson must break in order to get his water. Not finding any stick or other implement at hand, he used the bottom of one of his pails, and the thumping and splashing made so much noise that our friend did not hear the footsteps gradually approaching him, and, so much engaged was he, that he did not observe two men in blue uniform standing just behind him until he had filled his pails and turned to go to the house.

Had two ghosts suddenly started up before him, he could not have dropped his buckets more quickly.

"Bless me!" gasped Jackson. "Where in the world did you come from?"

Uncle Dan laid his hand on Jackson's shoulder telling him he was a prisoner.

"Yes, I kinder expected that for some little time," he answered, looking about in blank astonishment, as the soldiers, one by one, stole noiselessly from among the thick bushes.

"Do you belong to that house?" said Uncle Dan, pointing in the direction of the cabins.

"I did," replied Jackson, bowing politely to the veteran scout, "before you took me in charge."

"How many men are up there now!" asked Uncle Dan.

"There are but seven, now, sir."

"How many women?"

"Two, sir."

"Who are they?"

"My wife, sir, and the wife of Captain Tompkins."

"Wife of Captain Tompkins! When was he married?"

"Yesterday, sir."

"Is Oleah Tompkins your captain?"

"He is, sir," with a polite bow.

"Then, sir," said Uncle Dan with vehemence, "all I have to say is, that you have a d—d rascal for a captain."

Mr. Jackson bowed in acknowledgment.

"Where is Captain Tompkins now?"

"He went back to the command, sir, but will be here in a few minutes with more men."

"The infernal scoundrel!"

Mr. Jackson bowed politely.

"Bang!" came a musket-shot, and the ball whistled over the heads of the men grouped on the banks of the stream. The shot came from the direction of the cabins.

Uncle Dan gave the signal, and the thunder of twenty horses' feet coming down the hill instantly followed.

"Two of you stay and guard the prisoner, the rest follow me!" cried Uncle Dan, as he started up the hill, closely followed by his entire force, for every man was anxious to be in at the rescue, and every one expected that some one else would guard the prisoner, who, in consequence, was not guarded at all. Finding himself wholly deserted by the excited soldiery, Jackson hurried away down the stream. He looked injured and neglected, and slunk away, as in shame, from the men who so obstinately avoided his company.

Uncle Dan never paused in his headlong pursuit of the

flying enemy until he had reached the door of the cabin. Irene and Mrs. Jackson had been both surprised and terrified by the shouting and the discharge of firearms, but it was not until Uncle Dan stood in the doorway that either realized that Irene's rescue was the object of the attacking party.

With a wild cry, Irene sprang from the cabin into the arms of the old scout.

"Uncle Dan, Uncle Dan, take me home! Promise me you will take me home!" she cried as she clung to the veteran.

"You bet I will, my little angel?" replied the old man, brushing the gathering moisture from his eyes. "How long have you been here?"

"Night before last I was brought here."

"Is there any one with you in the cabin?"

"No one but a poor woman, who is frightened almost to death."

"Well, wait here till I get my men together, and then I will hear all about this rascally business."

When Irene went back into the cabin, it was her turn to comfort her companion with assurance of safety, but Mrs. Jackson was in an agony of dread as to the probable fate of her husband.

Uncle Dan had no need to recall his men, for they were already returning from the useless pursuit of the flying Confederates, who were now ascending the mountain side a mile away.

When he ordered them to bring up the prisoner, that had been captured at the creek, the soldiers looked inquiringly one at another; every one declared it was the business of some one else to have remained on guard.

It soon became evident that no one had been left behind to care for the red-headed rebel, and that he had resented this lack of attention by departing. Uncle Dan instructed his sergeant to make preparations for immediate return to Snagtown and then went into the house.

Mrs. Jackson met him with anxious inquiries if her husband had been killed.

"What kinder man was he—red hair?"

"Yes, oh yes! Is he dangerously wounded?"

"And red eyebrows?"

"Yes, yes, yes! Pray tell me the worst at once."

"And red eyelashes—long and red?"

"Yes, oh yes! Pray don't keep me in suspense."

"And a red face?"

"Yes, yes!"

"And was carryin' two buckets for water?"

"Oh, heavens! Yes. I know he is killed. Tell me where he lays that I may find him."

"Madam," said Uncle Dan, gravely," "that red man made his escape, as well as all the others."

The look of blank confusion and joyful amaze that overspread Mrs Jackson's face was singular to behold. The old scout, having thus summarily disposed of Mrs. Jackson, turned to Irene and drew from her the relation of all that had happened to her since the evening she had left. When she had concluded with her forced marriage, she burst into tears.

"The rascal!" said Uncle Dan, with energy. "Both a rascal and a fool. Where did he go?" he asked, after a moment's pause.

"I do not know," said Irene, weeping softly. "He left a few minutes after, and I have not seen him since."

"I don't know much about law," said Uncle Dan, after a few minutes' reflection, "but I know that ain't no wedding worth a cent."

"I did not agree to it, I did not consent, but the clergyman pronounced us man and wife," sobbed Irene.

"I don't care if he did, I heard a lawyer once say that marriage was a civil contract, and if any one was induced to marry by fraud, or forced to marry any one they did not want to, it was no good. Now, although I aint a lawyer, I know you aint married, unless you want to be."

Irene still sat sobbing before the fire by the broad fire-place, which Uncle Dan's own hands had built.

At this moment a soldier looked in and said:

"The rebs are comin' down the mountains re-enforced."

"Be quiet, honey, an' I'll see you are protected. Don't leave the cabin unless I tell you to."

Uncle Dan hastened out, snatching his rifle from the door, as he went, and looked up towards the mountains. Twenty-five or thirty Confederates, headed by Oleah Tompkins, were riding at a gallop toward them.

"They mean business, Uncle Dan," said a young man, who stood by the old man's side.

"Yes, an' 'twouldn't s'prise me if some of them git business," replied the old man.

"That is Oleah Tompkins at their head, Uncle Dan. You'll not shoot at him to hit?" said the youthful soldier,

"I never thought the time would come when I would harm a hair o' his head, but things air changed now, and as Randolph said about Clay, 'if I see the devil in his eye, I'll shoot to kill,'" replied Uncle Dan, examining the priming of his rifle.

"Fall in," commanded Uncle Dan,

The line was formed.

"Now wait till I fire an' then follor suit."

Oleah presented a tempting mark for any rifle, as he approached so fearlessly with his revolver in his right hand. Uncle Dan, though not without a twinge of conscience at what he was doing, leveled his deadly rifle at that head, which, when a child, had so often nestled on his breast.

Uncle Dan was a certain shot at that range, and every step Oleah took was bringing him to surer death. Unconscious of his danger, or perfectly reckless of consequences, the young Confederate urged his powerful black horse on. The old man held his heavy rifle in the palm of his right hand, the breech was balanced against his right shoulder, and his aim was as steady and true as if he were sighting a deer, instead of a human being he had known for years and loved from childhood.

"The d—d rascal!" he hissed between his clenched teeth. "He's ruined the gal, and now he shall die."

Just as his finger touched the trigger, Irene sprang from the doorway and struck the rifle from its intended mark. The ball whizzed two feet above the head of the Confederate captain.

"What do you mean?" said the old man, turning, in sharp surprise.

A roar of rifle-shots drowned any reply that Irene might have made.

Oleah had escaped the deadly bullet of the old scout, but some of the many shots, that immediately followed, struck him. The revolver dropped from his hand, his horse reared and plunged in terror, and then both rider and steed fell, a helpless mass, to the ground.

Then all eyes were astonished at the sight of a slender figure, with loosened hair streaming in the wind, hastening through the deadly shower of balls to the fallen man's side; and all ears were astonished by her wild cry:

"Spare, oh, spare his life! *He is my husband!*"

CHAPTER XXV.

AT HOME AGAIN.

When their leader fell, the Confederate cavalry wheeled about and galloped away toward the mountain. Uncle Dan ordered his men to cease firing, as Irene was directly between them and the flying enemy, and her life would be endangered by every shot.

Stunned, confounded, and nonplussed by Irene's sudden and unexpected action, the old man, without loading his rifle, hurried after her. She was kneeling by the side of the insensible soldier, holding his bleeding head on her knee. The horse was struggling in the last throes of death, the blood streaming from two wounds in his breast. Oleah had fallen clear of his horse and had struck his head in falling on a large stone.

"Speak to me, oh! speak to me, Oleah!" cried Irene, bending over him. "Oh, my love, it is I who have killed you! Save him, Uncle Dan. He must not die!"

"I fear he'll never speak again," said Uncle Dan. He said no more, for with one wild, long shriek the poor girl swooned on the breast of him whom not even the avowal of her love could thrill.

"Come here, some o' you fellars what's a loafin' about

there?" commanded the old scout, as half a dozen soldiers approached the place.

The men were soon at his side

"Now, some o' you pick up that gal, and the rest o' ye that fellar and take 'em to the house. Lift 'em gently as though they were babies. This has been a sorry job."

The soldiers obeyed, and Uncle Dan followed the group with both sorrow and amazement plainly visible on his features. They carefully laid Irene on the bed and called Mrs. Jackson to attend her, while Uncle Dan and another member of the company examined the injuries of Oleah. They found a gun-shot wound in his right side under his right arm. A rifle-ball had passed through the muscles of his right arm, between the elbow and the shoulder, but no bones were shattered and the wound was not a dangerous one. The cut on the head, caused by being thrown against the stone as he fell, seemed more serious, but an examination soon convinced them that it might not be fatal. They dressed the wounded arm and washed the blood from his head, and he began to show signs of returning consciousness just as Irene, recovered from her swoon, started up, crying:

"Where is he, where is he?"

"Here he is on the floor beside you," replied Mrs. Jackson. "Lie still until you are better."

"No, no," she replied, putting aside Mrs. Jackson's restraining hand. "Let me go to my husband! Lay him on the bed," she said to the men.

"What kind of a deuced change has come over that gal," thought Uncle Dan. "She hated him like pizen afore he got hurt, but now she loves him to distraction."

"Please, Uncle Dan," pleaded Irene, "have him put on the bed, he must not lie on that hard floor when he is wounded!"

"Boys, lift him up on the bed. She shall have her way."

Oleah, still unconscious, though breathing more freely, was placed on the bed. His head had been bandaged, and a soldier stood by his side dropping cold water on the wound from a cup.

"Give me the water," said Irene. "I am his wife."

As Irene took her station by his side, the wounded soldier

opened his eyes, and vacantly stared upon the group in the room. Irene bent over him, with her soul in her eyes; his eyes rested on her with no gleam of recognition for a moment, and then feebly closed again.

Uncle Dan had ordered a litter made and four men now entered with it, and reported that everything was ready for departure. Oleah was placed upon the litter, and Irene rode beside it, half the men preceding it and half following. Mrs. Jackson, at her earnest request, had been left at the cabin, and the guarded litter was not two miles on its way before her red-headed husband came from the woods, suave and smiling, and the two hurried away toward the gap between the Twin Mountains. When next heard of the Jackson family was at Colonel Scrabble's camp.

The movements of Uncle Dan were necessarily slow, and it was late at night when they arrived at the plantation. Irene with Uncle Dan rode forward to prepare the planter and his wife for Oleah's coming, the others following slowly. We will not attempt to describe the scene that followed— their joy at Irene's return, their astonishment at her story, their anxious alarm when she told them of Oleah's condition. She had hardly ceased speaking, when they heard in the hall the slow, heavy tread of men who carried a helpless burden. A fever had set in, and Oleah was in a critical condition. A messenger was despatched to Snagtown for the family physician, and Uncle Dan left his prisoner and returned to his command at the Junction.

For ten weary days and nights Oleah was unconscious or raving in the delirium of fever, and during all that time Irene was at his side, his constant attendant. When the fever had subsided and the man, once so imperious in his youthful strength, lay week and helpless as an infant, but conscious at last, she was still at this post.

It was on a cold, still Winter evening. The snow lay white over the landscape, but candlelight and firelight made all bright and warm within. As Irene returned from drawing the heavy curtains, he opened his eyes and fixed them on her, as he had done many times during his long illness but this was not a wild vacant stare, it was a look of recognition. His lips moved, but her ear failed to catch the feeble, fluttering sound. She eagerly bent her head. Again his lips moved.

"Irene!" was the faint whisper.

"Do you know me, Oleah, do you know me?" she asked, tears of joy shining in her eyes.

Only his eyes answered her. Stooping she pressed a kiss on his pale lips. With a smile of perfect content he raised his weak arm and put it about her neck.

But there were other anxious hearts to be relieved, and Irene left him for a moment, went swiftly through the hall, and her glad voice broke the silence of the room where sat father and mother and physician:

"He will live! He will live! He knows me now."

They hastened to the sick-room. The favorable change was plainly visible, though the patient could not speak above a whisper and only a few words at a time. The doctor issued peremptory orders to keep him quiet and to let him have as much sleep as he could get.

The recovery was slow and for several days yet not certain. The Winter was well nigh spent before Oleah was sufficiently recovered to be conveyed to the Junction. His young wife accompanied him.

Oleah was detained a few days before his parole could be signed and then he was allowed to return. During the time he was in the Union camp, the brothers were frequently thrown together, but not a word escaped their lips of welcome or recognition. Abner passed silently and coldly by and Oleah maintained the indifferent bearing of a stranger. Irene saw this complete estrangement and it embittered all her joy.

On the day Oleah was paroled and was about to return home, Abner's company was on drill. The sleigh passed the drill-ground and so near the captain that his brother might have touched him with his hand. Abner, seeing who was passing, drew his cloak about his shoulders and turned coldly away. Winter passed and Spring came with its blooming flowers and singing birds. And not only the flowers awoke, and bird songs thrilled the air, armies, that had lain dormant all Winter, were in motion and the noise of battle was renewed.

The farmers tilled the soil. Negroes, boys, and old men, and even women toiled at the plows, while fathers and brothers, and husbands and sons were engaged in grimmer work.

Oleah had been exchanged at last and had joined his company, leaving his young wife to use all gentle endeavor to comfort and cheer the father and mother, who watched with sorrowful anxiety the movements of both armies.

CHAPTER XXVI.

ANOTHER PHASE OF SOLDIER LIFE.

A long line of muddy wagons, and a longer line of muddy soldiers was moving southward. It was one of those dark, cold, rainy days in March, when the elements above, the earth beneath, the winds about, seem to conspire to make man miserable, and surely no men could have looked more miserable than the long line of muddy soldiers. Some were mounted, but the largest number by far were infantry and plodded along on foot. Various were the moods of the soldiers. Some were gay, singing, laughing, telling jokes; others were silent and morose, complaining and cursing their hard lot. The latter class were termed professional "growlers" by their comrades. One light-hearted fellow declared that any one, who would complain at their lot, would be capable of grumbling at the prospect of being hanged.

A fine, persistent rain had been falling nearly all day, and the men were cold and wet and tired plodding through the mud.

Two soldiers were toiling along behind an ammunition wagon, one with the stripes of corporal on his sleeves, the other a private.

"I don't mind fighting or being shot," said the private, a young man and evidently a new recruit, "but the idea of a man's dragging himself apart and scattering the pieces along in the mud in this fashion is decidedly disagreeable."

"No danger of that, said his companion, who was no other than the irrepressible Corporal Grimm.

"Isn't, eh? I tell you my legs are coming unjointed at the knees, and I'll soon be going on the stumps."

"Yer not used to this," said Corporal Grimm. "I tell ye, when ye get used to it, this is nuthin'. Why, when I was with General Preston, we traveled so fur and so long in the quicksand, and our legs became so loose at the knees, that we had to run straps under the soles of our boots and strap our legs tight to our bodies, or we would have lost 'em sure."

"Well, I shall have to go to strapping mine soon, I am certain," said the young soldier with an incredulous smile.

"Them was awful times when I was out with General Preston!" said the corporal, shaking his head in sad reminiscence.

Abner Tompkins was with this train, but having sprained his ankle, he was unable to ride his horse, and had been placed in a wagon. All day long it had rumbled and jolted over the hills of Southern Virginia, and he was tired, sick, and faint with the constant motion. He leaned against the side of the wagon and gazed out from under the cover. He saw a long line of slow-moving, muddy wagons, and to the right a long line of infantry, some of the men wet and weary as they were singing.

Passing one part of the line, he heard a not unmusical voice caroling:

"Oh, that darling little girl, that pretty little girl,
　The girl I left behind me."

Further a chorus of voices joined in:

"All the world is cold and dreary
Everywhere I roam."

These suddenly hushed, when the song was completed, and one poor boy, determined to rouse the drooping spirits of his comrades, was heard trying to sing "Annie Laurie."

This was soon interrupted by some wild fellow, who broke out with:

"Raccoon up a gum-stump, opposum up a holler"—

Next came "Rally round the flag, boys," roared out by half a hundred throats, and all the popular songs of the day were sung as solos, duets or choruses—all, except "Dixie," for this was not a "Dixie" crowd.

"Poor fellows!" sighed Abner, as he lay back on his couch in the wagon. "Enjoy your jokes and songs if you can; it is small comfort that awaits you. Your only beds will be wet earth to-night, your only covering the lowering clouds of heaven."

Night was fast approaching, and the division commander sent men ahead to determine a suitable location for encampment. A field, with wood and water close by, was selected, and the soldiers soon spread over it. Camp-fires gleamed bright in the darkness, pickets were stationed and guards thrown around the camp.

Abner, who was unable to walk without the aid of a crutch, gave his instructions for the night and then returned to the wagon, where he was to sleep. It was not an ambulance wagon, but simply a baggage-wagon, with a couch arranged within for the captain.

The wide, desolate field, with its hundreds of blackened stumps, gnarled snags, and drenched and matted grass, soon presented an exciting and not an uncheerful scene. The artillery and ammunition wagons were drawn up in a hollow square in the centre of the camp, and the baggage-wagons formed a circle about them. Then over all the broad acres of the field, from its farthest hilly border to the ravines beyond, hundreds of camp-fires blazed. The fences for miles disappeared, and roots and snags vanished as if by magic.

Abner was a patient sufferer, and, when the regimental surgeon came with his lantern on one arm and his box of instruments, medicines, and plasters on the other, he underwent, without a groan, the dressing and bandaging, firmly resolving not to have any more sprained ankles to be dressed, if he could avoid it.

"Captain—hem, hem!—Captain Tompkins," said a voice, as a head was thrust in the wagon front.

"Well, what will you have?"

"Are you alone?"

"Yes, come in."

Abner had lighted a small piece of candle, which he had placed on a box at the head of his couch.

A little round-faced man, with glasses on his nose, entered

the wagon and seated himself on a camp-stool near the box, on which the captain had placed his light.

"Well, Diggs, we have had a disagreeable day for marching."

"Yes, captain," said the little fellow, removing a greasy sutler's cap. "It has thoroughly satisfied me that I am not for the army. A soldier's life may suit coarser natures, but one such as mine, one that recoils from uncleanliness and confusion, and death by torture, should not be brought in daily contact with sights and sounds so repellant."

"I thought," said Corporal Grimm, who had just come to the wagon front, "that you had resolved to become a preacher."

Mr. Diggs turned towards the new-comer with an unuttered oath.

The corporal's laugh brought half a dozen soldiers to his side.

"Didn't you tell that preacher, that prayed a week for you, that you had talent for a preacher, and that you would be one if only you got out of that scrape?"

"What's the use of bringing up those old things again?" said Mr. Diggs, angrily. "I—hem, hem!—feel satisfied that my real vocation lies in the editorial field. I think I shall try my hand in the newspaper business."

"Better try preaching first. Maybe you can assist the chaplain next Sunday."

The little greasy sutler's clerk flew into a rage and left the wagon, cursing the fates that would not give him renown.

Diggs having gone, the rest also withdrew, but Abner was not yet to have the rest he so much needed. Scarcely had they gone before the entrance of the wagon was darkened again, this time by that strange person we have known as Yellow Steve. Abner had not seen him since the day he prevented the combat between himself and his brother in the forest, between Snagtown and the Twin Mountains.

"Well, sir," he demanded, "what are you doing here, more than two hundred miles from your usual place of abode."

"Forests and mountains everywhere are my usual place of abode, and have been for the last eighteen years."

"You have been a slave," said Abner.

"Yes, sir, and for eighteen years a fugitive. I have become accustomed to constant flying, to battling blood-hounds and their no less brutal owners, to all the mysteries of wood craft. Many are the bloodhounds that I have put to death, and have sent more than a few negro hunters plunging over the steep cascades and mountain sides to certain death. For eighteen years my life has been devoted to the liberation of my poor race, and I can number by hundreds the fugitives whom I have induced to leave their masters and have guided to where freedom awaited them."

"What are you doing here?"

"I am the sutler's steward, and, strange as you may think it, Captain Tompkins, I have come with the regiment on purpose to be near you. I have a story, a sad, dark story to tell you, that will strike you with wonder and horror. In these times life is uncertain and I must be near you when my time comes. I have w--- ...- it, and the manuscript can not be lost; my trunk, in ... sutler's camp, holds it."

The strange being was gone, and Abner was left alone to wonder.

CHAPTER XXVII.

A PRISONER.

The year 1862 passed, darkened by battle smoke, saddened by the groans of the dying, the tears shed over the dead. Abner Tompkins had been acting principally in Eastern Virginia, Maryland and Kentucky. His regiment had suffered severely in some of McClellan's hardest fought battles. His colonel had been killed at Fair Oaks on the 31st of May, 1862, and Captain Tompkins had been promoted to the vacant place.

It was the 2nd of May, 1863, and Abner and his command, now under General Hooker, having crossed the Rappahannock and Rapidan rivers, were advancing on Chancellorville, to meet a powerful Confederate force under Stonewall Jackson.

Yellow Steve, who was still the sutler's steward on the morning of the first day's fight at Chancellorville, came to the Colonel's tent, just as he was preparing to take charge of his regiment.

"Well, Steve," said Abner, "we shall have some work to do to-day."

"I should be surprised, colonel, if we don't," was the reply.

"Do you think those fellows over there will fight?"

"I think they will, their guns shine bright enough, and they look dangerous. I went over there this morning before daylight, and I can tell you, it will be nasty getting into that town."

"You over there, Steve? What do you mean?"

"I often go over to the rebel camp," said Steve, coolly.

'Do you know that is very dangerous?"

"I do not value my life very highly; it has not been worth a straw for eighteen years; all that ever was good within me has been crushed out by the very men who carry those bayonets over yonder. I have a feeling that my time has come and that you will know my story when the fight is over."

The long roll of the drum was heard calling to the field.

"I must be going now, Steve," said the colonel, buckling on his sword, "but I will see you when the fight is over, if I live."

Colonel Tompkins mounted his horse, and took his place at the head of his regiment. The order had been extended along the entire line to advance, Abner was ordered forward to support a battery on the extreme right, which was being thrown forward to drive a body of the enemy out of the woods. The battery unlimbered when within point-blank range, and, after the first three or four rounds, the enemy fell back. As the order to advance had been countermanded, the intrepid young colonel pushed his forces to the edge of the wood, pouring in a galling fire on the enemy. By this time the Eleventh Corps, to which Abner's regiment belonged, was fiercely engaged. The enemy poured forth twenty thousand strong and hurled themselves on the Eleventh, which was composed in great part of raw recruits.

The attack was fierce, and the Eleventh, being somewhat taken by surprise, were soon forced to fall back.

Colonel Tompkins' regiment had advanced three or four hundred yards beyond the main body of troops, and the falling back of the corps was not noticed until the enemy had them almost surrounded and were pouring in showers of grape and canister, while the face of the earth seemed ablaze with musketry.

"Colonel," cried the adjutant, galloping up to Col. Tompkins, "that infernal Eleventh is routed. They are in flight."

Abner's glance swept over the field. He was loth to give up the ground he had won, but they were almost surrounded. Things looked desperate. They must cut their way through and fly with the others or surrender. Rising in his stirrups, and waving his sword, the colonel shouted in thunder tones which were heard by the entire regiment:

"Yonder is our army. To remain here is death. Cut your way through, every man for himself!"

A wild cry went up, and the retreat commenced. As the colonel resumed his seat in his saddle a shell exploded in his horse's face, and, with one wild plunge, rider and steed fell to the earth, the horse struggling in death, the master struck senseless by a fragment of the shell; in a moment more rebel infantry were pouring over the place in quick pursuit of the flying soldiers.

Abner was only stunned by the shock and fall, and his men were scarcely driven from the field when he sat up and gazed around on the scene of desolation. The roar of battle could be heard in the distance; beside him lay his dead horse, and all the field was strewn with men and horses, dead and dying.

He wiped away the blood, that was flowing from a wound in his forehead, and tried to rise to his feet. A Confederate officer, seeing his endeavor, advanced and said:

"Are you badly hurt, colonel?"

"I think it is only a scratch," replied Abner, holding his handkerchief to his head, "but it bleeds quite freely."

"Let me assist you to bandage your head, and then we will retire to the rear." He bound Abner's handkerchief about his head, assisted him to rise, and offered him his arm.

"No, I thank you," said Abner, "I can walk alone; I am only a little stunned."

"I shall be compelled to take your sword, colonel," said the lieutenant.

"I am glad," said Abner, handing it to him, "that if I must surrender, it is to a gentleman."

Abner was conveyed to the rear of the Confederate army. During that day and part of the next the battle raged, but Hooker was finally compelled to fall back, with a loss of eleven thousand men; the enemy, however, suffered an irreparable loss in the death of Stonewall Jackson, who was mortally wounded and died in a few days after. The affair was kept secret in the rebel army as long as possible, and there is yet a difference of opinion as to how he met his death, some asserting that he was accidentally shot by his own pickets, others that he was killed by sharpshooters, while reconnoitering, and still others claim that he was assassinated.

The fourth day after the battle, several hundred prisoners, Abner among them, were brought before the provost-marshal, their names demanded and placed on a large roll. As Abner was standing in the ranks he observed a Confederate officer near him. There was something familiar about his figure, and Abner, looking up quickly, recognized his brother. A swift impulse swept over him, a longing to speak to him, to hear his voice, to break down—to sweep away, with passionate appeal, this monstrous barrier. But he smothered the impulse; his brother might think him imploring clemency at his hands, and *that* he would never do.

Oleah's look was only the indifferent glance of a stranger, and he passed on and made no sign.

It was no jealous rivalry that held these brothers apart. Abner felt no bitterness that his brother had won the gentle Irene's love; his feeling for her had not been the one overpowering love of a lifetime, and now he looked after Oleah with the brotherly affection, so long suppressed, welling anew in his heart, and deplored their hopeless estrangement, little dreaming that Irene had come to blame herself as the cause. But Irene was wrong; it was a deeper and deadly passion than love of her that had worked this evil miracle—a passion which had been roused in one son by the father's words, in the other by the mother's, which had grown in intensity, stirring up their very souls within them, and at last overcoming all other feelings.

Colonel Tompkins' name was enrolled on the prison list, and he was marched away with the other prisoners.

CHAPTER XXVIII.

OLIVIA.

Abner was kept but a few days at Chancellorville, when he was sent to Libby prison. Here he remained but a few weeks, when, from some cause, or no cause, unless the hope that change of climate would prove fatal, he was removed to Mobile. Here he was confined for four months during the hottest weather; but, Mobile being threatened, he was removed to a small town in the eastern part of Louisiana, about fifty or sixty miles north of New Orleans, and near the headwaters of Lake Ponchartrain; here he was confined in a small stone jail. The town was nearly all French, and the regiment stationed there were nearly all of French or Spanish descent.

The colonel of the regiment, Castello Mortimer, was a citizen of the town. He had formerly been one of the cotton kings of New Orleans; but, on the capture of that city, had removed to Bay's End, where he had a large cotton plantation. Colonel Mortimer was half Spanish and half French, a portly man, open-hearted and pleasant of countenance, with kindly black eyes and thick, iron gray hair.

He was regarded as a generous, whole-souled man, although he had his bitter prejudices. He was a most uncompromising rebel, and, although he knew very little about military tactics, was brave and chivalrous. He owned an untold number of slaves, and countless acres of cotton fields.

Colonel Mortimer had received his commission, not on account of his ability as a soldier, but on account of his wealth, and, as he was thought not fitted for active service, he was assigned to guard this out-of-the-way place, called Bay's End, and prisoners were brought and left there to be guarded and kept by him. Those brought to the colonel's camp fared well, considering the general treatment accorded prisoners. They were furnished with clean straw to sleep on, and their food, though not always the amplest in quantity, or the best in quality, was the best that, in the distressed condition of the country, could be afforded.

Here Abner lingered for two or three months. The glorious tropical Winter was coming on; the sun was losing his fiercer heat, and his rays fell with mellowed luster on the earth. The orange and citron groves made the air sweet with their perfume. The fields were yet white with cotton; but there were no slaves left now to gather it. A number of negroes, hired and forced, and whom the boon of freedom had not yet reached, were at work in and near Bay's End.

Colonel Mortimer was anxious about his cotton; as some of the negroes were constantly escaping and flying to the North, he kept a small body of soldiers detailed to watch them, while they worked in the fields.

Bay's End was a beautiful village, situated on rising ground, that overlooked distant bayous, lagoons, lakes and sluggish streams, where the alligator reveled in his glory. The colonel had selected the village, on account of its healthy location, for his country residence. He had here a spacious mansion, such as only a Southerner knows how to construct; and here, every Autumn, he came with his beautiful Spanish wife. But she had died years before, and the colonel's family consisted of only one daughter, now a young lady.

At the end of three months, after Abner's arrival at Bay's End, Colonel Mortimer appeared one morning at his cell door.

"Colonel," he said, "I shall be compelled to remove you from here. More prisoners are coming, and there is not room for all in this little jug."

"I hope, sir, that you will give me accommodations as good as I have at present," replied Abner.

"I shall be compelled to take you to my own house, every other place being occupied," said the fat, old colonel, with a merry twinkle in his black eyes.

"Surely, if I fare as well as my jailer, I can not complain," said Abner.

He followed Colonel Mortimer from the prison, and stood

still for a moment, looking about him in the glorious sunshine, up and down the shaded street, and at the beautiful orange groves in the distance. Never had nature seemed so beautiful to him before. For weeks at a time he had not seen the light of the sun, except through grates, for the rays that had struggled into his dungeon were shorn of their splendor. Now all the beauty of a tropical clime burst on him at once—the fields of cotton, the cloudless sky and the sweet scent of flowers, that continually bloom in this land of endless Summer.

"Oh, beautiful, beautiful!" murmured the prisoner, a moisture gathering in his eyes.

"What is beautiful?" asked the colonel, who was by his side; two soldiers walking in the rear.

"This world, which God has given us," was the reply.

"Yes, it is a beautiful world," said the rebel.

"But we know not how to appreciate it, until we have been for a while deprived of the sight of its beauties," answered Abner.

"Yonder is my home," said the Confederate, pointing to a large granite building. "It is not, perhaps, in strict accordance with military dicipline, to keep a prisoner in one's own house, but I have no other place for you."

"I wish your home was farther away," said Abner.

"Why, sir?"

"That I might longer enjoy the free air and sunshine."

The tender-hearted old colonel wiped his face vigorously with his red bandana, and the rest of the journey was made in silence.

On entering the house, the colonel took his prisoner into a reception room, opening from the hall, to wait until his prison room could be made ready.

"You will be granted some privileges here, that you have not had before," said the colonel. "You will be permitted to walk in the grounds once in every two or three days for an hour or so."

"I shall be very grateful to you for the favor, Colonel Mortimer," said Abner.

At this moment his quick ear caught the sound of a gay girlish voice on the stairway, and the swish of silken draperies. Then the door opened and a young girl entered. She cast a quick, surprised glance about the room, as one will, entering a room supposed to be vacant, to find therein a stranger. For a moment she hesitated.

"Come in, Olivia," said the colonel. "My dear, this is our prisoner, Colonel Tompkins. My daughter, colonel!"

A look of sorrowing compassion instantly clouded that sweet face—the sweetest Abner had ever looked on.

Olivia Mortimer was one of those Southern women, over whose beauty novelists wax enthusiastic, poets rave and painters dream and despair.

Abner forgot that he was a prisoner, forgot past hardships and future peril, forgot all but this beautiful, unexpected vision, with outstretched hand, and pitying eyes, and sweet, low voice, that made the heart throb wildly, that had kept its even beat amid the blasting of bugles and the sullen roar of cannon. He blushed like an awkward school-boy, as he bowed before her queenly little figure.

"I am very sorry to see you a prisoner," she said. "It must be very hard to suffer confinement; to know that the flowers bloom and the birds sing, without being able to partake of their joy."

The gentle words betrayed a heart, kind and womanly. Abner felt that to lay down his life at her feet would be the highest bliss a man might hope for.

"I assure you, Miss Mortimer, that prison life is not desirable, but I am more fortunate than most prisoners, while I have your father for my jailer, and his mansion for my jail, I can well endure my captivity."

"Colonel," said the old Confederate impulsively, "I have a notion to parole you and give you the freedom of the place. It will be pleasanter for you and easier for me?"

"For such a privilege, sir, I should be grateful indeed. I already owe much to your generosity, but this I can hardly realize."

"And I shall make Olivia your jailer," said the old colonel, with a quiet laugh, that caused his frame to quiver like agitated jelly.

"Then, sir, my imprisonment will be no punishment at all, but rather a lot to be envied," replied Abner.

"My dear, do you think you can guard a man who has led a thousand soldiers to the field of battle?" said the old colonel, with another quiet laugh.

"He don't look dangerous, papa, and I can find him sufficient occupation; busy people, you know, are not apt to get into mischief."

"Do you comprehend, colonel?" said Colonel Mortimer. "She means to make you a galley slave as well as a prisoner."

"Even such servitude, under such a mistress, would be a pleasure," answered Abner.

The old Confederate, being part French, was polite, being part Spanish, was chivalrous, and, when he had taken it into his head to treat his prisoner well, seemed unable to do enough for him. So Abner remained in the colonel's mansion, hardly realizing that he was a prisoner, treated rather as a guest. Since he had been brought to the house of the commander at Bay's End, Abner had greatly improved in his personal appearance. By chance he had retained a suit of undress colonel's uniform, which had not been soiled by the dampness of prison. He had been close shaved, excepting his light-colored mustache, and he had his hair trimmed by Colonel Mortimer's own barber. Still when in the presence of the Confederate's beautiful daughter, he always lost his self possession; his conversational powers, and, in fact, his common sense, seemed suddenly to desert him. He could only listen in silence, or make disjointed, incoherent replies.

Olivia sympathized with the poor prisoner, who was so far from home and friends. She did every thing in her power to cheer him, she misunderstanding his feelings and attributing his silence and sadness to the hardships he had suffered during his imprisonment and his long absence from home. She sang and played for him, she read to him, she walked and talked with him, revealing all her past history, telling him of the years she had passed in one of the New England seminaries, of her mother's death in her early girlhood, and of many incidents in her bright pleasant life, to which the war as yet had brought no bitterness.

It was several weeks, after Colonel Mortimer had brought

Abner to his home, that the shattered remnant of a Confederate regiment, passing through the village, paused to rest. There were not over three hundred men in the regiment fit for duty, and some of these were battle-scarred. Colonel Mortimer invited the commander of this brave little band to his house. He informed his prisoner and his daughter that a very brave and distinguished officer would dine with them that day—a young man, a brigadier-general—he could not recall the name, but they would meet him at dinner. Abner and his fair jailer were in the garden when the guest arrived, for, although it was in the month of February, the weather on this particular day was fine, and the garden was yet a pleasant resort.

They went together towards the house, and, passing the low, open window, saw the rebel general engaged in conversation with Colonel Mortimer—a young man, with fierce, black eyes, black hair and black moustache.

It was his brother. Abner turned suddenly pale. He detained Olivia for a moment, told her that he had been taken suddenly ill, begged her to make his excuses to her father, and left her at the door of the dining-room. The distinguished general dined, and, later on, left with the gallant remnant of his regiment. Olivia was too much rejoiced at the prisoner's rapid recovery to inquire into its cause.

CHAPTER XXIX

THE ALARM—THE MANUSCRIPT.

The fountain gleamed beneath the beams of the Southern moon, gentle ripples stirred the waves on the lake below, and the soft breezes wafted sweetest perfumes through the splendid gardens of Colonel Mortimer. Spring had come—Spring more than beautiful in this tropical clime.

Months had passed since last we saw Colonel Tompkins and his beautiful jailer, who now stand side by side by the splashing fountain. To him these months had seemed like a dream of heaven.

Never did he believe that such surpassing happiness could fall to the lot of any human being. Even now, at times, it did not seem real. When he paused to reflect, he thought it must be some delightful dream, that would pass and take with it all the brightness of life. Could there be on the face of this earth a being so lovely; a mansion, a village, a country so perfectly delightful? Was it not some wild imagination of some artist, that had turned his brain?

No, it was all real. Olivia was not paint and canvas, but flesh and blood; a living reality, though face and form were so beautiful; her voice was sweetest music, and her soul pure as her perfect face. Young as she was, Olivia had had many suitors, but the pale young officer from Virginia, with his handsome, melancholy face, had won her heart. Perhaps it was pity that first stirred her soul—pity for the poor prisoner so far from home and friends; pity for his former sufferings, and admiration for his brave record.

He had apparently succeeded in overcoming the mood that had held him silent and abashed in her presence, for now, as they stand in the pale moonlight and listen to the murmuring fountain, which seems, like their own hearts, to overflow for very gladness, the arm of the young colonel in blue clasps the yielding form of his jailer, and it is he who speaks, and she who listens in silence.

Darkness fell over the lake as they lingered. A light moved over the dark waters. The lovers saw it not. Another light and yet another appeared, first mere luminous points or stars, but gradually growing in size as they approached. No one, certainly not the inhabitants of Bay's End, would have dreamed of a floating battery of steamers crossing that shallow lake.

For days the Union forces had been busy damming up all the outlets of the lake, and the water had been gradually rising, occasioning considerable comment among the inhabitants.

Slowly the lights glided over the dark face of the waters. As they came nearer, they grew in size, and beneath them were defined the hulk of three monster gunboats, sweeping up towards the village. The sentry gave the alarm.

Simultaneously with the alarm came a great blinding flash

from one of the monsters of the water; then a ball of fire circled through the air, and an explosion shook the village to its centre. Another, another, and another shell, hurled from the gunboats, came curving through the air and exploded in the streets of the village.

Abner cast a quick glance around, seeking some place of safety for the terrified Olivia. The stone fence that bounded the grounds seemed to offer the most inviting retreat at present. Scarcely had he placed the frightened girl on the opposite side of the wall than a shell exploded in the fountain, tearing the water nymphs to pieces and scattering fragments far and wide; then a solid shot struck the mansion.

At this moment a rocket shot up skyward, leaving a long red tail, from the palmetto and orange groves at the north of the village, and wild cheers went up from a land force on that side. The bombardment from the gunboats ceased.

"What is it, what is it?" cried the terrified girl.

"Don't be frightened," answered Abner. "You will be quite safe here."

"But what is that awful noise? Is the lake blowing up? Is an earthquake coming?"

"No, it is gunboats bombarding the town."

"Then, let us hasten to the house. We shall be killed here," she cried.

"No, no, Olivia, that would not do," he answered, "for they will make the house an especial mark, it being the largest building in the village. Here is the safest place we can find for the present."

The wild yells of land troops, as they advanced on the village, again rose on the air.

The poor girl looked questionably at her companion, speechless with terror.

"They are soldiers, who have come around by land, and are advancing on the village."

"Oh, let me go! I must go home, I must go to my father!"

She struggled wildly in Abner's grasp, for he held her fast.

"Just listen to me one moment, Olivia," he entreated. "Can you not trust me? I tell you truly that the most dangerous place in town is at your father's house. Already a cannon ball has struck it, and if the present sortie is repulsed the cannonade will be instantly resumed, and it will be battered down."

"But my father is there!"

"No, he is in the village, forming his men to meet the attack. This is the only place of safety for you. They will scarcely throw any shells over here, and the fight will be on the other hill."

Bay's End was in a state of confusion. Colonel Mortimer was aroused by the first cannon shot, and was making ready for the attack. The long roll of the drum and the trumpets sounded, and the half-dressed Confederates fell hastily into line. Colonel Mortimer had the three field pieces in his camp turned on the gunboats, and they belched forth fire and smoke at the monsters, making the very earth shake. But their most deadly foe now was the land force, which was coming down in a solid column.

From behind the stone wall Abner could see the old Confederate colonel leading his men to meet them.

The Union forces advanced up the hill with fixed bayonets.

"Fire!" cried Colonel Mortimer.

A roar of fire-arms shook the air, and for a moment caused the advancing line to waver. The fire had but little effect, however. One or two of the soldiers fell, but most of the leaden hail swept over their heads.

"Forward!" commanded a voice among that line of dark blue coats, and they rushed up the hill.

"Fire!" came Colonel Mortimer's command again.

Not more than a dozen guns responded. All had been emptied in the first volley, and the enemy was now almost upon them.

"Stand firm!" cried the brave old colonel, waving his sword in the air. "Don't give way an inch! Shoot them down as they come!"

Drawing his revolver, he commenced firing at the line, and several of his officers followed his example. His men, taking courage, began to reload. The Union forces halted and poured a raking fire into the Confederate ranks. Men fell to the left and to the right of the old colonel, but he was as yet unhurt. About two hundred of his men, having reloaded, poured a destructive fire on the approaching lines, which made them recoil for a moment; but, rallying, they advanced up the hill again and poured three volleys in quick succession into the ranks under the brave old colonel, which settled the fortunes of the day, or night rather, though the moon shone almost as bright as day.

The Confederates fled, pursued by the glittering bayonets of their foes. Colonel Mortimer, with a mere handful of his bravest men, fell back towards his mansion. A detachment of soldiers pursued them and hemmed them in.

"Oh, my father, my father! he will be killed!" cried Olivia, as she saw the soldiers leaping the wall and surrounding the house. She broke away from Abner's restraining hand and ran towards the place, where the two opposing forces had met with clashing and thrusting of bayonets. Abner followed her, but no bird was more fleet than she, as she skimmed over garden and lawn and disappeared behind the house, from whence came the sound of defiant voices and the discharge of fire-arms, but she heeded them not.

When Abner reached the scene of struggle, he found that Colonel Mortimer had been thrown to the ground, and a bayonet glittered at his breast; then he saw a small, white hand thrust the bayonet aside, and Olivia threw herself between the soldier and the prostrate man. Abner sprang to the side of Colonel Mortimer and thrust back the astonished soldier.

"Colonel Mortimer surrenders as a prisoner of war," he cried, in his firm, ringing tones.

"Hold on!" cried the soldier, looking at the newcomer, "I be hanged if here ain't our old colonel. Hurrah, boys, here's Colonel Tompkins!" and the excited soldier, who was no other than Corporal Grimm, took off his cap, and gave three cheers, that were joined in by a hundred more men, who had gathered round.

The village was in possession of the Union forces, and nearly all of Colonel Mortimer's command were prisoners.

It was Abner's own regiment which had stormed the village.

"Well, well, I do declare," said Corporal Grimm, "this finding the colonel is a little romantic, and with a purty girl, too! It reminds me of an incident in my experience with

General Preston. Sergeant Swords, did I ever tell you my experience with General Preston?" and Grimm took the long suffering sergeant aside to relate it.

When Abner had told the story of the colonel's kindness toward him, the victors' politeness and kindness towards the old Confederate amply repaid him for the manner in which he had treated their colonel.

Abner was informed by Major Fleming that he was to take immediate command of the regiment.

He instantly ordered Colonel Mortimer paroled and given the freedom of the camp. He whispered to the beautiful, dark-eyed daughter that she need have no fear on her father's account, that he commanded the men, who held him prisoner. She clung to him and asked so sweetly for him to spare her papa that, had he been a monster, he could not have refused.

The night passed away, and daylight dawned before the dead and wounded had been gathered up. Some lay stark and stiff in some gully, ravine, or behind some trees, among the bushes and between the rocks, and it required time to find them.

The next morning a courier reached Abner, with an urgent message from a wounded man, who was dying and wished to see him.

"Who is he?" asked Abner.

"A steward of one of the sutlers, who came on this expedition as cook. He was a colored fellow," answered the messenger.

A look of intense interest came over Abner's face.

"Where is he?" he demanded.

"Follow me and I will show you," said the messenger.

Leaving the affairs, that were engaging his attention, to the management of Major Fleming, Colonel Tompkins hurried away. In one of the lowly huts of the village he found Yellow Steve, the strange negro, lying on a pallet. He had been wounded by a musket ball in the breast, and his life was fast ebbing away. He had but a few hours to live at most, for the wound was such the surgeon pronounced recovery impossible.

"I am dying, colonel," said the negro, "but I thank God

that I have seen you at last to give you this." He put his hand in the breast-pocket of his blouse and drew forth a sealed package. "I could not have died without giving you this. I have hunted for you everywhere since you were captured. I have been in almost every camp in the South. I should have been satisfied to give it to your brother Oleah, had he not shown the same haughty spirit of one who has been the cause of his own ruin as well as mine."

Abner noticed that the packet had been much worn, as if it had been carried a long time in some one's pocket. It was addressed, in a very plain but evidently unknown hand, to himself.

"You will understand," said the negro, "the seal is not to be broken, nor the contents examined, until I am dead. I want no one, least of all you, to know my dark secret while there is yet life within this poor body. I have suffered enough during my miserable existence without having your curses heaped upon my dying head."

Abner assured him that the packet should not be opened while he lived, and left, promising to return.

His multifarious duties demanded his attention, and when he returned to the hut *Yellow Steve was dead*.

It was late that night when Abner found time to return to his head-quarters. He drew his chair close to a lighted lamp, and, breaking the seal of the packet, he drew forth the manuscript and read.

CHAPTER XXX.

YELLOW STEVE'S MYSTERIOUS STORY.

"My name is Jeff. Winnings, and I was born in the State of South Carolina, a slave owned by Wade Hampton. My father, I have been told, was a Seminole Indian. I have little recollection of my mother, as I was torn from her, when but little more than two years old, and sold to a man in Kentucky. Here I lived until the age of twelve, when, my master dying, his property was divided, and I was taken by a son of his to Missouri, in the county of Pike. I found this man an excellent master, he always treated me kindly, and, as I picked up a little knowledge of books, he encouraged me and furnished me means to improve my mind after my day's work was done.

"It was through his kindness, that I, a slave, learned to read and write, which now enables me to record the history of my dark career, far darker than heaven made my face. I lived with him until I was eighteen years of age, and was at one time well known about Bowling Green, Missouri, as Yellow Jeff. Then my master became financially embarassed, and I, with his other slaves, was sold at a sheriff's sale.

"A professional negro-buyer, one of the most detestable class of men that God ever created, purchased me, and I was taken to North Carolina and sold to Mr. Henry Tompkins—"

"Great God!" gasped Abner, the manuscript falling from his hands. "Was that man connected with my Uncle's murder?" He sprang to his feet and paced the floor, but finally forced himself to pick up the manuscript and resume.

"Mr. Tompkins was a man of very hasty temper and, although he was of Northern birth, he was a harsh master.

"Among the slaves he owned was a beautiful quadroon, named Maggie, and an attachment sprang up between us. I loved her with all my heart, and she loved me as earnestly. White people, who think that the tender emotions are only for their own race, are much mistaken. I, who had the blood of two savage nations in my veins, loved as wildly, fiercely, and yet as tenderly as any white man that ever lived. Maggie loved me as fervently as I did her. The little education, I had picked up from my master in Missouri, made me the hero in the negro quarters. Oftentimes, in the balmy Southern nights, when the day's work was over, have I taken my banjo and sat by the side of my pretty quadroon, pretty to me, whatever she may have been to others, and played those old, long-forgotten songs.

"Our overseer was hard on us, and the tasks we accomplished were wonderful—they seem impossible now for even negroes to have performed. Yet darkness never found me too tired to take my accustomed place by Maggie's side. When I was twenty-one, I was a strong, athletic man. No one on the plantation could equal me for strength or activity. Two or three times had the overseer tied me to a post and used his whip on me for some very trifling matter. On such occasions I felt the rising in my heart of that wild thirst for blood, which afterward proved my ruin. I was called 'Indian Jeff,' 'Proud Jeff,' and 'Dandy Jeff,' and the overseer, who seemed to have a special grudge against me, used to declare that he would whip the pride out of me.

"I could have borne all their beatings and ill treatment, and have lived peaceably the life of a slave, until death or Abraham Lincoln's proclamation had set me free, had not my master given me a blow, that was worse than death. When I was twenty-one, Maggie and I were married, in sight of heaven, though the law said negroes can not marry, and were as happy as persons in perpetual bondage could be. She sympathized with me and I with her. I can not see now how we could have been so happy then. There was no promise in the future, but slavery, toil, and the lash. Our only hope of release was death, yet we were happy in each other's love.

"We laughed at the threatened lash and sang at our work from morning until night. I toiled in the cotton fields, and Maggie was employed in the planter's mansion. It was cotton-picking time, a few months after our marriage, and, the crop being unusually large, my master sent my wife to work in the field. She came gladly and asked permission to work by my side. I also pleaded for this privilege, promising to do the work of two men, if our prayer was granted.

"Our master ordered us away to the field and said that the overseer would arrange that. Scarcely had the overseer set eyes on my beautiful quadroon wife than I trembled. I saw an evil purpose in his dark eye. He refused our request and placed us on opposite sides of the field. I went to work sullenly and, although I kept busy, I did but little, trampling under foot more cotton than I picked. We had been in the field all day, and the sun was setting, when I heard a shriek from the opposite side of the field. The voice I knew well to be Maggie's, and in an instant all my wild Indian nature was on fire. I flew across the field to find the overseer beating my wife. Some terrified negroes whispered the cause to me, as I paused, horror-stricken. The overseer had offered some indecencies to her, which she had resented, and now he was punishing her.

"They tried to hold me back, but they might as well have tried to stop the fires in a volcano. One spring and one blow from my fist laid the villain senseless on the ground, and snatching up my wife, who had fainted, I hurried away to our lowly cabin.

"I expected punishment, but not such as came. The next morning both Maggie and myself were put in irons, and I was compelled to stand by while a contract of sale was read, conveying her to a Louisiana sugar-planter. Again that wild cry of my heart for vengeance rang through every nerve, and I uttered a fearful oath of vengeance as I saw them bear her away. Her shrieks have rang in my ears ever since.

"For my threat I was tied to a tree, and the lash laid on my bare back by my master, Mr. Henry Tompkins. During the flogging I turned on him, and swore I would have his blood and the blood of his whole family. It only augmented my own suffering, however. When Henry Tompkins was exhausted, he ordered me to be released, and I went sullenly away. No words except threats had escaped my lips, and they could not have wrung a groan from me had they cut me into pieces with the cowhide.

"For a few days I remained about the place, planning revenge. I went about my work until an opportunity offered, and then ran away. I knew how vigorous would be the pursuit, and selected a mountain cave, which I believe to be unknown to any one but myself. Here I lived for about three weeks, frequently hearing the bay of the bloodhound and the shout of the negro-hunter. They evidently gave it up at last, and one night I came from my hiding-place and went to my master's house. I knew the place well. I found an ax, and I went in at the front door.

"I will not describe, for I can not, what I did. With the name of Maggie on my lips, and the Indian devil in my heart, I perpetrated a horrible murder. The baby, a little girl, I spared and picked up with some of its clothing and carried it away with me. The rest were all struck down by my avenging ax. As I was leaving with the baby, my conscience already smiting me for what I had done, a groan came from the eldest child, a boy. Stooping, I found he was not dead, but that my ax had fractured his skull. He was between ten and twelve years of age and slender. I snatched him up, and, having set fire to the house, I put the baby in a large basket and set off with the wounded boy and the baby girl.

"How I reached the cave, without discovery, no one, not even I, know. The burning mansion doubtless aided me, by calling off all pursuit. Here I remained for a week or two, living I know not how. The boy recovered from the blow, but he was a idiot and had no recollection of his former life.

"I had no heart to kill him or the baby now; I had had blood enough, and for some time was puzzled what to do with the baby and the idiot. There was a colored freeman, known as 'Free John,' living near, with his wife. I knew I could trust them, and, one night, I told them all. I knew that Henry Tompkins had a brother in Virginia, and to him I resolved to take the children.

"My friends went ahead in their ox-cart, leaving bits of leaves on the road to indicate which way they had gone. I started after them, with the idiot by my side and carrying the baby in my arms. I had found on some of the baby's clothes the name Irene, which I was careful to preserve, as they might lead to her discovery; a plan I had decided upon when I should be far enough out of the way. When in the State of Virginia, about twenty-five miles from Mr. Tompkins' the boy ran away from me, and I did not see him again for years. We had traveled mostly by night and found hiding-places in the cane-brakes during the day time.

"I finally reached the vicinity of Twin Mountains, where I found Free John, and we remained there for two or three days, as we both were nearly exhausted with our long, hard travel. One day, while at his hut, an old hunter, called Uncle Dan, stopped in for a moment and saw the little, tired, dirty baby. He looked at it curiously and asked some questions, which Free John's wife answered, but that very night I carried it to the mansion of Mr. Tompkins and left it on his porch. He raised the child, and now she is the wife of his son, and her husband does not know that she is his own cousin. The boy finally wandered to the same place and lived there and at the cabin of Dan Martin, until he was accidentally killed by the Union soldiers. He went by the name of Crazy Joe, on account of his persistently calling himself Joseph.

"John Smith, or Free John, and his wife, Katy, are now living at Wheeling, Virginia, and can attest the truth of my story, if it becomes necessary to prove Irene Tompkins' heirship to her father's estate.

" Since that night, I have been a wanderer through the South, and have assisted hundreds of my race to reach the North and freedom. I have become accustomed to danger and accomplished in woodcraft.

"I have searched the South over, and a hundred times risked my life trying to find my Maggie. Only a few weeks ago, I learned that she had died, years ago, of a broken heart. When you read this, pronounce me a fiend if you will, but remember that I was once human. I was maddened, desperate. It was the curse of slavery that caused the horror I have related; but now, thank God! when you read this, and I am no more, the curse is lifted from the land. For the first time in many years I write my real name,

"JEFF. WINNINGS."

CHAPTER XXXI.

THE RECONCILIATION.

The large clock in the hall chimed out the midnight hour as Abner finished reading the manuscript. He sat for a long time reflecting on what he had read. The great family mystery, and with it many other mysteries, was now cleared up, and like many other things, seemingly inexplicable until fully explained, it seemed so simple and so plain that he wondered he had not guessed it before. Irene was really his own cousin, and poor Crazy Joe was her brother.

Late as it was, he copied the confession in full, intending, when he reached New Orleans, to send it to his father. He did mail it, but afterward learned that it never got through.

The next day the entire force, with all the prisoners, recrossed the lake and went to New Orleans. Olivia, at her earnest request, accompanied her father. On reaching the city, they were allowed to occupy their own residence, and one would scarcely have thought that Colonel Mortimer was a prisoner, so little was his freedom curtailed.

The long Summer of 1864 passed, and Abner's regiment still remained in New Orleans. But when Sherman had almost completed his devastating raid through the South Atlantic States—many of which, South Carolina especially, still bear traces of its march—Abner was ordered to join the army of the Potomac, then about to invest Richmond.

On the evening before his departure, Abner sat in the parlor of Colonel Mortimer, with Olivia by his side. "To-morrow," he said, "I must leave you; but I leave you now, feeling more hopeful than when we last talked of parting. Victory will soon crown our arms, and when Spring opens the next campaign, it will witness the surrender of General Lee and all the Confederate armies. Then, when the angel of peace shall have spread its white wings over this land, I shall return to claim you for my wife."

"Do you forget, when you speak so confidently of your victories," said Olivia, sweetly and sadly, "that you speak of our defeat? With all my love for you, I must remain a Southern girl, and the cause of the South is my cause. I love my sunny South, and I feel as all Southern people feel."

"My darling, I am sure that every true Northern man and woman will regard this unhappy war as a family quarrel, and victory something to be thankful for, but nothing to gloat over. May we not rejoice together, when peace shall come, when the iron heel of martial law shall be removed from your city? Then I shall be free to claim you. Will you remain in this city until I shall come for you?"

"But have you asked papa about that?" she asked, smiles brimming over her beautiful eyes. "I don't believe that he will give me up."

"That's all attended to."

"And does he consent?"

"Rather reluctantly, but he consents, nevertheless," replied Abner.

"Yes," said the old colonel, entering the room, "I could do no better, seeing I was his prisoner."

The next day, Abner, with his regiment, steamed down the river toward the Gulf. The steamer passed through the Florida Straits, and after a very rough voyage, which was the one event of the war that did not remind Corporal Grimm of any one of his experiences with General Preston, they landed on the coast of South Carolina, and thence set across the country to join General Sherman. They came up with him at Columbia, the capital, on the 18th of February, 1865, the day after its capture, and Sherman at once started for North Carolina, entering Fayetteville, March 11, 1865. Abner was at Raleigh, the capital of North Carolina, when the final crisis came. Lee's army surrendered April 9, 1885—Oleah Tompkins, Colonel Scrabble, Seth Williams and Howard Jones with the rest. Raleigh was taken April 13th; Mobile and Salisbury, N. C., on the same day. The Confederacy was conquered, the war was over, and all good people rejoiced in the prospect of peace. But a wail went out over the Nation at the news of the assassination of Abraham Lincoln.

Abner's regiment was ordered to Washington, to pass the grand review and be mustered out. The grandest army the world ever knew passed down Pennsylvania avenue on the review.

Cheerful news had come from home. Old Mr. Tompkins was rejoicing that peace had come to the country, and that he might return to his home.

On the evening of his discharge, Abner was, with his fellow-officers, making arrangements for the next day, when a messenger entered with a telegram addressed to him. He took the message and opened it. It contained the brief sentence:

"*Your father is dead.*"

No more horror can be crowded into four words. The color left the young man's cheek as he leaned against the table for support. His associates, learning his bad news, considerately left him alone. Abner was almost stunned with grief. Now that he was so near home, after a separation of three long years, it seemed too cruel for belief. There was nothing to detain him, and he started by the first train for the Junction. As he was borne swiftly homeward, his thoughts dwelt sadly on the father whom he should never meet again on earth. He never knew before how deeply he had loved him. His every word to him, when he was a child, his fond caresses, and his kind, fatherly indulgence came to his mind. As the iron wheels roared on, he read the telegram over and over again, but could gain no information from it. It contained simply those four brief words, and no more.

The Junction was reached at last, and he saw the family carriage there with the old coachman waiting. The old carriage had lost its stately splendor; it was faded, dilapidated and worn. He hastened to Job, half hoping he might find the telegram a mistake, but Job confirmed it. His father had died suddenly two days before, but the funeral had not taken place yet; they were waiting for him. He had died of heart disease, and had dropped dead from his favorite chair in the lawn. Abner stepped in, and Job drove off, the carriage rattling and creaking, and the faded skirts flapping noisily on the side.

From Job he learned that most of the negroes had left the old plantation, since the war had brought them freedom, that the place was greatly changed since the last time he had seen it. The houses were dilapidated and many of the fences down. It was late in the night before he reached the home of his childhood; but, dark as it was, he could see the sad change that time and neglect had made on the dear old place.

In the hall his mother met him, weeping and calling him her dear son, and begging him never to leave her again—a promise which he readily made. Irene also was there to greet her long-lost brother.

It was not until the third day after the funeral that Abner told his mother and Irene of Yellow Steve's confession. They had not received the copy he had sent, and listened to him with wonder and sorrow that the news came too late to benefit Crazy Joe or to relieve the mind of Mr. Tompkins. Then he told his mother of Olivia, and it was decided that he should start the next day to bring home his bride. New Orleans, at this time, was not a pleasant or an altogether safe place of residence; hence his haste.

He went that evening alone to the grave of his father. The young leaves were green on the trees, the flowers of Spring in full bloom, and birds were singing in lofty boughs.

It was growing late as he approached the grave. Just before reaching it, he paused and looked in astonishment. A man, dressed in faded gray, with one arm in a sling and a bandage around his head, stood by the fresh mound. His once fierce black eyes are misty now with tears.

What a tempest of emotion swept over Abner's soul as he recognized in that travel-stained, wounded man his only brother! He went toward him with outstretched arms and cried: "Brother!"

Oleah looked up, and with an exclamation, half joy and half sorrow, was clasped, over his father's grave, in the arms of that brother, from whom he had so long been estranged.

Abner and Oleah were reconciled.

* * * * * *

It is twelve months later, and the old Tompkins mansion has recovered some of its ancient splendor. The fences have been rebuilt, the long-neglected trees pruned, the doors are on the barn again, and the laborers' houses repaired.

A merry crowd of our old friends are gathered at the mansion and just in the act of sitting down to a dinner, given by Mrs. Tompkins in honor of her oldest son's wedding, which took place a week before at New Orleans. Many of our old friends are seated around that table. There is Howard Jones, with a scar of a saber cut on his face, but merry as ever. By his side sits Seth Williams, with an armless sleeve dangling at his side, but the same jolly Seth as of yore. Our friends of both armies are met here, though all have laid aside their uniforms and appear in citizen's grab. Corporal Grimm is as anxious as ever to relate to everybody his experience with "General Preston," and Sergeant Swords is ready to second Grimm in any thing. Colonel Mortimer is there, erect and soldier-like, and our friend Diggs also, a representative of both parties. The little fellow is dressed with the utmost care, his shirt front and high collar aggressively stiff, and his glasses on his round, silly face. He confides to every one that he has tired of the patent medicines and photography, and that he intends to start a country newspaper, which eventually shall startle the world.

There are the brothers, Abner and Oleah, with all their old brotherly affection renewed, and Irene and Olivia, types of the two classes of beauty. It has been arranged that Oleah and Irene are to live on her father's plantation in North Carolina, while Abner and Olivia remain on the old homestead.

The good minister, whose saving prayer had proved so effective in Diggs' case, is seated at the head of the table. Mrs. Tompkins, in widow's weeds, is at the foot. She has lost her brilliant beauty and her political ambition; she thinks that the happiness of the world depends on domestic peace, and that this can be secured only by perfect unanimity of feeling between husband and wife.

Olivia Tompkins is happy in the love of husband and father and her new-born babe, and she has come to the same conclusion.

To see the happy mingling and general good feeling of those who wore the gray and those who wore the blue, it is hard to think they once were enemies. We had almost forgotten Uncle Dan, who has retired to his cabin on the Twin Mountains, but he is with the others, always the same Uncle Dan, whether hunter, scout, or wedding guest. They sit at the common table—the soldier of the North and the soldier of the South—as though they were, as they are, of one family.

Dear reader, we have written late into the night, and now, as the faces of these friends, whom we have followed so long and learned to love so well, fade from our sight among the shadows, let us rejoice that the time has come, when this great Nation, North and South, is united once more in the firmest bonds of friendship—one brotherhood.

[THE END]

OUT OF THE MIRE,

many a family has been raised by the genuine philanthropy of modern progress, and of modern opportunities. But many people do not avail of them. They jog along in their old ways until they are stuck fast in a mire of hopeless dirt. Friends desert them, for they have already deserted themselves by neglecting their own best interests. Out of the dirt of kitchen, or hall, or parlor, any house can be quickly brought by the use of Sapolio, which is sold by all grocers.